THREE WORLDS

Memoirs of an Arab-Jew

Avi Shlaim

ONEWORLD

A Oneworld Book

First published by Oneworld Publications in 2023
Reprinted, 2023

Copyright © Avi Shlaim 2023

ISBN 978-0-86154-463-9
eISBN 978-0-86154-464-6

Typeset by Geethik Technologies
Printed and bound in Great Britain by Clays Ltd, Elcograf S.p.A.
Frontispiece credits: Chapter 1 © Sabah Arar/Getty, Chapter 2 © Chronicle/
Alamy, Chapters 3–13 from Avi Shlaim's personal collection.
Plate section credits: Shlaim family home, Hotel Cecil, Wedding Party, Yusef Basri, Baghdad
police report, Uncle Isaac Obadiah and Doris from Avi Shlaim's personal collection. Balfour
Declaration and Theodor Herzl courtesy of Wikimedia Commons. David Ben-Gurion courtesy
of Paul Goldman, released into public domain. Mohammed Amin al-Husseini and Rashid
Ali al-Gaylani in Berlin © Sueddeutsche Zeitung Photo / Alamy; Coronation of Faisal I ©
UtCon Collection / Alamy, Tents at Pardes-Hanna © Matteo Omied / Alamy, Regent of Iraq
with Nuri al-Said © World History Archive / Alamy. Kinahan Cornwallis © Hulton Archive /
Keystone / Getty. Menachem Begin © AFP / Getty. Shlomo Hillel © Ya'acov Sa'ar / Government
Press Office Israel. Mordechai Ben-Porat © Ya'acov Sa'ar / Government Press Office Israel

Every effort has been made to trace copyright holders for the use of material
in this book. The publisher apologises for any errors or omissions herein
and would be grateful if they were notified of any corrections that should
be incorporated in future reprints or editions of this book.

Map of Baghdad 1944 courtesy of the Wellcome Collection
Map of the Middle East pre-1967 © Neil Ketchley

Oneworld Publications
10 Bloomsbury Street
London WC1B 3SR
England

MIX
Paper from
responsible sources
FSC
www.fsc.org   FSC® C018072

To the women who accompanied me on the journey:
Mouzli, Aida, Dalia and Vilma.

Contents

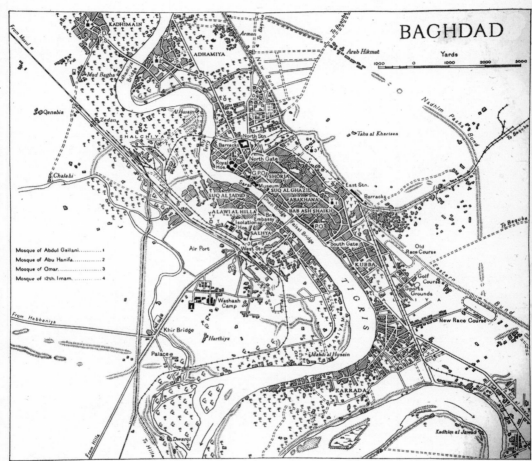

FIG. 79. *Plan of Baghdad*

A map of Baghdad in 1944

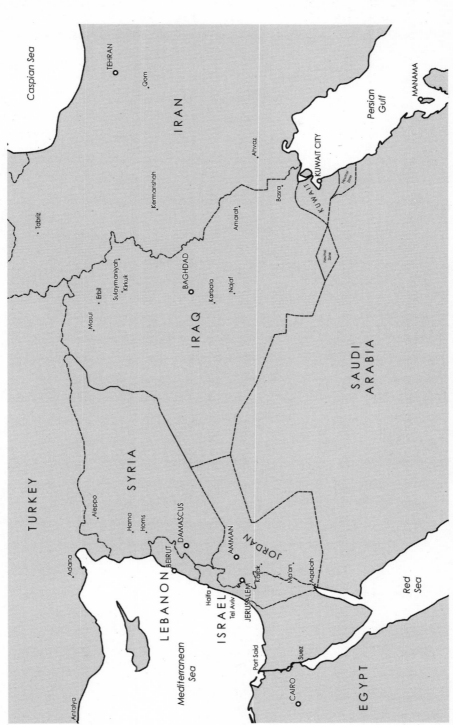

Map of the Middle East before 1967

Prologue

ONE HOT SUMMER DAY, MY FATHER APPROACHED AS I WAS hanging out with friends outside our block of flats in the Israeli town of Ramat Gan, east of Tel Aviv. Unlike my companions and me, in our shorts and sandals, my father wore a three-piece suit, white shirt and tie. He addressed me in Arabic – a foreign tongue. My reply had to be in Arabic too. Shame overwhelmed me and my cheeks turned red. Answers to my father's questions were muddled, monosyllabic, barely audible. What I wanted to say to him was that, while it was all right for us to speak Arabic at home, when I was in company he needed to speak to me in Hebrew. However, in the presence of my peers, I could not bring myself to say anything. Even later at home, I could not articulate these inhibitions. I just wanted the ground to open up to devour me. Difficulties in communicating were to characterise my relationship with my father for the rest of his life. As a child I never considered how humiliating this incident must have been for him.

This was in the mid-1950s when I was about ten years old. I had been born in Baghdad in 1945 to a Jewish family, three years before the birth of the state of Israel. My family had moved from Baghdad to Israel in 1950 when I was five. At home we spoke Arabic; the language of the young Jewish state was Hebrew, adapted for the modern age from Biblical Hebrew. My sisters and I picked it up very quickly at school and spoke it both with our friends and to each other. My father, in his mid-fifties, was still struggling to learn an immensely difficult language.

It was only to be expected, therefore, that he would speak to me in Arabic – but for me this was acutely, almost painfully, embarrassing.

1

Israel had been established by Jews from Europe and prided itself on being part of the West, of what was at the time commonly called the *Free World*. It saw itself, and it presented itself to the rest of the world, as an island of democracy in a sea of authoritarianism. We were Jews from an Arab country that was still officially at war with Israel. European Jews tended to look down on us as socially and culturally inferior. They also despised the Arabic language and what they considered to be its strange guttural sounds. Not only was Arabic the language of 'the enemy', it was cast as ugly and primitive.

An impressionable young boy, I picked up and internalised the beliefs and biases of my new environment. I wanted to turn my back on my Arab heritage, on the culture and customs of the Diaspora, and to morph into a Hebrew-speaking 'new Israeli'. Speaking Arabic did not sit well with the new identity I was adopting. This seemingly minor episode encapsulates the emotional turmoil that plagued me throughout my childhood in Israel. Nor was it simply a matter of language. Switching from Arabic to Hebrew was only one dimension of the fundamental change that my parents, my two sisters and I underwent following our arrival in Israel.

Meir Tweig Synagogue in Baghdad

ONE

ARAB-JEWS

IF I HAD TO IDENTIFY ONE KEY FACTOR THAT SHAPED MY early relationship to Israeli society, it would be an inferiority complex. I was an Iraqi boy in a land of Europeans. Perhaps surprisingly, in my early years, this did not engender a rebellious streak. On the contrary, the status quo seemed the natural order of things: I unquestioningly accepted the social hierarchy that placed European Jews at the top of the pile and the Jews of the Arab and African lands at the bottom. Nor did I believe that I had any special abilities or talents that Israeli society failed to recognise. I entirely lacked the burning sense of injustice that may propel some marginalised children to prove themselves. I saw myself as an ordinary boy with some handicaps and limitations and no prospect of a bright future. I was lazy, apathetic, alienated from my environment but at the same time resigned to my fate. The notion of pulling myself up by the bootstraps was totally alien to my whole way of thinking.

At that time, I had no idea that being an Iraqi in Israel might have advantages as well as disadvantages. The main advantage for me, in later life, was the ability to transcend national stereotypes and to take a more balanced, if not detached, view of the Arab–Israeli conflict. This is no ordinary conflict. It is one of the most bitter, protracted and intractable conflicts of modern times and spawns intense passions and partisanship on both sides of the divide. Israeli schools and the media to this day promote a skewed version of the conflict in which Israel can do no wrong and the Arabs can do no right. Arab schools and the Arab media similarly purvey a black-and-white picture which casts the Palestinians as the innocent victims and the Jews – a term often used interchangeably with Israelis – as selfish, cruel and unscrupulous villains, as uniquely evil.

Both sides believe fervently in the justice of their cause. Both adhere to a narrow narrative of history which, like most nationalist narratives, is often simplistic, selective, self-righteous and self-serving. Having lived as a young child in an Arab country, I was aware of the possibility of peaceful Arab-Jewish coexistence. I could see Arabs not just as an enemy but as a *people*, worthy of recognition and dignity. My Iraqi background thus helped me, as I grew up, to develop a more nuanced view, based on empathy for all the parties locked into this tragic conflict.

In this respect I was not typical. A significant number of Iraqi Jews who moved to Israel became Arab-spurning, right-wing nationalists. In my youth I flirted with right-wing ideas, as I shall describe later. There is no way of telling how I might have developed politically and ideologically had I stayed in Israel. In any case, the right-wing phase in my life was short-lived. Distance from Israel bred in me a more independent and reflective attitude towards Israeli society. The years I spent as a university student in England, in the aftermath of the June 1967 war, enabled me to see beyond simple certainties and to acquire a more critical perspective on nationalism in general, and a more sophisticated understanding of the diverse ingredients that make up the Arab–Israeli conflict. Nationalism, it gradually dawned on me, lies at the heart of most international conflicts. The trouble with nationalism, as Marilyn Monroe wrote in her scrapbook, is that it stops us thinking.

This book is a personal story of a young Iraqi-Jew told by a professional historian. It recounts my early life up to the age of eighteen, in Iraq, Israel and England, but from the vantage point of a scholar of the Arab–Israeli conflict. Virginia Woolf observed that many memoirs are failures because 'they leave out the person to whom things happened.'

Here the impressionable little boy and the troubled teenager are at the centre of the story, but the backdrop to the drama is filled in by the mature scholar. My personal experience is used to illustrate and illuminate a much bigger story, the story of the Jewish exodus from Iraq following the establishment of the state of Israel in 1948. The result is an autobiographical fragment, a family story and, hopefully, a glimpse into the rich and lost world of the Iraqi-Jewish community.

I aim to recover and reanimate a unique Jewish civilisation of the Near East which was blown away in the first half of the twentieth century by the unforgiving winds of nationalism. The detached lens of academic analysis does not suffice here, and so I delve into a more intimate history: my family's. We were an upper middle-class Iraqi-Jewish family displaced from Iraq by the combined pressures of Arab and Jewish nationalism, by the push of Iraqi xenophobia and the pull of the newly born Jewish state. We were part of the mass exodus of Jews from Iraq to Israel in 1950. Our departure from our homeland was due to forces that were completely beyond our control, and even beyond our comprehension. This book began as an attempt to make sense of my early life and to piece together the fragments of my family's history. It ended up as a narrative of family drama during an exceptionally turbulent period in the history of the Middle East.

Our family fortunes mirrored that of an entire community, one that was uprooted from a world in which it felt at home to one in which it had to make painful adaptations. Our family story is placed within the broader context that framed it: the history of the Jewish community in Iraq. The story revolves around the settled and mostly contented life we led alongside Muslims in Iraq; the anguish and pain of displacement; the problems of adjusting to a new life in 'the Promised Land'; my poor performance at school in Israel which led my parents to send me to study in England; and the three mostly unhappy years I spent in London in what amounted to a second 'exile'.

What lends our story some broader interest is the fact that we belonged to a branch of the global Jewish community that is now almost extinct. We were Arab-Jews. We lived in Baghdad and we were well-integrated into Iraqi society. We spoke Arabic at home, our social customs were Arab, our lifestyle was Arab, our cuisine was exquisitely Middle Eastern and my parents' music was an attractive blend of Arabic and Jewish.

What do I mean by the term Arab-Jew? I do not mean Arab as a national identification in the sense of pan-Arabism, a nationalist ideology as young as Zionism. I use the term as a shorthand for describing a shared cultural heritage and language.

For all I know, my family tree may stretch back to the exile of the Jews from Judea to Babylon two and a half millennia ago. Psalm 137 of the Bible expresses the yearnings of the Jewish people during their Babylonian exile to return to Zion (one of the biblical names for Jerusalem as well as the Land of Israel as a whole): 'By the waters of Babylon, there we sat down, and there we wept, when we remembered Zion.' For my family, however, Zion held little lure. We had struck deep roots between the two rivers of Babylon and we had no reason to want to tear them up.

We were Iraqis whose religion happened to be Jewish and as such we were a minority, like the Yazidis, Chaldean Catholics, Assyrians, Armenians, Circassians, Turkomans and other Iraqi minorities. Relations between these diverse communities before the age of nationalism, despite inevitable tensions, were better characterised as a dialogue rather than a 'clash of civilisations'. Baghdad was known as 'the city of peace' and Iraq was a land of pluralism and coexistence. We in the Jewish community had much more in common, linguistically and culturally, with our Iraqi compatriots than with our European co-religionists. We did not feel any affinity with the Zionist movement, and we experienced no inner impulse to abandon our homeland to go and live in Israel.

In one respect, however, we were not a typical Iraqi-Jewish family: on my mother's side we were subjects of the mighty British Empire. My maternal great-grandfather had left Iraq as a young man to go to Bombay, where he had made his fortune and become a British subject.

He returned to Iraq to retire and built a synagogue that was named after him. My maternal grandfather was a British subject by birth who moved from Bombay to Iraq with his parents when he was 16. He later worked as an interpreter for the British consulate in Baghdad. Two of his three sons were recruited by the British Army during the Second World War and served as officers in the intelligence corps. The whole family lived in Iraq, a state founded by the British Empire, after the First World War, on the ruins of the Ottoman Empire. And in the end the family was forced to leave the country because, among other reasons, by facilitating the Zionist takeover of Palestine, Britain had helped to fuel Muslim hostility towards the Jews throughout the Muslim world. My father's family were all Iraqi Jews.

My paternal and maternal grandmothers, who came to Israel with us, felt great nostalgia for the old Iraq and frequently referred to it as *Jana mal Allah*, 'the Garden of Eden'. For them Iraq was the beloved homeland while the Land of Israel was a place of exile. Their true feeling could have been expressed by a reversal of Psalm 137: 'By the waters of Zion, there we sat down, and there we wept, when we remembered Babylon'. Their personal predicament pointed to a fundamental paradox at the heart of Zionism. Zionism emphasised the historic connection of the Jewish people to its ancestral homeland in the Middle East, but it spawned a state whose cultural and geopolitical orientation identified it almost exclusively with the West. Israel saw itself, and was regarded by its enemies, as an extension of European colonialism in the Middle East, as being 'in' the Middle East but not 'of' it. In this Eurocentric state, it was impossible for people like my grandmothers to feel at home.

My mother, who died aged ninety-six in Israel in 2021, often talked about the many close Muslim family friends who used to come to our house in Baghdad. One day, when she was over ninety, I asked her whether we had any Zionist friends. She gave me a look that implied this was an odd question, and then said emphatically: 'No! Zionism is an Ashkenazi thing. It had nothing to do with us!' This, in essence, had been my elders' view of Zionism before we were catapulted into Israel, its principal political progeny. Zion was a small, faraway country of which we knew little. Our migration to Zion was one of necessity, not an ideological choice. It is no exaggeration to say we were conscripted into the Zionist project. Moreover, migration to Israel is usually described as *Aliyah* or ascent. In our case the move from Iraq to Israel was decidedly a *Yeridah*, a descent down the social and economic ladder. Not only did we lose our property and possessions; we also lost our strong sense of identity as proud Iraqi Jews as we were relegated to the margins of Israeli society.

In my later career in England, as a specialist on the international relations of the Middle East and as a public intellectual, I took issue with two dominant narratives: Samuel Huntington's 'clash of civilisations' thesis and the Zionist narrative about the Jews of the Arab lands. The former implicitly rules out the possibility of a Jewish-Arab identity. The Zionist narrative maintains that antisemitism is inherent in Islamic religion; that Islam has been relentlessly persecutory towards the Jews; that hostility to Jews is endemic to all Arab countries; that the Jews of these countries faced the threat of annihilation in another Holocaust; and that the infant state of Israel valiantly came to the rescue and offered them a safe haven. The Zionist narrative further asserts that Arab antisemitism is an unmoveable impediment to a peaceful settlement of the conflict between Israel and its Arab neighbours. In this reading, the migration of the Jews from Arab lands to Israel is attributed primarily to the persecution and prejudice they allegedly encountered in their country of origin; and their hard-line political positions once in Israel are traced to their lived experience among the Arabs. It was only in recent years, however, that I began to reflect on the extent to which my own personal experience helped to shape my worldview and led me to challenge the 'clash of civilisations' as well as the Zionist narrative.

Samuel Huntington's 'clash of civilisations' thesis was one of the buzzwords of the early 1990s. The Harvard professor believed that after the end of the Cold War and collapse of the Soviet Union, the world would revert to its normal state of affairs, characterised by cultural conflict. The most important distinctions among people, he argued, were no longer political or ideological but cultural. Human beings are divided along cultural lines – Western, Islamic, Hindu, and so on. Islamic culture was presented as basically hostile to the West. People in the Islamic world were said to reject the values of the West. Their primary attachment, Huntington claimed, was to their religion rather than to their nation-state. And their religion was incompatible with liberal Western ideals such as individualism, pluralism, freedom and democracy.

The now largely discredited 'clash of civilisations' has been a major influence on the approach of some Zionist historians to the Arab–Israeli conflict. These historians view the conflict as rooted in Islamic dogma and hatred of the Jews. Echoing Huntington, they place the emphasis on the religious and spiritual dimension of the conflict.[1] What Huntington and these Zionist historians have in common is an Orientalist mind-set. They deal in stereotypes of the East. They explain Muslim hostility towards the West, and by extension Arab hostility towards Israel, as the inevitable product of their religion and culture rather than of specific historical circumstances. The clash is said to be between Judeo-Christian civilisation and Islam. An essentialist view of what it is to be Muslim leads to a reductionist account of the Muslim approach towards the outside world in general and towards Jews in particular. This kind of analysis is hopelessly ahistorical. It collapses the diversity of the Muslim world into one angry, ignorant monolith. And it fails to put into the equation the very real, not imagined, grievances that Muslims have against the Western powers and Israel.

This simplistic Eurocentric worldview has a parallel in the world-view of some radical Islamic activists. Radical Islamists maintain that the story of Arab and Jew is the story of a fundamental clash of reli-gion and culture. According to them, the Jews were never part of the fabric of Arab society; they were aliens, a hostile element, even a fifth column in *Dar al-Islam*, the House of Islam. The state of Israel is seen by them as an illegitimate entity, planted by the colonial powers in their midst with the aim of dividing and weakening them. Both Zionists and

Islamists thus use the history of Muslim–Jewish relations selectively to serve their respective secular and religious agendas. Both groups urge mistrust of the enemy and call for constant mobilisation in the struggle for supremacy and domination.

The story of my family does not sit well with either the Zionist or the Islamist narrative of the Jewish experience under Islamic rule. At a deeper level it conflicts with the 'clash of civilisations' premises that underpin both narratives. The story of my family is thus not only interesting in and of itself; it contains possible implications for our understanding of the course of modern Middle Eastern history. More specifically, it serves as a corrective to the Zionist narrative which views Arabs and Jews as congenitally incapable of dwelling together in peace and doomed to permanent conflict and discord.

Zionism was a nineteenth-century European movement: it offered a solution in the form of a Jewish state in Palestine to the Jews who suffered discrimination and persecution in Europe. In Iraq, by contrast, there was an old tradition of religious tolerance and a long history of relative harmony between the different segments of society. The Jews were neither newcomers nor aliens in Iraq. They were certainly not intruders. The Jewish connection with Babylon goes back to the time of Abraham the Patriarch who migrated from Ur, south of the city of Babylon, to the land of Cana'an. Jews lived in Babylon since 586 BC when King Nebuchadnezzar destroyed their kingdom in Jerusalem and drove them into exile. Centuries later, Babylon became the spiritual centre of the Jewish Diaspora and the seat of its most distinguished religious academies, Nehardea, Sura and Pumbedita (modern Fallujah). It was there that the Babylonian Talmud was compiled, and Jewish *halacha* law was codified.

The Jews were thus firmly settled in Babylon long before the rise of Islam in the seventh century CE. After Iraq became a majority-Muslim state, the Jews remained an integral part of Iraqi society. At the time of the First World War, the Jews constituted a third of the population of Baghdad and it was often described as a Jewish city. After the war, Jews continued to play a prominent part in the social, economic, literary, intellectual and cultural life of the Kingdom of Iraq. It was precisely that prominence that fed Muslim antagonism towards them in the age of nationalism and growing sectarianism.

Under the Ottoman Empire the Jews had the status of a protected minority with the same rights and obligations as the other minorities. One of the saving graces of the Ottoman Empire was the considerable autonomy it extended to its minorities. Although Islam was the official religion of the empire, Islamic law was not imposed on the non-Muslim communities. The Jews flourished under this pluralist system and they also benefitted from the *Tanzimat*, the reforms of the late nineteenth century. They had representatives in the Ottoman parliament, and they played a prominent part in the finance, trade and commerce of an empire that stretched from the Gulf of Aden to the eastern edge of Europe. In the modern Kingdom of Iraq, which was formed from three Ottoman provinces following the collapse of the Ottoman Empire, the Jews continued to enjoy the same rights as the other minorities.

In Europe, by contrast, the Jews were the minority seen above all as 'the other' and therefore constructed as a problem. Europe had what was often referred to as the 'Jewish Question'. The Nazi 'Final Solution' to this question led to the extermination of six million European Jews. Unlike Europe, the Middle East did not have a 'Jewish Question' – antisemitism was a European malady that later infected the Near East. Antisemitic literature had to be translated from European languages because there was so little of it in Arabic. In political terms, as Edward Said pointed out, Europe's nineteenth-century Jewish question became the twentieth-century Palestinian question.

Iraq's Jews did not live in ghettos nor did they experience the violent repression, persecution and genocide that marred European history. It was not without reason that Mark Mazower called his history of Europe's twentieth century *Dark Continent*. It took Europe much longer than the Arab world to accept the Jews as equal co-citizens. In Iraq, there were stresses and strains and one infamous pogrom against the Jews in June

1941. The overall picture, however, was one of religious tolerance, cosmopolitanism, peaceful coexistence and fruitful interaction. Undeniably,
the status of the Jews of Islam could be contentious at times. But it is
both confused and confusing to lump all these issues together under
the umbrella of 'the Jewish Question'.

My family did not move from Iraq to Israel because of a clash of
cultures or religious intolerance. Our universe did not collapse because
we could not get along with our Muslim neighbours. The driver of our
displacement was political, not religious or cultural. We became entan-
gled in the conflict between Zionism and Arab nationalism, two rival
secular ideologies. We were also caught in the crossfire of the conflict
between Jews and Arabs over Palestine. This conflict developed in the
aftermath of the First World War and intensified in the wake of the
Second World War. In 1948 the Iraqi army participated in the Arab
war against the newly proclaimed state of Israel. As a result of the Arab
defeat, there was a backlash against the Jews throughout the Arab world.
Zionism was one of the primary causes of this backlash. It gave the Jews
a territorial base for the first time in over two thousand years. This made
it easier for Islamic fundamentalists and Arab nationalists to identify
the Jews in their countries with the hated Zionist enemy and to call for
their extrusion. What had been a pillar of Iraqi society was increasingly
perceived as a sinister fifth column.

For the Zionists the top priority all along was to bring as many Jews
as possible from all over the world to build up a state of their own. Their
goal was an independent Jewish state spreading over as large a part of
Palestine as possible, with as many Jews and as few Arabs as possible
within its borders. Zionism was the negation of the Diaspora. Until the
Second World War the activities of the Zionists had focused primarily
on the large Jewish population centres of Europe. The Jews of the Middle
East were regarded as inferior 'human material' who could make only
a limited contribution in the process of state-building. The Holocaust
led to a reversal of Zionist attitudes in this regard. By wiping out the
principal human reservoir for their project, it forced the leaders of the

Zionist movement to turn their attention to the East. In other words, as a result of the Holocaust, the Jews of the Middle East became for the first time a vital element in the Zionist project of building a sustainable Jewish-majority state in Palestine.

In the course of the 1948 Arab–Israeli war, over 700,000 Arabs left or were driven out from their homes in Palestine. In Arabic this fateful year is called the *Nakba* or the catastrophe. In Hebrew it is called the 'War of Independence'. For the Zionists 1948 was not just a military triumph but a historic landmark, the attainment of statehood and sovereignty, the moment when the Jews were written back into world history. Consequently, we have two radically different national narratives about 1948. One focuses on the dispossession and displacement of the native population by the Zionist aggressors. The other asserts the right of the Jews to national self-determination in their ancestral homeland. Both claim the moral high ground. What is undeniable is that the creation of Israel involved a monumental injustice to the native population. Palestinians are the main victims of the Zionist project. More than half of their number became refugees and the name Palestine was wiped off the map. But there was another category of victims, less well known and much less talked about: the Jews of the Arab lands. The twin currents of Arab nationalism and Zionism made it impossible for Jews and Muslims to continue to coexist peacefully in the Arab world after the birth of Israel.

My memoir is about the second category of the victims of the Zionist movement as reflected in the history of my family. I repeat, we were Arab-Jews. There is no better way to define our identity prior to our displacement. Yet the term Arab-Jew is fiercely disputed in Israel. You can freely describe yourself as a French-Jew, a Russian-Jew, a Romanian-Jew or even as a German-Jew, despite the grim association between Germany and the Holocaust. But if you describe yourself as an Arab-Jew, as I do, you immediately encounter opposition. The hyphen is significant. Critics of the term Arab-Jew see it as confusing and conflating two separate identities. As I see it, the hyphen unites: an Arab can also be a Jew and a Jew can also be an Arab.

Some Israelis deride the notion of an Arab-Jew as an ontological impossibility. Jews and Arabs are habitually depicted as oppositional figures, locked in a timeless conflict. On the Arab side, the extremists also subscribe to this straightforward, bipolar view. Time and again we are told that there is a clash of cultures, an unbridgeable gulf between Muslims and Jews. The 'clash of civilisations' thesis has become entrenched, supplying ammunition for rejectionists on both sides of the Arab–Israeli divide.

The story of my family in Iraq – and that of many forgotten families like mine – points to a dramatically different picture. It harks back to an era of a more pluralist Middle East with greater religious tolerance and a political culture of mutual respect and cooperation between different ethnic minorities. My family's story is a powerful reminder of once thriving Middle Eastern identities that have been discouraged and even suppressed to suit nationalist political agendas. My own story reveals the roots of my disenchantment with Zionism. It shows how my experience made me sceptical of Zionist discourse and why, many years later, it helped to turn me into a revisionist Israeli historian, a member of the small group of what used to be called 'the new historians'.

In this sense, my memoir is a revisionist tract, a transgressive document, an alternative history, a challenge to the widely accepted Zionist narrative about the Jews of the Arab lands, who after the mass emigration to Israel in the 1950s became collectively known as *Mizrahim*. I argue that the history of the Mizrahim has been deliberately distorted in the service of Zionist propaganda. This history may be divided into two parts: pre-1950 in the Ottoman Empire and its successor states, and post-1950 in Israel. Pre-1950, Arab-Jewish history was part and parcel of the history of the Middle East as a whole. It is impossible to make sense of this history without the regional context. Post-1950, Arab-Jewish or Mizrahi history becomes part of Israel's history and as such divorced from its wider regional environment. Zionists are only interested, obsessively interested, in the first phase of Arab-Jewish history; they are profoundly uninterested in the second. Interest in the first phase is driven not by the search for truth but by the propaganda need to portray the Jews as the victims of endemic Arab persecution, a portrayal that is then used to justify Israel's own atrocious treatment of the Palestinians. A rich, fascinating, and multi-dimensional history is thus reduced to the quest for ammunition to use in the ongoing war against the Palestinians.

This trend reached its climax with the manufacture of the narrative of the 'Jewish Nakba'. According to this narrative, the forced exodus of 850,000 Jews from Arab countries after 1948 amounted to a catastrophe, a 'Jewish Nakba' at least on a par with, if not more devastating in its consequences than the Palestinian Nakba. Variously called the 'Forgotten Exodus', the 'Forced Exodus', or the 'Double Exodus', the purpose of this narrative is to create a false symmetry between the fate of the two communities.[2] This narrative is not history; it is the propaganda of the victors. Honest history has to acknowledge the part played by all the governments concerned in causing this man-made tragedy. The main difference is that the Palestinian refugees, for the most part, were ethnically cleansed by the Israeli armed forces whereas the Arab-Jews, with a few exceptions, were given by the Arab governments the option of leaving or staying.

My book is both a personal record of a complex past and an essay with a political argument. It is a critique of Zionism from a perspective that is rarely heard outside Israel. The three worlds of the title of the book are Baghdad, where I lived up to the age of five; Ramat Gan, from the age of five to fifteen; and London, from the age of fifteen to eighteen. The backdrop to the story is a seismic period in Jewish history which saw the spread of Nazi propaganda in Iraq, the Nazi genocide of European Jewry, the partition of Palestine, the birth of the State of Israel, the origin of the Palestinian refugee problem, the mass exodus of Jews from Iraq and other Arab countries to Israel, and Ashkenazi–Sephardi tensions in the early years of statehood, tensions that in some ways persist to the present day.

The trauma of antisemitism lies at the heart of the master narrative of universal Jewish victimisation. This is Jewish history as a never-ending

litany of harassment, discrimination, oppression and persecution, culminating in the Holocaust. American-Jewish historian Salo Baron
disparagingly termed it 'the lachrymose conception of Jewish history'.
The true history of Jews in Europe, he argued, amounted to more than
tragic suffering. But even if one concedes, for argument's sake, that the
lachrymose conception describes European Jewish history, it does not
do justice to the history of the Jews in the Near East. Recalling the era
of cosmopolitanism and coexistence that some Jews, like my family,
enjoyed in Arab countries before 1948 offers a glimmer of hope. Amid
the dismal wreck of the contemporary Middle East, it's the best model
we have for a better future.

Picnic with King Faisal I and Gertrude Bell

TWO

INVENTING IRAQ

THE RISE AND FALL OF EMPIRES IN THE TWENTIETH CENTURY had far-reaching consequences for Jewish life in the Middle East. British colonialism shaped the politics of modern Iraq and determined the fortunes of Iraqi Jews, including my family. Under the Ottoman Empire, which had ruled the region for the previous five centuries, the Jews had the legal status of *ahl al-dhimma*, a 'protected people', or dhimmies for short. They were subjected to a host of discriminatory regulations, including an annual poll tax, but in return they enjoyed the protection of the central government. The Ottoman polity was despotic, ramshackle, inefficient and corrupt but it had one redeeming feature, namely, the autonomy it afforded its various religious and ethnic minorities to run their own affairs. The empire was Muslim, but it guaranteed in law the religious and cultural autonomy of all its minorities. Under the millet system, each confessional community was allowed to govern itself in accordance with its own laws: the laws of Muslim Sharia, Christian Canon law or Jewish Halacha.

The First World War brought a sudden end to Ottoman rule in the region. By entering the war on the side of Germany in 1914, the Ottoman Empire signed its own death warrant. Britain's principal ally in the war in the Near East was Hussein the Sharif of Mecca, the guardian of the Muslim holy places, a direct descendant of the Prophet Mohammad and the head of the House of Hashem. In secret negotiations in the course of 1915, Britain promised to support the establishment of an independent Arab kingdom to be headed by the venerable Sharif if he mounted an Arab revolt against his Ottoman overlords. The Sharif of Mecca broke a taboo by allying himself with infidels against fellow Muslims. He kept his side of the bargain by deputising his son, Prince Faisal, to lead the Arab Revolt, closely cooperating with T. E. Lawrence, better known as 'Lawrence of Arabia'. But his British allies had no intention of honouring their commitments. Britain and France imposed a victors' peace, carving up the Middle East into spheres of influence.

The First World War dismantled two empires: the Austro-Hungarian Empire and the Ottoman Empire. The successor states of the former became independent states whereas the successor states of the latter were denied independence and placed under European colonial rule with the new-fangled device of mandates; the League of Nations awarded France the mandates for Syria and Lebanon while Britain received the mandates for Iraq and Palestine. The justification for the mandates was that the Arabs were not capable of ruling themselves and that they were not ready for democracy. In theory, the idea was to prepare a country for independence and then to hand over power. In practice, the mandates were a cover enabling the greedy colonial powers to pursue their own political and commercial interests.

Britain needed a stable and friendly Iraq because of its large oil reserves, and the attractive trade routes to India it provided. But the British occupation generated ill-will among the tribes and the Shi'i Muslim majority. By 1920, this provoked a full-scale nationalist revolt, which could be suppressed only by deploying a large number of troops at considerable cost to the British Treasury. Colonel T. E. Lawrence pointed out to his government that 'The Arabs rebelled against the Turks in the war not because the Turk Government was notably bad but because they wanted independence. They did not risk their lives in battle to change masters, to become British subjects…but to win a show of their own.'

Lawrence and Gertrude Bell, the representative of the Colonial Office in Iraq, proposed an alternative to direct rule: exercising British influence indirectly through a dependent and therefore loyal Arab political elite – an 'informal empire'. As well as being persuasive proponents of this, Lawrence and Bell were also great fans of Prince Faisal. Bell first met Faisal at the Paris peace conference in 1919 and was immediately impressed by his good looks, intelligence, evident sincerity and good humour. Some thought she had a crush on him. The fact that Faisal was not an Iraqi but hailed from the Hijaz in the north of the Arabian Peninsula posed a bit of a problem. However, Winston Churchill, the Colonial Secretary, was persuaded that Faisal offered hope for the 'best and cheapest solution'.

Prince Faisal's leadership of the Arab Revolt had won him a substantial nationalist following. In March 1920, the Syrian National Congress promulgated the Arab Kingdom of Syria. This was a self-proclaimed, unrecognised state that began as a 'fully and absolutely independent... Arab constitutional government'. The new state was to include Syria, Lebanon, Palestine and portions of northern Mesopotamia. Faisal was elected as king and declared head of state. The constitution defined his role as a constitutional monarch in a democratic system of government. The following month, however, the League of Nations gave France the mandate over both Syria and Lebanon while Britain was entrusted with the mandates over Iraq and Palestine.

The French were as heavy-handed in dealing with political rivals in their sphere of influence as the British were in their sphere. The French were no friends of Arab nationalism, viewing the Arab Revolt as British imperialism in an Arab headdress and Faisal as the unwitting stalking horse of a duplicitous British policy calculated to undermine France's position in the Levant. Britain's conduct in the Syrian affair was typical of a great power under pressure: to preserve the alliance with another great power, it let down a minor ally. Neither France nor Britain were friends of democracy. The French called Britain 'Perfidious Albion', a fully deserved moniker. France, however, was no less perfidious. The three-cornered dispute came to a head in July 1920 when French forces marched on Damascus, banished Faisal into exile, and took over the government of the country. This is how the modern state of Syria was created: with a republican regime, under French control, and on the ruins of the dream of a united and independent Arab kingdom led by the Hashemites. The episode refuted the self-serving colonial claim that the Arabs were not ready for democracy: the Arabs established a democratic regime with a constitutional monarchy and the colonial powers stole it from them.[1]

After Faisal was driven by the French from Damascus, he was back on the royal job market and the British manufactured for him a throne in Mesopotamia, recently renamed Iraq. Faisal's ascent to the throne in 1921 had to be carefully stage-managed because he was an outsider with no local power base. To make matters worse, he was a Sunni in a country with a disenfranchised Shi'i majority – the Shi'is suspected that the British were sponsoring Faisal in order to further entrench Sunni rule. Almost all Iraqis rejected Faisal, including the Kurds, but this did not deter the British kingmakers. First the decks had to be cleared. The Naquib of Baghdad, who was eighty years old, was disqualified on the ground that he was too old. The British deported Sayid Talib Pasha, a prominent nationalist leader from the province of Basra, on trumped-up charges. His crime was that he aspired to establish home rule for his country. To confirm Faisal as the monarch of the newly invented polity, his British champions organised a one-question plebiscite and rigged the result, claiming that 96 per cent of Iraqis voted for Faisal to be their king. Many more elections would be rigged in the Arab world in later decades, but the British imperialists had the dubious distinction of being the first.

The coronation of Faisal, on 23 August 1921, was a peculiarly British affair, orchestrated by Gertrude Bell wearing her CBE star and three war ribbons. Bell designed the flag, the heraldic coat of arms and later on the national anthem. Faisal was crowned by the British High Commissioner for Iraq, Major-General Sir Percy Zachariah Cox, GCMG GCIE KCSI

KBE DL, whom the Arabs nicknamed Kokus. Sir Percy, in white uniform with all his ribbons and stars, announced from a dais set up in the courtyard of the Baghdad Serai that Faisal had been elected king by 96 per cent of the people of Mesopotamia –Long Live the King! In front of the dais, sitting in blocks, were British colonial administrators, Iraqi ministers and local deputations. The national flag was broken on the flagstaff and the band played 'God Save the King' – the Iraqis had no national anthem yet. There followed a twenty-one gun salute.[2]

A photograph of the coronation shows a dignified but nervous-looking Faisal sitting on a large wooden throne and a group of rather tall British officials standing behind him on the dais. There were none of the cheering crowds that attended Faisal's inauguration in Damascus the previous year. The contrast was stark: in Damascus Faisal was the democratically elected constitutional monarch; in Baghdad he was the thin façade for foreign rule. Colonial Secretary Winston Churchill viewed Faisal as a vassal, indelicately pointing out that he who pays the piper calls the tune.

The British not only handpicked the first ruler of Iraq, they also designed the political system of the new state in such a way as to conceal their own dominant role. As Faisal was not an Iraqi, the British had to find a suitable temporary residence for him. This task fell to Gertrude Bell, who was given a new title as the Oriental Secretary in the British High Commission in Baghdad. In her inimitable style, Bell sailed along the River Tigris in a skiff, searching for a home fit for a king. From the offers on her shortlist, Faisal chose Qasr Shashoua, a large castle built on the riverbank by a wealthy Jewish tea merchant named Sha'ul Shashoua. The magnificent residence, reputed to be the most beautiful villa in Baghdad, was rented from its owner until a proper royal palace could be built. In Qasr Shashoua, as the grateful tenant of a local Jew, the new monarch settled down and assumed his royal duties. Ms Bell helped him furnish it, establish the protocol for the royal court and appoint ladies-in-waiting for his queen. During this crucial phase in the history of the country, Bell worked indefatigably to help the novice king in all matters large and small. In a letter to her father, Ms Bell half-jokingly remarked, 'I'll never engage in creating kings again; it's too great a strain...'[3]

From now on the British steered Iraq in close collaboration with the Hashemite monarchy and an oligarchy of pro-British politicians led by Nuri al-Said. Anyone who did not serve their imperial interests was marginalised. Nuri had been an officer in the Ottoman army, but had switched sides and fought alongside Prince Faisal in the Arab Revolt against the Ottomans in the First World War. Nuri was to serve fourteen terms as prime minister before meeting his grisly end in the revolution of July 1958.

Gertrude Bell, who used to go horse-riding with Nuri on the banks of the Tigris River, had many close friends among the Iraqi political elite and very considerable influence in shaping the country's fortunes. In the early years of Faisal's reign, she was sometimes referred to as the 'uncrowned queen of Iraq'. In this Anglo-Hashemite political system there was a pompous parliamentary façade but no democracy and no peaceful means for bringing about political change. Thus, from the beginning, an anti-British sentiment was evident in Iraqi politics. Britain's fundamental mistake was to erect an upside-down pyramid which gave the Sunni elite a monopoly of power and marginalised the Shi'i majority. This British-made state exacerbated Iraq's inherent structural problems and brought no freedom, no peace and no happiness to its people.

Equally arbitrary and equally calculated to suit Britain's own political, strategic and commercial interests, was the delineation of Iraq's borders. These borders took little account of the divisions within Iraq along linguistic or religious lines. The main groups were the Kurds in the northeast, the Sunnis in the central area around Baghdad and in the northwest, and Shi'is in the south. In addition, there were several minorities, including Assyrians, Armenians, Turkmen and Jews. Originally, Iraq was going to be made up out of two Ottoman provinces: Basra and Baghdad. But later the oil-bearing province of Mosul was added to Iraq, dashing Kurdish hopes, based on the Treaty of Sèvres of 1920, for an autonomous Kurdish state. The logic behind the enterprise was cleverly summed up by one observer: 'Iraq was created by Churchill, who had the mad idea of joining two widely separated oil wells, Kirkuk and Mosul, by uniting three widely separated peoples: the Kurds, the Sunnis and the Shiites.'[4]

The three provinces were very different and had never previously been governed together. Cobbling them together by imperial fiat ensured that the new polity was fragmented and fractured from the beginning. As we say in Arabic, something that starts crooked, remains crooked. In Iraq's case the original fault-lines of the polity remained in place and, if anything, became more pronounced with the passage of time. The Kurds resented Britain for reneging on its promise of independence, the Shi'is for marginalising them and the Sunnis for curbing their nationalist aspirations. The army, which the British trained and equipped, became the breeding ground of nationalist opposition to the British overlords and their local protégées.

A major cause of resentment during the mandate era was the British practice of divide and rule between the three major segments of the population: Kurds, Sunnis and Shi'is. The Sunnis were the smallest of the three communities, but they had the lion's share of power, privilege and patronage – during the mandate, government departments and state institutions were run predominantly by Sunnis, aided by their British advisers. Another source of frustration for Iraqi nationalists was the British policy of giving preferential treatment to ethnic and religious minorities, notably Christians and Jews. These minorities were favoured because they were less likely to be drawn to nationalist causes than the rest of the population. The British also favoured the Assyrians on the border with Syria, and the Bedouin tribal Sheikhs in the countryside.

Of all the Jewish communities in the Ottoman Empire, the one in Mesopotamia was the most integrated into local society, the most Arabised in its culture and the most prosperous. When the British created the Kingdom of Iraq, they found a vibrant Jewish community led by the Chief Rabbi and committees of notables; merchants who controlled much of the import and export trade with extensive links to Bombay and Calcutta in India; and bankers and *sarrafs* or moneylenders who provided much of the finance to keep the wheels of commerce turning. Although they constituted only 2 per cent of Iraq's population, they controlled 75 per cent of its imports. The Baghdad Chamber of Commerce in 1935 consisted of nine Jews, four Muslims and two Britons.[5] In short, the Jews were the backbone of the Iraqi economy.

The first Iraqi minister of finance was a cosmopolitan Jew, Sir Sassoon Haskell (1860–1932), better known by his Ottoman honorific title, Sassoon Efendi. Scion of an ancient and aristocratic Jewish family of great affluence, he had received his primary education in the Alliance Israélite Universelle in Baghdad and his higher education in economics and law in Constantinople, Vienna and London. He knew nine languages: English, Arabic, Turkish, Persian, Hebrew, French, German, Greek and Latin. In his early career he served as a deputy in the Ottoman parliament, then in 1925 he was elected as a deputy to the first Iraqi parliament and re-elected until his death, earning the informal title 'Father of Parliament'. As minister, he established the kingdom's financial and budgetary structures and laws. Gertrude Bell considered him the ablest minister in the government, the most selfless and the most far-sighted. Haskell was opposed to the Zionist takeover of Palestine and to the goal of turning it into a Jewish state, foreseeing that a Jewish state in Palestine would create a Jewish problem in the rest of the lands of the former Ottoman Empire.

Few Jewish families, apart from the Sassoons, belonged to the old aristocracy of the new kingdom. My family belonged to the upper middle class of affluent Jews. My mother attended a Jewish school for girls in Baghdad and made friends with the daughters of Sassoon Efendi, Hilda and Rachel, the latter later marrying one of my mother's relatives. As indicative of Sassoon Efendi's wisdom, my mother pointed out that it was he who had insisted that Britain pay Iraq's oil royalties not in rupees but in gold coins. She upheld him as a prime example of the contribution that the Jewish community had made to the building of the Iraqi state.

The Jewish middle class included not only merchants and financiers but members of the free professions like doctors, lawyers, academics and journalists. Below them was a substantial layer of lower middle-class Jews, and lower down the social hierarchy there were poor Jews, many of whom lived in the Abu Sifain neighbourhood. Jews, like the rest of Iraqi society, could be found in most professional occupations such as plumbers, electricians, carpenters, cobblers, tailors and hairdressers. Jewellery making with gold and silver was a Jewish speciality. In the north of the country there were some Jewish farmers, but they were a tiny fraction of the total Jewish population. Some businesses, like those producing kosher food, had only Jews among their clients. In most other spheres, however, interaction between Jews and Muslims was a normal feature of everyday life.

Baghdad, which regained its status as a capital city after five centuries of Ottoman rule, had a mixed population of Sunnis, Shi'is, Christians and Jews, all Arabic-speaking. The Jews were the largest group with a continuous record of living in Mesopotamia. Their lineage stretched as far back as Babylonian times, predating the rise of Islam by a millennium. They excelled in every aspect of national endeavour, playing a prominent part in the development of the Iraqi health, education and transport systems. Their influence was evident in every branch of Iraqi culture, from literature and music to journalism and the media. Banks – with the exception of government-owned banks – and all the big markets remained closed on the Sabbath and on the other Jewish holy days.

After the fall of the Ottomans, the Jews in Iraq welcomed the arrival of the British, believing it would bring security and stability to the fractious country, expand commercial opportunities and uphold the same rights that were enjoyed by the Jews in the rest of the British Empire. Although they initially favoured direct British rule, the Jews quickly rallied behind King Faisal and joined in his project of building a new state.[6] Shortly after Faisal's ascent to the throne, the Iraqi-Jewish community organised a grand reception in his honour. It was held in the great synagogue in the presence of many of the city's notables. Faisal kissed the Torah which was brought out for him from the Ark of the Covenant, and in his speech he thanked the Jews whom he described as 'the living spirit of the population of Iraq'.[7]

In the 1920s Iraqi Jews developed what was often referred to as an 'Iraqi orientation' which meant living as equal citizens and playing an active part in developing Iraq for the benefit of all its inhabitants.[8] The appointment of Sir Sassoon Haskell to one of the top government positions reinforced this orientation.

Faisal did not disappoint his Jewish subjects. He was an enlightened monarch who genuinely believed in equal rights for all his subjects and in trying to merge all the different sections of the population into a united Iraqi nation. In his speeches Faisal repeatedly stressed that there was no difference between Muslims, Christians and Jews: they were all Iraqis and they all belonged to the Semitic race. His father had educated him to respect the Jews, who are referred to in the Qur'an as 'the people of the book'. Gertrude Bell encouraged Faisal to reach out to his Jewish subjects, to visit their schools and synagogues, and to praise the part they played in the project of nation building publicly. At the same time, she encouraged the Jews to look to Faisal for their protection and welfare.

The 1924 constitution enshrined the principle of equality before the law regardless of religion and race and included measures to enable minorities to preserve their religious and cultural autonomy. The Jews were granted representation in both houses of parliament in proportion to their population. They were allowed to rise to senior positions in the civil service in line with their educational attainments, professional qualifications and managerial skills. For the most part, however, prominent Jews avoided involvement in pan-Arabism, an ideology that espoused the unification of the Arab states. There were several reasons for this. First, they belonged to a non-Muslim minority and as such did not fit in easily into radical, anti-British, pan-Arab sentiment. Second, although they were involved in party politics, mainly on the left-wing and liberal side, they preferred to keep their distance from mass movements and region-wide political struggles.

Nevertheless, the prominence of the Jews in the economy and in the bureaucracy cast a shadow over Muslim–Jewish relations. Success in financial and other spheres gave rise to jealousy that could translate into active antagonism. Some Muslims regarded the Jews as traitors to the national aspirations of the Iraqi people. Others, especially on the extreme right-wing fringes of Iraqi politics, went even further by denouncing the Jews as the agents of British imperialism. The Jews were well aware of their vulnerable position, but they felt they had few political alternatives. As far as they were concerned, the British were not just the all-powerful rulers of Iraq but also the champions of minorities and the representatives of Western culture.[9]

The end of the British mandate in October 1932 brought formal independence but only minor changes in the way the country was run. Like the nationalists, King Faisal was disappointed with an agreement that did not bring about genuine self-rule. But having been booted out by the French from his throne in Damascus, he was wary of provoking a showdown with his British masters, preferring to proceed step by step towards the goal of real independence. For the time being, he continued the delicate balancing act between the British and the more extreme Iraqi nationalists. But time ran out on him. On 8 September 1933, King Faisal died unexpectedly and mysteriously while undergoing a general medical check-up in a clinic in Bern, Switzerland. He was only fifty years old. The official cause of death was a heart attack. No autopsy was conducted; his body was hurriedly embalmed and flown back to Baghdad. Many questions were raised about Faisal's sudden death, especially as the Swiss doctors maintained that he was healthy and that there was nothing wrong with him when he arrived. His private nurse reported signs of arsenic poisoning before his death. Although my mother was only nine years old at the time of the king's death, she remembers people weeping in the street and singing a song which cursed Switzerland. Many Iraqis of that generation, including my mother, believed that it was the British who had secretly ordered the poisoning of the popular king because he had outlived his usefulness.

The death of King Faisal was a tragic milestone in the history of Iraq, marking the end of a liberal, religiously pluralist era. Iraqi politics became increasingly dominated by the deeply authoritarian and staunchly pro-British Nuri al-Said. Nuri was a wily character, frequently referred to as the 'old fox'. He personified the innate conservatism of the Iraqi ruling class. Such was Nuri's dominance that the next twenty-five years in Iraqi history were often referred to as *Ahd Nuri*, or Nuri's era. During the first decade of the kingdom, Nuri was a powerful ally of the Jews, but his attitude would change in the aftermath of the Second World War, partly because of Jewish involvement in the Iraqi Communist Party, partly because of the Zionist offensive in Palestine.

Faisal was succeeded by his only son, Ghazi. Ghazi was twenty-one years old when he ascended the throne. He hated the British because of their betrayal of his grandfather, Hussein the Sharif of Mecca, and their betrayal of the Arabs by issuing the Balfour Declaration. Unlike his worldly father, Ghazi was an inexperienced and unbalanced young man, immature and debauched, assiduous in pursuit of pleasure and sport but neglectful of his public duties. He held some half-baked but strongly expressed pan-Arab views and dabbled in Nazi ideology and the notion of racial purity. My mother spoke of Ghazi as a huge disappointment compared to his father, and as a scoundrel who got mixed up in bad company, notably the Nazis and Haj Amin al-Husseini, the leader of the Palestinian national movement. During Ghazi's short reign, the nationalists became more outspoken and more assertive in Iraqi politics.

Following the rise to power of the Nazi party in 1933, German propaganda stepped up in Iraq. The Germans had their eyes on Iraq's oil and their propaganda machine skilfully pandered to anti-British and anti-Zionist feelings. Admiration for Germany spread through the country; German replaced French as the second foreign language after English in some schools. The Ministry of Education encouraged the formation of the *futuwwa* (the Youth), a paramilitary brigade modelled on the Hitler Youth, which took to harassing Jews on the streets of Baghdad.

Nazi militarism made a strong impression on members of the younger generation who aspired to set up a Nazi movement in Iraq. Hostility towards the Jews, whatever its sources, had found a new and toxic ideological justification. The German ambassador, Dr Fritz Grobba, who was an Arabic speaker, made many friends among the local politicians and the journalists. He bought a Christian-owned newspaper, *al-Alam al-Arabi*, the Arab World, and he serialised there an Arabic version of Adolf Hitler's autobiography, *Mein Kampf*. Ghazi befriended Grobba. Secular and religious nationalists, previously sidelined by the British, now found in Grobba a sympathetic ally.[10] With Grobba's encouragement the army voiced ever more strident anti-Jewish and anti-imperialist sentiments, and began to intervene in the political arena against civilian governments it considered insufficiently patriotic. In 1936, with the tacit support of the king, four army officers nicknamed 'the Golden Square' overthrew the civilian government. This was the first coup d'état in modern Arab politics.

On Ghazi's watch, xenophobia in the country at large, in the media and in government circles resulted in a move to cancel the special status and privileges which his father had granted to minorities. In the new age of Sunni triumphalism, minorities were vilified. The Iraqi army dealt harshly with the Assyrians, culminating in a massacre of hundreds of innocent civilians in 1933. Towards the Kurdish rebels the central government in Baghdad adopted an iron fist policy, which involved great brutality and the use of the air force to bomb civilian centres. Although the position of the Jews was unlike that of the other minorities, they too faced mounting restrictions and discrimination. Ghazi imposed a tax on Jews whenever they left the country. The purpose of this measure was to sever the link between the Jews of Iraq and the rest of the world, especially in Palestine. Other measures were intended to restrict the influence of the Jewish community at home. Hundreds of Jews were dismissed from the civil service in the name of reform and budget cuts and informal quotas were put in place to limit the number of young Jews admitted to state schools and colleges. The government actually took the lead both in spreading European-style antisemitism and in enacting anti-Jewish measures.

King Ghazi met a premature death in an accident in 1939 when the sports car he was driving crashed into a tree in the grounds of *Qasr al-Zuhur*, the Palace of Flowers. At the time many Iraqis took the view that Nuri al-Said had instigated Ghazi's murder at the behest of the British. The German embassy fed the rumours that British intelligence was implicated in the alleged regicide, but no convincing evidence could be adduced to support this conspiracy theory. The Jews breathed an audible sigh of relief. Ghazi's son Faisal was promptly proclaimed king and given the title of Faisal II but, as he was a four-year-old infant, he was to rule under a Regency Council headed by his uncle, the pro-British Prince Abd al-Ilah.

Abd al-Ilah was the son of Ali, King of the Hijaz and elder brother of Faisal I. Abd al-Ilah was a shy prince, lacking in self-confidence, inarticulate, weak and indecisive. He was taller than his relatives and more fair-skinned, a trait thought to have been inherited from his Caucasian grandmother. He loved horses and the countryside, and he developed a keen interest in farming. Abd al-Ilah was proud of the role that his family had played in leading the Arab Revolt during the First World War and he was moved by a genuine desire to do well by his country, but he simply was not up to the task. His political skills were limited, he lacked charisma and he was widely regarded as a British stooge.

German propaganda continued to play a major part in disseminating anti-Jewish sentiment in Iraq, especially among the young, during the Regency. Another external factor, which increasingly impinged on the position of the Jewish community in Iraq, was the Zionist struggle to establish a Jewish state in Palestine. The Zionist movement was a settler-colonial movement, which had its roots in late nineteenth-century Europe, as a response to the problem of European antisemitism. Although Zionism was a rebellion against the European treatment of the Jews, its leaders appealed to the self-interest of the European great powers. Theodor Herzl, an assimilated Viennese Jew and the father of political Zionism, made this promise in 1896: 'For Europe we shall serve there as the vanguard of civilisation against the barbarians.' Apocryphally, the rabbis of Vienna decided to explore Herzl's ideas and sent two representatives to Palestine. This fact-finding mission resulted in a cable from Palestine in which the two rabbis wrote: 'The bride is beautiful, but she is married to another man.'

To make its way in the harsh world of international politics, and to overcome the predictable and inevitable opposition of the Palestine Arabs, the Zionist movement allied itself to Great Britain in the First World War. Its first diplomatic triumph was the Balfour Declaration of 2 November 1917, which pledged British support for the establishment of a national home for the Jewish people in Palestine. This was a classic colonial document. At that time, the Arabs formed 90 percent of the population of Palestine; the Jews constituted 10 percent and owned only 2 per cent of the land. Yet the British supported national rights for the Jews and only religious and civil rights for the Arab majority. To add insult to injury, the Balfour Declaration referred to the Arabs as 'the non-Jewish communities in Palestine'. Britain had no legal, political or moral right to turn over the land of one people to another, but after receiving the mandate over Palestine from the League of Nations, it had the power to do so. With the support of the mandatory power, the Zionists began the systematic takeover of Palestine. The centrepiece of mandatory policy was to deny representative institutions so long as there was an Arab majority. The idea was to delay the granting of independence until there was a Jewish majority capable of running the country along European lines. Although this was never acknowledged, a national home for the Jewish people in the country could only come about at the expense of the native Arab population. No room could be made in Palestine for a second nation except by dislodging and displacing the first.

The conditions that gave rise to Zionism in Europe were largely absent in the Orient. The nationalist idea at the core of European Zionism found few adherents among the Jews of the Arab lands. In Iraq Zionism was not a home-grown product but a foreign ideology propagated by emissaries from Palestine. Some of these emissaries were Ashkenazi Jews and some were Iraqi Jews who had migrated to Palestine in small numbers in the interwar period. Although the emissaries were well received by senior British and Iraqi officials, Iraqi Jews seemed largely indifferent and even hostile. When the Zionist Committee was given permission to function, a delegation of Jewish leaders met with the High Commissioner to express their opposition. The Zionists were unable to enlist the support of any influential local Jewish leaders.[11]

On one of the anniversaries of the Balfour Declaration, Sir Arnold Wilson, who served as Civil Commissioner in Baghdad from 1918 to 1920, wrote to the Colonial Office about a discussion he had had with several members of the Jewish community at the time:

> They remarked that Palestine was a poor country and Jerusalem a bad town to live in. Compared with Palestine, Mesopotamia was Paradise. This is the Garden of Eden, said one; it is from this country that Adam was driven forth – give us a good government and we will make this country flourish. For us Mesopotamia is a home, a national home to which the Jews of Bombay and Persia and Turkey will be glad to come. Here shall be liberty and opportunity. In Palestine, there may be liberty but there will be no opportunity.[12]

The views conveyed to the Civil Commissioner were representative of the Jewish community at large. A small minority, consisting mainly of orthodox Jews, were attracted to the idea of going to live in the ancestral Jewish homeland. The majority, on the other hand, saw Iraq as their homeland and Arab culture as their culture even though Judaism was their religion. They were committed to Iraq and they viewed the idea of a Jewish state in Palestine as both unrealistic and disturbing.

This highly complex political environment, with its currents and crosscurrents of Iraqi conservatism, British colonialism, Arab national-ism, Zionism and Jewish-Iraqi anti-Zionism, shaped the life of my family in Baghdad until 1950. At this point, these currents morphed into tidal waves, laying waste to the world we had known before and plunging us into the new state of Israel. Looking back now, I can still barely grasp the profound effect of the Balfour Declaration's sixty-seven words and how they upended the life and fortunes of my family decades later.

Yusef and Saida Shlaim

THREE

IRAQI ROOTS

MY FATHER AND MY MOTHER HAD A STRONG SENSE OF BELONGING and a deep emotional attachment to Iraq. They had extended families, many friends, a support network, wealth and a high social status. Before the birth of Israel and the first Arab–Israeli war, the thought of leaving the country for good would have been inconceivable.

Although they were both Iraqi patriots, my parents were an odd couple: both came from Jewish families, but they were ill suited, having been brought together in an arranged marriage in Baghdad in 1942. The age gap between them was twenty-three years: my father was forty-one and my mother was only seventeen years old at the time of their marriage. Arranged marriages were the norm among Iraqi Jews in those days but this particular marriage was not entirely part of the norm: my mother was coerced by her family to marry a man old enough to be her father. Once the formal union was forged, both sides did their best to make it work. My father was a kind, gentle and generous man. My mother was resilient and realistic, quick to seize opportunities and always disposed to look at the bright side of life. As my father was very wealthy, she had ample material compensations for the sacrifice of freedom she had been forced to make. Moreover, the young bride gave birth to three children in rapid succession and this took up a fair share of her time and energy without curtailing her sybaritic lifestyle.

My father was born in Baghdad in 1901. He was an Iraqi Jew. His name was Yusef Shlaim. Yusef was the Jewish variant of the Arabic Yusuf and of the English Joseph. Shlaim was probably a German name that went back several generations. According to a story I heard from my mother but was not able to verify, my father's ancestor was a young German-Jewish doctor who went to help the Jews of Baghdad to cope with an epidemic at some point in the nineteenth century. The epidemic was said to affect mainly the poor Jews in the crowded Abu Sifain district of Baghdad. In the course of his work, the doctor treated a local Jewish girl, fell in love with her, married her and settled down. According to this story, the doctor travelled to Baghdad with two other Jewish volunteers who had recently completed their medical training, but only he stayed. The other two went back to Germany after completing their humanitarian medical mission. We do not know the first name of the doctor who stayed, nor do we know the exact German spelling of his surname – it may have been Schleim or Schlayyim. A search by a German graduate student of mine under all these variants bore no fruit. This led me to wonder whether the entire story might have been baseless. My father never mentioned a German ancestor. When I pressed my mother on the source of the story, she admitted that the source was not my father but one of his relatives. With regret, I relegated my paternal German ancestor to the realm of conjecture.

My father's father was an Iraqi Jew named Abraham and I was named after him – Abraham, or Abi for short. Abraham had four brothers and one sister. He married Lulu Beitchati, who was illiterate, not at all uncommon in the Iraq of those days though the ratio of illiteracy among Jews was considerably lower than among the Muslims. Abraham was a moderately wealthy man who owned land in the farming village of Dora on the outskirts of Baghdad and lived off the rent. His tenants were peasants who used primitive methods to cultivate the land. They took for themselves two thirds of the yield and paid Abraham the other third either in cash or in kind. This ensured that Abraham and his family had a regular supply of olive oil, dairy products, melons, watermelons and other fruit and vegetables.

Abraham had three sons and two daughters: Yusef (my father, the eldest son), Ezra, Itzhak, Rosa and Ragina. He used to ride to Dora on horseback to collect the rent from his tenant farmers and he carried on him a money belt. On one of his rounds, in 1914, robbers shot him dead and stole all the money. Abraham left behind a widow and five little orphans without a regular source of income. At this point, with the breadwinner lost, my father Yusef, as the eldest son, had to leave school and go out to work to support his family.

I do not recall a single occasion when my father talked about the past, either to me or to anyone else. Nor do I have any written records to help me piece together his story. How I wish I could interview him for this memoir, check facts and dates and get his perspective on his life and times. But he died of a heart attack on 3 December 1970, when I was twenty-five years old, and he left no records behind. At that time, I had just been appointed a temporary lecturer in International Relations at the University of Reading. My elder sister Lydia and our cousins, the children of Ragina, made arrangements for the funeral. Lydia, whose name was changed to Dalia after our arrival in Israel, informed me of the death of our father by means of an air-mail letter which reached me over a week later. She did this deliberately to spare me the filial duty of flying back to Israel to sit *shiva*, the Jewish ritual of seven days of mourning for the dead. Dalia's intentions were good, but her actions increased rather than reduced the pain of bereavement. I had to cope with the loss on my own, lacking any support. My grief was intensified by feeling that I had never properly known my father. Having been denied the chance to grieve for him properly, I would sink into a mild depression every year around the date of his death for many years after.

My main source of information for this early period in my father's life was my mother, and her account contained many lacunae and not a few internal contradictions. According to her, my father was not a good pupil at school, partly because he suffered from poor eyesight which his parents failed to diagnose. After his father was killed, the teachers at school stopped bothering with him, saying that the boy had no father and that his mother was ignorant. They were therefore not particularly sorry to see young Yusef leave school.

At the tender age of fourteen, my father embarked on what gradually turned into a highly successful and lucrative career as a businessman. He had a Jewish partner of roughly the same age, named Shouwa' Obaid. They bought and sold building tools and materials: cement, cement mixers, iron bars, doors, bricks, tiles, bathroom equipment and kitchen sets. They worked hard, developed their business, seized every opportunity that came their way and prospered. Soon their small shop could not accommodate the expanded volume of merchandise, so they rented a big storehouse – *khan* in Arabic. After the end of the First World War, in 1918, the British Army offered for sale on the open market all kinds of surplus items including scrap iron, machines, tools, cranes, water tanks and construction equipment. My father and his partner bought the equipment at very low prices and turned over a tidy profit. Their business expanded steadily. In time, they also became commission agents in Baghdad for European companies involved in construction. The British company Twyford, who specialised in bathroom sets, chose them as its agent in Iraq. German and other European companies also used them to export their goods and the young partners continued to prosper.

By making top-grade British and European products available for sale in their *khan*, my father and his partner acquired a large circle of customers that included senior public figures and cabinet ministers. King Faisal I was their most illustrious customer; his aides ordered supplies from them to build the Qasr al-Zuhur. This was the permanent residence that Faisal I had built for himself and his family after his temporary sojourn in Qasr Shashoua and this was where King Ghazi met his death. Government ministers would buy plots of land and build luxury villas on them for their families. They would get my father to supply the building materials for their homes, on their account. The credit facilities he extended were extremely generous and more often than not, the ministers failed to pay the money they owed or made only partial payments, but my father didn't insist.

Supplying goods without insisting on payment was a form of bribe. In Iraq of those interwar years, the practice was common, based on the tacit understanding that 'you scratch my back and I scratch yours'. The ministers would incur an obligation, and this disposed them to use their official position to return the favour when the opportunity arose. Return favours could take the form of purchasing supplies for their ministry at inflated prices, issuing import licences or granting exemption from certain categories of taxes. According to my mother, many Jewish merchants resorted to this kind of subtle or not-so-subtle way of bribing Muslim ministers and senior officials.

The successful partnership between my father and Shouwa' Obaid ended not because of changes in the economic or political climate but as a result of family problems. Obaid had a son who turned out to be a bounder whose vices included drinking, gambling and using the services of brothels. Eventually, the behaviour of the son was bound to spill over from the home to the business. In the end, the two partners went their own way by mutual agreement and without any acrimony. The business partnership ended but the friendship endured. As the French say, *tout casse sauf l'amitié* – 'everything breaks except friendship'.

On his own, my father continued to prosper. In 1939, he built for himself a large, well-appointed and strikingly elegant house. A German expatriate architect friend designed it for him. The house was near the YMCA and Orosdi-Back, the famous Jewish-owned upmarket department store, and opposite the Meir Taweig synagogue in the prosperous district of Bataween, which sprawls across central Baghdad. The house was located not far from the Tigris River which flows through the middle of the city and adds to Baghdad's architectural beauty with its array of old-fashioned bridges. The house had three floors, about ten rooms, three luxurious bathrooms and a large garden of manicured lawns, lush flower beds and tall palm trees.

By the time the house was completed, my father had won a reputation as one of the most eligible bachelors of the Jewish community in Baghdad. He was in his late thirties, wealthy, well connected and now the proud owner of a dream villa. All this made him a target for Jewish matchmakers who apparently bombarded him with proposals to wed young women whom they claimed would make suitable brides. My father, however, politely declined all the offers and bided his time. Eventually, without the help of matchmakers, my father set eyes on my mother and they got married in 1942. He chose her but she did not choose him: she was coerced by her family into this marriage. The reluctant bride moved into the large house and this became the family home until we were forced to leave Iraq in 1950.

My exploration of my family's roots took a dramatic turn in 2014 when I discovered that we had a connection with the Holocaust. A distant relative, of whose existence I had not been aware, took the initiative to get in touch with me. The relative was Keren Efrat Elimelech, neé Shlaim, the granddaughter of Haskell, my father's uncle. One day, in May 2014, Keren left a message for me on the telephone of the Middle East Centre at St Antony's College, Oxford. I called her back and we had two long conversations to compare notes about our common ancestors. From our conversations, I gained the impression that Keren was a religious Jew and an Israeli patriot who had time on her hands and was anxious to find out as much as she could about the history of her family. She had heard about me from a couple of relatives and got in touch to find out more. She was especially intrigued by the German provenance of our family. I told the little I knew about the putative German-Jewish doctor and expressed my frustration at not being able to obtain any details or dates.

As it turned out, Keren was in fact able to tell me more than I could tell her. Her own research suggested that there was a large Jewish clan that went by the name of Shlaim in Germany, that it was a peripatetic family, with branches not only in Iraq but in Iran, India, Czechoslovakia and other European countries. Keren's father, Mansour, had visited the Jewish cemetery in Prague and located the grave of some members of the family. One gravestone, bearing the Star of David like all the others, had the name of a Josef Shlaim whose date of birth was 1913. Next to Josef's lay the grave of a woman named Elka, possibly his wife. Joseph had four children, listed at the bottom of his gravestone, two on each side. Two of the names were Hugo and Rudolf. Each child had a different date of birth but the date of death for all of them was 1944. This suggested to Keren that the whole family had perished in the Holocaust. She had gone to Jerusalem to visit Yad Vashem, Israel's official memorial to the victims of the Holocaust. The names of her relatives appeared in their records, but no further details were available.

Keren's father had taken photos of the tombstone on his mobile phone and she promised to forward these to me by email, but never did. All my subsequent attempts to contact her were unsuccessful: she did not answer my emails or return my phone messages. I could only speculate on her reasons for breaking off contact. One possibility is that I was of no further interest to her but then one brief email would have sufficed to say so. A more plausible explanation is that I must have offended her in some way. Keren had not read any of my books although two of them were available in Hebrew editions. When she had asked me about my work over the phone, I had explained that I am a revisionist Israeli historian, one of the so-called 'new historians', and that I challenge the standard Zionist accounts of the causes and course of the Arab–Israeli conflict. Foolishly perhaps, I followed up by emailing to her one of the very few articles I had published in Hebrew, an article on 'New History and the First Arab–Israeli War'.

In 2017 I was invited by the Palestinian Embassy in Prague to speak at a conference they were organising to mark the centenary of the Balfour Declaration. At my request the conference organiser forwarded my inquiry about my namesakes to Suzana at the Jewish cemetery. Suzana was unable to find the names in the database; she needed more information. On 13 November 2017, I sent her a note with all the information I had received from Keren. More questions followed: which cemetery was it? Was it the one in the Old Town, or the one in Vinohrady? Was I sure it was a Jewish cemetery? Did I have the names of all four children? Was I one hundred percent sure it was the year 1944? As I was unable to answer these questions, the quest for my German ancestors' burial place reached a dead end.

One consequence of this somewhat frustrating quest was to prompt me to reflect on my own attitude to the Holocaust. Until my encounter with Keren, my feeling about the Holocaust was not dissimilar to that of most people: utter horror at the thought that such barbaric acts could even be contemplated, let alone perpetrated in the heartland of Christian Europe in the middle of the twentieth century. The Holocaust was the most horrendous phenomenon in modern European history but until that point it had not been part of my personal history. The Jews of the East had largely been protected by the accident of geography from the horrors of the Nazi genocide.

The discovery that five members of my own family could have been among the six million Jews exterminated by the Nazis did not change anything in the grand scheme of things, but it certainly influenced the way I felt about this tragic chapter in the history of my people. One immediate effect was to make me realise that by placing Israel's conduct in the 1948 war under an uncompromising lens, I had not made sufficient allowance for the fact that this war had occurred only three years after the Nazi genocide. I had underestimated the desperate Jewish need for a safe haven as a result of this trauma. The Palestinians were unquestionably the victims in the 1948 war: they lost their homeland and 750,000 of them became refugees. Yet, in Edward Said's apt formulation, they were the 'victims of victims'. Both victors and vanquished, as he poignantly put it, were inter-linked as 'two communities of suffering'. Several years would pass before I turned my attention to other victims of the Zionist project – the Jews of the Arab lands.

The other effect of the discovery of my personal connection with the Holocaust was, paradoxically, to make me more critical of Israel. The Holocaust has frequently been used by Israel's friends to explain its obsession with security and to justify its harsh treatment of the

Palestinians. Israel's more extreme critics, on the other hand, have occasionally denounced Israel's treatment of the Palestinians as no better than Nazi Germany's treatment of the Jews. Such comparisons are far-fetched: for all its sins, Israel has not engaged in genocide. But nor is it justified to use the Holocaust as moral blackmail to silence legitimate criticisms of Israel's treatment of the Palestinians. Dehumanising 'the other' is bound to have terrible consequences whoever 'the other' may be. Israel's systematic dehumanising of the Palestinian people certainly has had dire consequences; it prepared the ground for their oppression and brutalisation.

The Holocaust stands out as the archetype of a crime against humanity. For me as a Jew and an Israeli therefore the Holocaust teaches us to resist the dehumanising of any people, including the Palestinian 'victims of victims', because dehumanising a people can easily result, as it did in Europe in the 1940s, in crimes against humanity.

Mas'uda ('Saida') née Obadiah

FOUR

SAIDA'S STORY

My mother was born in Baghdad on 31 July 1924. Her father's British nationality – obtained by his birth in Bombay – extended to his wife and four children. My mother's maiden name was Mas'uda Obadiah, Saida (meaning joyful) for short. When we moved to Israel in 1950, she changed her name to Aida. She died in 2021 aged 96 in Ramat Gan, our hometown in Israel. She had two passports: one British, one American. Although she lived in Israel most of her life, she never acquired Israeli nationality. My mother used to tell anyone who would listen that the date of birth in her British passport was wrong. According to her, her father had bribed a British consulate employee with six bottles of whisky to put her down as three years older. She was rather vague about what possible advantage this could bring to her father.

As ever, my mother was an entertaining narrator – but not always a consistent one. But far be it from me to complain: her memory was phenomenal and forms the foundation of my attempt to reconstruct my family's past. In this chapter and the next I set out to tell Saida's story as I heard it from her over the years, as accurately as I can. My mother's life exemplifies the rich experience of what it meant to be an Arab-Jew both before and after the birth of the State of Israel.

Saida's maternal grandfather, Haskell Saltoun, hailed from a rich family of landlords, inheriting from his father a small fortune in the shape of forty keys to forty houses. The father told Haskell that their family should be able to live from the rent for these houses alone for seven generations without having to do any other work. Unfortunately, the patriarch failed to anticipate that his eldest son and heir would develop a taste for gambling.

In those days nearly all marriages in the Jewish community were arranged by the parents, often with the help of a matchmaker. The Jewish community was rather puritanical: girls were shielded from contact with men and even with boys. Despite these rules, there was always the risk of lapses and chance encounters. Haskell's mother was worried that he might meet someone who wasn't up to scratch by the family's standards, and she decided to leave nothing to chance. She arranged for him to be engaged to his orphaned cousin Habiba when she was only twelve years old, though the actual marriage did not take place until four or five years later.

Haskell's gambling habit began following the death of his father. He used to play cards in the evenings in his palatial home with members of the prominent Muslim families in Baghdad such as the Pachachis and the Haidaris. His friends liked him because his pockets usually bulged with money. Haskell, for his part, often contrived to lose in order to ingratiate himself with his guests; being a Jew in the company of upper-class Muslims apparently reinforced his naturally generous instincts. Whenever he ran short of money, he would sell a house. Ultimately there were no houses left. He was forced to earn a living and became a *saraf*, a moneylender. Despite the decline in his fortunes, Haskell retained his extravagant lifestyle and his easy-going disposition.

Saida's paternal grandfather, Isaac Shalom Yusef Obadiah, was born in Baghdad but as a very young man went to India and settled in Bombay, home to a large Jewish community, most of whose members hailed from Iraq. It was common for Baghdadi Jewish merchants to go east in search of new markets and new opportunities. In Bombay they maintained their Judeo-Arabic dialect, set up their own synagogues and communal institutions, and tended to marry within their own community. One of the best known and wealthiest Iraqi-Jewish families in Bombay were the Sassoons. From Baghdad they had moved to Bombay in the eighteenth century and became known as 'The Rothschilds of the East.' While the Rothschilds were bankers, the Sassoons were global merchants and manufacturers, reigning over a commercial empire that spanned Shanghai, Hong Kong, England and many more countries.[1]

Isaac joined the Sassoon family business, got on well with them and married the niece of his boss, Dawud Sassoon. The wife turned out to be, as my mother put it, 'not entirely normal'. After giving birth to a baby, she sank into post-natal depression. Washing the baby under a tap, she inadvertently drowned the infant. Her family put the distraught mother in a mental asylum where she died tragically young.

Isaac visited Baghdad in 1880 in search of a second wife. By now extremely prosperous, he set the matchmakers to work. They presented to him a parade of young women but none of them caught his eye until a visit to the Mani family where the grandmother, her daughter, and her granddaughter, Mas'uda, were baking *mahbooz*, date cookies. Mas'uda, who was sixteen or seventeen at the time, was hard at work with a rolling pin. She was very pretty, with dark hair and green eyes, and her cheeks were red from the heat of the oven. Isaac fell in love at first sight. On the spot, he offered to marry Mas'uda, to take her back to India with him, and to compensate her family for letting her go. The grandmother turned to Mas'uda and asked her whether she wanted to go to India. Without a moment's hesitation, Mas'uda replied 'Yes, yes!' The grandmother berated her for agreeing so readily to abandon them, but the deal was clinched on the spot to the delight of the matchmaker. Mas'uda's three brothers, Yehuda, Moshe and Menashe, did not witness the happy scene. Perhaps it was just as well for, as Isaac was later to find out for himself, they were, in Saida's words, 'fat, lazy, malevolent and good for nothing'.

At that time there were fifty-five synagogues in Baghdad so there was no shortage of places to pray, but Isaac was motivated to make a personal contribution to his community so he bought the home of Rabbi Aharon

Smooha and had it turned into the site for a synagogue. The synagogue was named Neve Shalom, the Oasis of Peace. Its more popular name was *slat s'hak shalom*, the Synagogue of Isaac Shalom. It was located in Mahalat El-Keshel, near al-Shorja in central Baghdad. Like most other synagogues in Baghdad, it was intended to serve not just as a place of worship but also as a community centre and a school for teaching Hebrew to Jewish children. Isaac stipulated that every year fifty rupees would be donated from the revenue of the synagogue to the Yeshiva of Ezra the Scribe near Basra, Yeshiva being an academy for the advanced study of Jewish texts.

According to Saida, her grandfather set out in the deed he deposited in the *tapo*, the land registry, that the synagogue would belong to the Jews of Baghdad so long as they used it as a place of worship, but ownership would revert to his descendants afterwards. Unable to verify this claim, I used to dismiss the notion that we were the legitimate heirs to a substantial piece of real estate in Baghdad. My mother, however, was not one to let go lightly of what she regarded as her absolute and indisputable right to the property. She must have told me the story of the synagogue and the alleged caveat in the deed a thousand times. Moreover, she insisted that because I was the only member of the family living in Britain and because I was a respected professor at Oxford, it was my duty to initiate legal proceedings to recover our synagogue. The pressure to act steadily intensified until eventually I relented – only to discover that, as Iraq had been at war with Israel since 1948, the Iraqi state would not consider any legal claim from a resident of Israel.

After the visit to Baghdad in 1880, Isaac Shalom Yusef Obadiah returned to Bombay with his young wife, Mas'uda. In Bombay he continued to prosper. His business specialised in the export of merchandise from India to Iraq, and he and his second wife enjoyed a luxurious lifestyle in a grand villa, with a horse-drawn carriage and a retinue of Hindu servants. They used to holiday in Pune, a holiday resort with cool weather near Bombay, with other members of the Sassoon family, taking with them a singer and a violinist, Nahum al-Kamanjati (*Kamanja* is the Arabic for violin).

Mas'uda smoked a water pipe or hubbly-bubbly (known as a hookah), unusual for women in those days. She had a splendid hookah made of gold and lavishly decorated. One day it disappeared. The police were called in; they lined up all the servants, and when no one owned up to the theft, they ordered them to crouch and stand up repeatedly without a break. This was a form of torture. It went on until an elderly woman servant collapsed from exhaustion and confessed that she had stolen the hookah and hidden it on the roof. A short prison sentence was both her arbitrary punishment by the police and a harsh warning to the other servants. Cruelty always lurked beneath opulence in Bombay.

Isaac and Mas'uda had four boys: Meir, Abdullah, Salman and Joseph. The eldest son was Meir, Saida's father and my grandfather. He was born in Bombay on 16 September 1882. His full name was Meir Isaac Shalom Obadiah. Having made his fortune and lived in India for over fifty years, Isaac decided to sell his business, realise his assets and return to Baghdad to retire. His wife was especially keen to return to Baghdad to re-join her family. When Isaac died, he bequeathed to his four children his enormous wealth. As the eldest son, Meir managed the inheritance. My mother depicted the sons as feckless, indolent and gluttons to boot. For a fair number of years, Meir and his brothers led a life of leisure. They lived in the large parental home, kept a pleasure boat on the river, ate well and consumed large quantities of Arak, a distilled Levantine spirit of the anise drinks family with an alcohol content of 40–63%. They threw parties for which they hired famous singers and spent money prodigally. According to one apocryphal story the brothers spent their days lying in hammocks tied to trees in the garden, and every now and again a servant would come around with a bottle of Arak to refill their glasses.

During this carefree phase of his life, Meir met and rather reluctantly married Mouzli Haskell Saltoun. He was an eligible bachelor, well-educated and wealthy, and most Jewish parents would have been thrilled to have him as their son-in-law. Many young women were presented to him by matchmakers, but none satisfied his exacting requirements. One day they introduced him to Mouzli, a tall girl with curly black hair, not particularly pretty but clever, lively and amusing. He was informed that Mouzli came from a good home and would be a devoted wife and mother. Meir had just come from his boat where he enjoyed singing, playing the accordion and sipping Arak. Drunk, he didn't judge Mouzli by his previous high standards. By chance, he knew her father, Haskell Saltoun – a great boon. Haskell, as noted earlier, was a genial, easy-going and malleable character. Meir used to call him *mai bali wa'ash ikhalif*. Roughly translated, this meant: 'No worries, it's OK, it doesn't matter'. When Mouzli was introduced to him, he said: 'Oh, she is the daughter of *mai bali wa'ash ikhalif!*' He assumed that Mouzli would be as sweet-natured and mild-mannered as her father and he was persuaded to get engaged to her.

Meir soon realised he had made a terrible mistake. His fiancée was difficult and argumentative. He informed the Rabbi that he had had second thoughts and wanted to annul the engagement. The Rabbi panicked: in Baghdad in those days an engagement entailed a signed document, analogous to a marriage contract. He ruled that if Meir wanted to annul the engagement, he would need to pay Mouzli's family five hundred gold coins, as specified in the document, to compensate them for the disgrace. Reluctantly, Meir took out five hundred gold coins, gave them to his maternal uncle, Menashe Mani, and asked him to hand them over to the Rabbi with a curse.

Walking along the river towards the Rabbi's home, Menashe passed a man on a boat in the river, shouting 'One dinar to Basra! One dinar to Basra!' Menashe reflected: 'Am I building a home or destroying one? This money is not for a marriage but for a divorce.' Instead of delivering the money with a curse, he bought a ticket to Basra whence he went by boat to India and disappeared. Meir did not have another five hundred gold coins to spare, so he went ahead with the marriage to Mouzli. Following the birth of three sons in rapid succession, fifteen years into the marriage, Mouzli gave birth to a baby girl whom they named Mas'uda.

At some point after Meir got married, Abdullah, one of his brothers, caught up with him and asked 'Where is my share of our father's legacy?'

Meir replied that he had spent most of it in bringing up Abdullah and their other two brothers. Abdullah rejected this explanation and took Meir to court. The judge ruled in Abdullah's favour. As by this time Meir had no money left, the bailiffs came to seize the contents of the house, including Mouzli's sewing machine. This infuriated her. She remonstrated with the judge, telling him that the sewing machine belonged to her – it was a wedding present from her parents. The judge was unmoved. He was Jewish and his first name was Sha'ul. Mouzli addressed him not as 'Your Honour' but as *sha'ul al-aswad* – black Sha'ul – and shouted: 'Doesn't your wife own her sewing machine?!'

Stripped of the remnants of his inheritance and his worldly goods, Meir had to find a job. His forte was in languages: he spoke Arabic, English, French, Turkish and Persian. He had moved with his parents from Bombay to Baghdad when he was about sixteen, and in Baghdad he attended the Alliance school for boys, which in those days taught the main languages of the Ottoman Empire. Meir spoke Arabic with an Indian accent, but his command of English was impressive. He was hired as an interpreter in the British consulate in Baghdad. Eventually, Meir resigned from his post there and got a job as an accountant in one of the ministries of the Iraqi government.

A nationalist wave sweeping through Iraq since the 1930s brought his career to an end. Meir was told that if he wanted to keep his job, he had to give up his British nationality. This involved an agonising choice. At first Meir was inclined to stick with his job and lose the passport. But on second thought, he decided to hold onto his passport. He left the civil service and regretted nothing. On the contrary, he gave a party to celebrate his defiance of the powers that be and his success in retaining his British passport, an object of great pride. He displayed the document alongside the celebratory cake, drank generous libations of Arak and sang English songs as he played his accordion.

Meir didn't stay unemployed for long. He joined his younger brother Joseph, a commodity trader with an import-export business. He had links with merchants in Asia and Africa and used to buy from them various goods such as tea, coffee, sugar and spices. Joseph had a list of prices, and his Iraqi clients would place an order and pay on delivery. The brothers prospered, buying new villas for their families.

Saida recalled her childhood in Baghdad with great nostalgia. She considered herself a lucky child, pampered by her extended family. As the only girl, she was the focus of much attention. Her father doted on her. She had three considerably older brothers and seven maternal uncles some of whom travelled on business and brought her sweets, all kinds of toys and fashionable clothes. She was also encouraged to pursue any leisure activities she liked. As an infant, she would plunge into the water at every opportunity – the origin of her passion for swimming. At the age of five, she began to have swimming lessons with the teacher who had previously coached her brothers. She was increasingly adventurous in the waters of the Tigris, jumping off bridges, doing stunts and participating in competitions. On top of this, she pursued horseback riding and dancing.

Unlike the men in the family, Mouzli did not display much physical affection towards her daughter. She was caring, but not demonstrative. As a cook, Mouzli did not distinguish herself either. The meals she cooked were fairly basic; the staple diet was chicken and rice. When serving the chicken, she would give the breast and legs to the men and the wings to little Saida. When Saida protested mildly against this discrimination, her mother replied that she was a girl and not a boy so she needed wings in order to fly away from home, to get married and bring up her own family.

Saida received her education at the Laura Kadoorie School for Girls in Baghdad – the most renowned 'Alliance' school. Alliance was the short name for the *Alliance Israélite Universelle*, a Paris-based Jewish organisation founded in 1860 by wealthy French Jews to bring the light of the West to their co-religionists in the East. It sought to combine heritage with modernity and to excel in both general and Jewish studies. The motto of the organisation was the rabbinic injunction 'All Jews bear responsibility for one another.' Its schools emphasised European languages, especially French, and modern sciences. The main language of instruction was French, the language in which History, Geography, Maths and the sciences were taught.

The Alliance used secular education as a vehicle for social mobility. It had an explicit '*mission civilisatrice*': to lift the Jews from what some regarded as the backwardness of the Arab lands. In 1864, the first Alliance school for boys was opened in Baghdad. In 1893 a school for girls was opened. The values of the organisation were openness, tolerance and equality of opportunity, and as such it did not exclude non-Jews. As the reputation of the Alliance went up, a few Muslims and Christians began to send their children to its schools. In this Westernised, cosmopolitan environment, Saida received her elementary and secondary education. One of her early memories was a visit to the Laura Kadoorie school by King Faisal I in the company of the Chief Rabbi and other leaders of the Jewish community. Faisal made a point of visiting every Jewish school in Baghdad in his quest to embrace minorities and to forge a unified Iraqi nation.

In Saida's recollection, the Alliance was a happy and progressive school with particularly high standards in languages: the French teachers came from Paris, the English teachers from London, and some of the Arabic teachers from Beirut, one of the cultural centres of the Arab world. Saida did not excel in her studies, however. She was more interested in sporting activities, dancing, clubs, parties and having fun. She left school at the age of seventeen with varying degrees of competence in four languages. Because she had been taught in French, she spoke it fluently, with no trace of an accent. Well into her nineties she would show off by declaiming Archimedes' principle in French.

The Alliance Israélite Universelle was at odds with the Zionist movement which emerged in Europe towards the end of the nineteenth century. Zionism demanded that the Jews leave their homes and join in the project of building an independent Jewish state in the Middle East. The Alliance, on the other hand, sought to maintain Jewish communities as integral members of their respective societies. As a result, the two movements found themselves in a tug-of-war over the Jewish communities throughout the Arab and Muslim worlds. [2]

Growing up, Saida was unaware of this battle of ideologies gradually pulling the global Jewish community apart. Her school promoted Iraqi patriotism like any other school, with the girls all singing a paean to the goodness of Faisal I as 'the best king in the world'. In 1933, when Faisal died in suspicious circumstances, she and her classmates all wept, calling for Bern to be burned to the ground and the destruction of Switzerland.

The Alliance's school for boys inculcated similar values and its alumni seized the professional opportunities offered by the British mandate and its successor state, ending up as civil servants, administrators and accountants. Two of Saida's brothers became officers in the intelligence corps of the British Army. By this time, a more assertive Iraqi nationalism was on the move – and a revolt was in the making. No one knew then how consequential it would be for the future of Arab-Jews.

Saida in Trafalgar Square

FIVE

THE BRITISH CONNECTION

IN 1941, SAIDA WAS SIXTEEN YEARS OLD. WAR RAGED IN EUROPE, and its horrors approached Baghdad, a world away from her former sheltered existence. As xenophobia hit fever pitch across the country, British citizens and Jews suddenly found themselves facing new dangers – and Saida was both. Lurking in the shadows of the new Iraqi nationalism, Rashid Ali al-Gaylani prepared to seize the reins of power once more. He was anti-British, pan-Arabist and pro-Nazi. He hoped that an Axis victory would help Iraq to achieve full independence. The Regent, Abd al-Ilah, had pressured him to resign as prime minister in January 1941, after he had refused to sever ties with Mussolini's Italy. Rashid Ali would not take this defeat lying down.

Rashid Ali was enthusiastically supported by four army officers known as the 'Golden Square'; they rejected the monarchy and the politicians imposed by Britain from 1921 onwards. As Nazi Germany intensified its propaganda in Iraq, anti-British sentiment became intertwined with antisemitism. For the Golden Square, the British were foreign colonisers – and the Jews were their imperialist agents. Iraq was part of a larger Arab nation to which the Jews did not belong.

Anti-Jewish propaganda was also circulated by a group of Arab refugees from Palestine. At their head was the Grand Mufti, Haj Amin al-Husseini, the leader of the Palestinian national movement, who had fallen out with the British because of their sponsorship of a national home for the Jewish people in Palestine. In 1939 Haj Amin had arrived in Iraq and begun to denounce the local Jews for their alleged collaboration with both the British and the Zionists. He did not distinguish between Zionism – a settler colonial movement – and Judaism – a religion. He spoke of the Jews of Iraq as 'the internal enemy'. His message was picked up and recycled by right-wing newspapers and rabble-rousing politicians. Therefore, while antisemitism in Baghdad was clearly on the increase, it was more of a foreign import than a home-grown product.

The forced resignation of the nationalist government exacerbated mistrust of Britain and the royal family. Rashid Ali, together with the members of the Golden Square, made plans to assassinate Abd al-Ilah and seize power. On 31 March, Abdul-Illah discovered the plot; he and the rest of the royal family fled to Jordan, which was ruled by another branch of the Hashemite family. The following day, the Golden Square executed their coup d'état. Two days later, the 'National Defence Government' replaced the government of the Regent with Rashid Ali once again becoming prime minister. One of the first acts of the new government was to send an Iraqi artillery force to confront the RAF base in Habbaniya and to begin a siege.

Field Marshal Archibald Wavell, the commander-in-chief of the British forces in the Middle East, and Sir Kinahan Cornwallis, the British ambassador to Iraq, favoured negotiations with the rebels but Winston Churchill saw this as tantamount to appeasement and overruled them. For the embattled empire the stakes were high. The Mediterranean fleet depended completely on oil sent from Mosul to the refineries in Haifa down a 600-mile-long pipeline. In the words of *Time* magazine, this was the 'carotid artery of the British Empire'. [1]

Iraq was also an important land bridge between Egypt and India. Fearing a pro-Nazi bridgehead in the Middle East and the loss of control over Iraq's oil fields, Churchill ordered forceful military action. Following his orders, an Indian army contingent landed in Basra while British-led

Arab Legion troops (Habforce), were sent across 1,000 kilometres of desert from Jordan. The two forces converged on Baghdad in a pincer movement. By the end of May, Britain had completed the reoccupation of the country in what amounted to a reversal of the independence the country had gained, at least nominally, back in 1932. The British termed their action 'The Thirty Days' War'. The purpose of the military intervention was to effect regime change. On 29 May, Rashid Ali, the Grand Mufti, and forty of their supporters panicked and fled to Iran and from there to German-occupied Europe, leaving behind a serious power vacuum. A wag in the Foreign Office, invoking an old Iraqi children's story, promptly dubbed them 'Ali Baba and the Forty Thieves'. On 31 May, Cornwallis negotiated an armistice with the Iraqi forces.

During the brief interregnum that followed, disaster struck in the shape of a violent pogrom against the Jewish community in Baghdad, which became known by its Arabic name as the *farhud*. Literally, the word means 'the breakdown of law and order'. The man who bore the largest share of the responsibility for this catastrophe in the Iraqi capital was Cornwallis, a giant of a man, well over six feet tall, aloof and arrogant and rather devious. Once the British forces reached Baghdad, they were placed under his command rather than their military superiors, and the ambassador was an appeaser.

On the morning of 1 June, the Regent returned to Baghdad and set about the task of forming a loyalist government. Two days earlier, Habforce, the British motorised column from Jordan, had arrived at the city's outskirts, about five kilometres short of the centre. Cornwallis ordered Habforce to stay where they were, not to cross the Tigris, and not to enter the city. The Indian army force, en route from Basra, was ordered by Cornwallis to halt its advance and camp thirteen kilometres from Baghdad on the west side of the Tigris. The reason behind these strange orders was Cornwallis's desire to avoid the impression that the Regent had returned to power due to British military intervention. The presence of British bayonets in Baghdad, he argued, would lower the dignity of their ally. [2] Yet that was the stark reality: there was no way the unpopular Regent, who was widely regarded as a British stooge, could have returned to power without the support of those British bayonets.

Keeping the army at arm's length was a fatal miscalculation. It resulted in chaos because there were no policemen on the streets to keep the peace. Moreover, the armistice that Cornwallis had signed allowed the Iraqi army to enter the capital as long as it remained on the east side of the Tigris. The east side included downtown, the *souks*, the commercial centre and the quarters in which most of the Jews lived. Civilians were thus abandoned to the tender mercies of defeated but still armed and angry soldiers seeking revenge. The Jews were an obvious target because they were perceived as the friends of the British. As Elie Kedourie, the Jewish-Iraqi-British scholar pithily put it: 'It was thus as supporters of the British that the Jews of Baghdad were murdered and looted.' [3]

Suspicions that the Jews were disloyal to their country were fed by a misunderstanding. A group of Iraqi soldiers crossing the Khirr Bridge to the west side of Baghdad saw a small group of Jews in festive clothes, walking in the opposite direction. Since it was Sunday, not the Jewish Sabbath, the soldiers assumed that the Jews had dressed up in order to welcome the Regent. That Sunday happened to be the first day of the holy Jewish festival of *Shavuot*. *Shavuot* marks the end of the wheat harvest and also commemorates the anniversary of the day God gave the Torah to the people of Israel assembled at Mount Sinai. For the feast the Jews dressed up in their finest clothes, mostly white, and celebrated in the streets on their way to the synagogue. The soldiers attacked the Jews, killing one and wounding sixteen others, and sparking a wave of riots. An innocent celebration of a Jewish festival became the spark for a barbaric pogrom. An angry mob armed with knives, sticks and axes set upon the Jews on buses, in the streets, and in their houses in Jewish as well as mixed neighbourhoods. In the evening, a bus full of Jews was stopped by a frenzied mob and its passengers were dragged out, slaughtered and mutilated.

At night, soldiers, civilians and armed young men attacked more Jewish homes. They murdered, raped, looted and set houses on fire. The next day saw more rioting and arson with the arrival of people from out of town. Most of the newcomers were slum-dwellers from the other side of the Tigris River and Bedouins who had settled on the outskirts of the city. Whereas the first day featured vicious anti-Jewish atrocities, the second day saw peasants and paupers from the periphery coming to loot and accordingly heading for the well-to-do Jewish areas.

In two days of anarchy, 179 Jews were killed and several hundred more injured. The dead were buried in a mass grave and the wounded taken to hospitals; 586 shops and 911 houses were looted. The damage was estimated at several million pounds at the time. The riot was not quelled until the evening of the second day – suppressed very quickly once the Regent gave the army the order to shoot. The delay in issuing the order was apparently caused by his fear of antagonising the fiercely anti-British Iraqi armed forces; he had awaited the arrival of Assyrian troops from Kirkuk who were uncontaminated by Nazi propaganda and were loyal to him. The operation claimed the lives of around one hundred non-Jews, mostly unarmed looters.[4]

The *farhud* shook the entire Iraqi-Jewish community to its core. For some it marked the destruction of the Jewish Iraqi paradise. Such a vicious assault on the Jews was completely unexpected and unprecedented. There had been no other attack on the Jewish community in recent centuries. It was contrary to the teachings of the Qur'an and violated the Sharia laws about the treatment of *ahl al-dhimma* or 'protected minorities'. The 'Iraqi orientation' that had taken root since the 1920s was now called into question. Serious doubts were raised about the possibility of Muslim–Jewish coexistence in their common homeland. The leaders of the community were obliged to engage in honest soul-searching.

At first it seemed that the dream of integration into Iraqi society had been irretrievably shattered by the events of 1–2 June. But after the initial shock had worn off, the majority of the leaders – the Chief Rabbi and the elected council of sixty members – regained hope that life could return to normal. They discouraged the many members of their community who wanted to emigrate in the immediate aftermath of the *farhud* and stressed the importance of reintegration. Not long after the event, the leaders came to see the *farhud* as an aberration, as the product of peculiar circumstances in the interregnum between the demise of a fascist regime and its replacement by a more benign one.[5] Prosperity, boosted by the war economy, reinforced the belief in the possibility of a better future.

While the older generation of Jews tended to follow their leaders, the younger generation was much more sceptical. For them the *farhud* was not just a passing episode but proof of unalterable Muslim hostility. The rebels were divided into two main groups: the supporters of Zionism and the supporters of Communism. Both groups were profoundly dis-illusioned with Great Britain because the British army had stood at the gates of Baghdad while innocent civilians were being looted and killed. And both groups shared the premise that life for the Jews was unbearable in Iraq as it was then constituted. For the Zionists, the only answer was for Iraq's Jews to join the Zionist movement and emigrate to Palestine. The Communists thought that in order to be able to live in Iraq as equal citizens, a radical reform of the regime was required. They believed that the triumph of Communism in Iraq would put an end to discrimination against all minorities, including the Jews.

Although Saida was only a teenager at the time, she had vivid mem-ories of the *farhud*. Her story throws some light on the complex politics that lay behind the terrible tragedy that unfolded before her eyes. As the *farhud* was to assume such importance in the collective memory of Iraqi Jews, and as there are conflicting interpretations of these events, her recollections are worth relating in some detail. Besides this, nearly all the accounts of the *farhud* that are available to us were written by men. The Jewish community did not want to report the experience of women, especially those who were raped, and their stories were rarely told. Saida and her mother offer a rare female perspective.

At the heart of the existing literature lies a critical question: did the Iraqi Jews see the *farhud* as a continuation of a long and melancholy history, similar to that of the Jews of Europe, from the Middle Ages to the Holocaust? Some commentators maintain that the antisemitism displayed by the Muslims in 1941 was just another link in the long chain of hatred and persecution, a kind of Arab equivalent to *Kristallnacht* in Nazi Germany. Mark Cohen, a Princeton professor and a leading expert on Muslim–Jewish relations, examined the relevant Jewish-Iraqi memoirs of this period and concluded that their authors did not share this view. For them the *farhud* was not an antisemitic episode but rather the product of complex external political factors. In their eyes the *farhud* was not a link in a long chain of hatred and persecution but the beginning of a new chapter in their history.[6]

Saida's first-hand testimony has a bearing on this debate. It touches on various aspects of the *farhud* besides antisemitism. Her account brings to the fore the anti-British sentiments prevalent in Iraqi society at the time, sentiments that helped to spark both the nationalist revolt of Rashid Ali al-Gaylani and its bloody aftermath. In a sense, Saida's experience provides one small piece of evidence in support of both Mark Cohen's and Orit Bashkin's view that the *farhud* was not simply a manifestation of deeply held and widely shared Muslim antagonism towards the Jews but a more complex phenomenon.[7]

When Rashid Ali seized power, one of the last acts of the outgoing royalist government was to issue an announcement calling on all foreign nationals to seek protection in the nearest foreign embassy. Saida's parents had recently bought a large and beautiful mansion in the Karrada district on the east bank of the Tigris River. At the back of the house was a large garden with lawns, daffodils, marigolds, chrysanthemums, hollyhocks, wallflowers and a cluster of palm trees. None of her brothers was married yet and all of them lived in the family home. The parents did not heed the outgoing government's call. They were reluctant to abandon their new home and they also felt that because they were old, they were not likely to be harmed. The brothers would have chosen to go to the British embassy, but it was far away on the west side of the river whereas the American embassy was on their side. They decided to go to the American embassy instead. The parents asked the brothers to take their teenage sister with them, fearing she would be vulnerable if she stayed at home. So all four siblings trooped off to the American embassy and stayed there for a month until the crisis subsided.

One specific reason for the parents' concern for the safety of their daughter was that in the Karrada, not far from their house, was the Royal Military Academy, a school for officer cadets. The training period lasted six months and on graduation the cadets earned the rank of 'Naib Thabit' or Deputy Officer. The daily drill of the cadets, under the supervision of a ferocious-looking sergeant-major with a handlebar moustache, took them past my grandparents' house. It had not taken the cadets long to spot the pretty schoolgirl who lived in the house. When they approached, the sergeant-major would scream an order to turn all heads to the left but the cadets would swivel their eyes to the right in the hope of catching a glimpse of her.

Although the defenestration of the royal family was followed by a period of great anxiety and stress, Saida had a merry time in the embassy. At this young age, she had an enviable knack for making the most of any new situation. The American hosts, from the ambassador down, behaved with unfailing courtesy and consideration towards their uninvited guests. The guests included a number of Iraqi Jews, but the majority were American citizens who owned businesses in Baghdad or worked for the oil companies. The embassy allocated one building for the women and one for the men. The food was adequate, but some commodities were in short supply because of the emergency. One owner of a department store was able to arrange special deliveries of food. No one complained except one young woman who loved food and kept demanding more. When asked why she was so needy, she replied: 'I am Sandy, not Gandhi!' Every evening a show was put on for the benefit of the guests. Saida's older brother Isaac helped to entertain the guests and the embassy staff by putting on a false moustache and mimicking Adolf Hitler.

A young and handsome American diplomat in his mid-twenties took a shine to Saida. His name was Elmore Evans. In the afternoon, when most of the guests relaxed in the gardens of the embassy, Elmore gave Saida private English lessons. They got on well together. He liked her, she liked him and they enjoyed each other's company. By Saida's account, they flirted but did not kiss. One day Elmore said to his attentive sixteen-year-old pupil: 'My God, I want to tell you the most beautiful thing in the world, but I can't because you are too young.' What he probably meant was that he was in love with her and that had she been a bit older, he would have proposed marriage.

Saida's parents were not allowed to stay at home during the emergency. Rashid Ali's government announced that all foreigners were going to be moved to prison camps for the sake of public safety. The announcement did not mention Jews specifically, only foreigners in general. A few days later policemen turned up at the house to arrest Saida's parents. Mouzli protested that that she was an Iraqi, not a foreigner. The policeman said to her: 'You should be ashamed of yourself for marrying a foreigner, and not any old foreigner but an Englishman!' Mouzli retorted: 'Well then, take my English husband and let me go home to my Iraqi family.' The policeman said: 'This kind of talk will get you nowhere.'

Mouzli and Meir were taken to a camp where tents had been hastily erected to accommodate the foreign internees. The conditions in the camp were spartan but not degrading. With the horrors of the twentieth century behind us, the spectre of camps call to mind the worst violations of human rights. But these camps, although focused on 'containing' the foreigners, did not display the cruelty we are now familiar with. Detainees were fed, watered and never subjected to physical abuse. They were not harassed or mistreated in any way. When a woman needed to go to the toilet, she had to be escorted by a policeman. Escorting Mouzli was an unpopular duty because she was fierce, feisty and argumentative. Each policeman tried to wriggle out of this duty when it was his turn and there was some amiable banter between them on the subject. At night there was a blackout to make it difficult for RAF pilots to identify Iraqi targets. RAF pilots were hardly likely to bomb any civilians, let alone British subjects, but her rebellious spirit prompted Mouzli to switch on the lights, deliberately and defiantly. When reprimanded by a policeman, she told him she wanted the British planes to come and kill all of them. When Britain reoccupied the country, all the foreigners were released and allowed to go back to their homes.

Saida and her brothers left the American embassy on 31 May and went to the home of their uncle Haroun, the brother of Mouzli, because he lived in Bab al-Sharji, then considered a safer neighbourhood. Saida and her brothers heard the screams of the victims and saw the flames but did not witness the atrocities. The following morning, Uncle Haroun's driver took them back to the American embassy where they stayed another two days until the riots were quelled by the police and order was restored. After the dust had settled, Saida learnt that the British had troops outside Baghdad but had not used them. The rumour mill suggested that the secret motive of the British was to turn the Jews into scapegoats for the national humiliation that they themselves had inflicted on the Iraqi army and the Iraqi people. In later life, Saida's suspicion fell on Sir Kinahan Cornwallis. The way she put it to me was that Cornwallis wanted to give the angry populace a chance to let off steam, but she thought that he probably did not anticipate the scale of the death and destruction that was to be visited upon the Jews as a result of his orders to the army. At the very least, she thought, the episode displayed callous indifference on his part to the fate of the Jews.

Saida recounted that many Muslims in the mixed neighbourhoods went to great lengths to help their Jewish neighbours and friends in their hour of need. Protection was given either by taking the Jews into Muslim homes or by standing outside the homes of the Jewish neighbours and preventing the rioters from attacking. It took a lot of courage, Saida added, to stand at the gate of a Jewish home and to say to the angry mob, 'You cannot come in here!' Tributes to the courage shown by Muslims during the *farhud* are found in numerous first-hand testimonies of Jewish survivors. Famously, the Muslim wife of an Iraqi colonel stood in front of her Jewish neighbour's gate with her husband's loaded gun and threatened to shoot anyone who came near them.

Saida's other noteworthy comment concerns the people who were not driven by hatred of the Jews but saw in the state of anarchy that prevailed an opportunity to loot and pillage. She illustrated this with a story of a shabbily dressed man who lived in a shack with no running water or electricity. He picked up an expensive radio from a Jewish-owned store and took it to his shack. As there was no power supply, the radio remained silent. Infuriated, the man banged the radio and shouted, 'Come on, sing! You sing for the Jews so why can't you sing for us?!'

Following the restoration of the monarchy and the appointment of a pliant government, the British became once again the ultimate arbiters of the country. They determined the composition of the cabinets and purged the army and the higher echelons of the civil service of anyone suspected of pro-Nazi or anti-British sympathies. The new Iraqi government, under Nuri al-Said, appointed a commission of inquiry into the events of 1–2 June 1941 and offered compensation to the victims. Eight of the assailants, including army officers and policemen, were condemned to death. This was part of a series of steps taken by the government to boost the confidence of the Jews, but the Jewish community remained apprehensive. They did not trust the police and feared a recurrence of the violence. Army officers and soldiers continued to lurk in Jewish neighbourhoods to extract money and to threaten retribution against anyone who gave information to the authorities about members of the armed forces who had taken part in the atrocities. Saida remembered the pervasive sense of insecurity and danger lurking wherever she went. She and her Jewish school friends began to wear *abayas*, the loose black overgarment worn by Muslim women, in order to conceal their Jewish identity. They also imitated the dialect of Iraqi Muslims, fearing their very voices would give them away.

War had more 'mundane' consequences as well. Saida did not sit her national examinations, as they were postponed. The following year, her family forced her to leave school and to get married. What happened to my father during the *farhud* was rather more obscure to me, until my cousin, Fouad Hamama, told me that my father was well protected during and after the event by his Muslim friends. In 1950, aged twelve, Fouad left Iraq illegally on his own to go to Israel and there he was given by the immigration officer a Hebrew name: Herzl Yonati. *Hamam* in Arabic means dove; in Hebrew it is *yona* – *yonati* in Hebrew means my dove. Herzl was the name of the visionary of the Jewish state and it indicated pride in Zionism.

Fouad was the son of Ragina, Yusef's sister. After the *farhud* Fouad was sent by his parents to stay with his uncle Yusef because their neighbourhood, poor and Jewish, was considered unsafe. Moreover, his uncle's house was guarded by two policemen, one on the street outside and one on the roof. This unusually high degree of protection, Fouad explained, was due to my father's close friendship with the Muslim chief of the Baghdad police. The two friends used to play cards together and go out to nightclubs. They also spent quality time with a troupe of German women dancers whose shows in cabarets had to be licensed by the local chief of the police. Since my father did not speak either German or English, conversation must have been rather limited.

How my father felt about the reoccupation of his country by the British is not known. What is clear is that his business suffered a serious setback. After the outbreak of the Second World War, he focused his energies on accumulating as much galvanised iron (iron coated with a layer of zinc) as he could. This earned him the sobriquet *malik al-zinku* – the king of galvanised iron. During the war this material was in great demand, especially by the British forces stationed in Iraq. Father's aim was to establish a monopoly so he could name his price for the product. After the British reoccupied the country, however, they imposed strict control over the economy and rigorous rationing of many strategic items, including all types of iron and steel. My father's wholesale store fell under the new regime. He could sell iron only to the British forces and at a price they fixed – the old price. His dream of becoming the emperor of galvanised iron was shattered. The man who imposed all the restrictions was the arrogant proconsul, Sir Kinahan Cornwallis, whom my father, like my mother, used to curse. As his name was difficult to pronounce, they chose an Arabic designation for him: *kalb ibn al-kalb* – a mutt born from mutts.

One member of our family was happy to collaborate with the British: Saida's elder brother Isaac or, to give him his full name, Isaac Shalom Meir Obadiah, a businessman who received commissions from British companies for distributing their goods in Iraq. Honesty, as I would discover later, was not one of his most striking qualities. He acted as the agent for a major British company in Baghdad. The company owned a large building in Baghdad which Isaac sold to a Jewish friend of his at well below its market price, pocketing a substantial bribe himself. When the bosses of the company found out about the side-deal, they fired their crooked local agent. Unashamed, with the proceeds Isaac bought a luxury villa in the Karrada district near the River Tigris and continued his dubious wheeling and dealing.

One of Isaac's lucrative lines of business was the sale of Scotch whisky. Following the outbreak of the Second World War, he needed to make a trip to Scotland to meet with his suppliers and this necessitated a visit to the British consulate in Baghdad to attend to the formalities. A clerk must have told the consul that there was an Iraqi man in the waiting room who spoke good English and who might be useful to them. Before long the consul himself came down and interviewed my uncle at some length. Many of the questions were about his qualifications and language skills. At the end of the interview the consul said: 'Mr Obadiah, we would like to offer you a commission.' 'That would be very nice,' replied my uncle, thinking the consul meant a business commission. It was on the tip of his tongue to ask 'How much?' but he did not utter the words. The consul went away and came back with a wodge of forms printed with the letterhead 'War Office'. As he was filling the forms, it gradually dawned on my uncle that the commission he was being offered was to become an officer in the British Army. He hesitated for a moment but then decided to go through with it. And that is how he became a lieutenant in the British Army. Once in the army, Isaac was assigned to the intelligence corps without any military training. No training was needed because his job was essentially that of an interpreter, especially for senior British officers at meetings with their Iraqi counterparts who spoke no English.

One day a British major-general arrived in town. He had to be escorted to a series of meetings with senior Iraqi officers and Isaac was detailed to interpret for him. On the way to the first meeting, Isaac took a deep breath and said to the general: 'Excuse me for pointing this out to you, sir, but in this country people would not respect you if your assistant is just a junior officer'. The general turned to him and said: 'Lieutenant Obadiah, when we return to base, go to the office and get yourself the temporary rank of a captain.' After the general went back to England, Isaac was ordered to revert to lieutenant. He made a fuss and threatened to resign from the army, telling the colonel who commanded his regiment that there was no justice in the British army and that there was discrimination against foreigners. The colonel, an Irishman who had risen from the ranks, was sympathetic to this argument; he encouraged Isaac to tell their commanding officer what he'd just told him. Isaac did and as a result he was allowed to keep the rank and insignia of a captain.

Thus it was that Isaac attended Saida's wedding in the dress uniform of a British army captain. The marriage itself had been forced on Saida by her family. She was only seventeen years old, a schoolgirl with a busy social and sporting life and no desire to be tied down. In those days most marriages in the Jewish community in Baghdad were arranged. Nor was it unusual to marry off young women to much older men, especially if they were wealthy. But in this case the marriage was not just arranged but imposed by the family on a reluctant teenager. The initiative came from my father-to-be, Yusef Shlaim, a 41-year-old bachelor who saw Saida at a party and was dazzled by her beauty, not realising how young she was. Yusef was a business associate of some of Saida's uncles and it was through one of them that he broached the delicate subject. The uncle consulted with Saida's parents, brothers and other uncles, and the consensus was in favour of accepting the offer.

One twist in the story was Saida's friendship with a handsome Muslim boy named Niazi and the fear that she would bring disgrace upon the family. He and Saida met in a horse-riding club and had a few surreptitious conversations in its less exposed corners. The dalliance between the teenagers was reported by an eyewitness to Saida's parents. By marrying Saida off, the family intended to nip in the bud her friendship with a Muslim and to protect the honour of the family. Business partnerships and playing cards with Muslims were one thing, intermarriage was another. It was an absolute taboo. Saida's father was the only member of the family who expressed reservations about the proposed match, arguing that the man in question was too old for her. But her father was outnumbered. For her mother Mouzli, who was more money conscious, the wealth of the suitor was the overriding consideration. She was excited by the thought that her daughter would marry a rich man and the owner of a magnificent residence that was the envy of the community. Another attraction was that the parents would not have to provide the customary dowry – the going rate at the time for families of their socio-economic class was 5,000 dinars. With her habitual sarcasm Mouzli turned on her husband and demanded to know: 'How else would we marry off the poor girl? With your father's millions?'

Saida was not allowed any say in the matter; she was simply informed that she was going to marry a man she had never met. All her protests were in vain. In the end she went on a hunger strike, locking herself in her room and refusing to come down for meals. Yet she did not go entirely without food. Her brother Salih had just come back from a business trip to Mosul and brought with him large bags with all kinds of nuts and dried fruit, which he kept in his room. Whenever Saida felt the pangs of hunger, she would sneak into Salih's room and help herself to the goodies. The hunger strike collapsed after a couple of days.

Getting married meant Saida would not have to go back to school to take exams. Isaac encouraged his sister to yield to the pressures of the rest of the family. He told her that if she married a rich man, she would be able to send her children to be educated in England. This argument could not have been very persuasive at the time, but it backfired on Isaac

later. When I was failing in school in Israel, at a time when my father
was unemployed, Saida insisted that her brother assume responsibility
for my education in England.

Saida did not meet her husband face-to-face until their engagement
party, or henna night as it was called. The party was a sumptuous affair
with lavish food, drink and entertainment and no expense spared. It took
place in the large mansion of Saida's parents in the Karrada which her
brother Isaac had bought with the proceeds of his dodgy side-deal. The
three floors of the house, the two roofs and the garden were decorated to
create a festive atmosphere. A list of about a hundred guests included the
families and extended families of the bride and groom, Saida's school-
mates, friends and acquaintances, and a few British army officers who
had been invited by Isaac and Salih. Among the guests were also several
diplomats from the American embassy who had offered a refuge to the
bride and her brothers the previous year, during the Anglo–Iraqi war.

Saida's fingers were covered with henna, a dye that fades after a few
days and which is supposed to bring good luck, and each guest was also
given a dab on the hand. Three famous Baghdadi women singers were
engaged to entertain the guests. One of them was Afifa Iskandar, an
Armenian Christian, considered to be one of the best female singers in
Iraqi history. Nicknamed the 'Iraqi Blackbird', she was rumoured to be
the lover of the mayor of Baghdad. Another was Salima Murad, popularly known as Salima Pasha, a Jewish singer whose fame had spread
far and wide. Despite being Jewish, she was the most popular singer in
Iraq at the time; Nuri al-Said, a former Ottoman officer, had given her
the honorific Ottoman title 'Pasha'.

Salima sang modern Arabic songs rather than the traditional *maqam*,
and she soon became part of the Iraqi musical canon. Salima was well
integrated into Iraqi society, having married another famous singer and
actor, Nazem al-Ghazali. He was a Muslim and she took the rare and
highly controversial step of converting to Islam. This was not strictly
necessary because Islam allows men to intermarry women of the other
Abrahamic religions – while a Muslim woman is formally forbidden to

marry a non-Muslim man regardless of his religion. A Muslim man is allowed to marry a Christian or a Jew, who are dignified by the Qur'an as the 'People of the Book'. Salima Pasha never visited Israel but stayed in Iraq until her death in 1974.

A small fortune, and a precious ring, were needed to entice the legendary Salima to sing at this private party. She arrived at midnight from the al-Jawahiri Club, where she performed every night, but once she got to the party, she stayed until dawn. She was accompanied by the al-Kuwaiti brothers who composed many of her songs. They were Jewish musicians, inseparable like Siamese twins, hailing from Kuwait as their name suggests. From Kuwait they had moved to Basra, and from Basra to Baghdad where they became superstars. Da'ud played the oud and Salih the violin. They composed songs that were innovative but rooted in tradition, hence their great popularity. They performed regularly in the al-Hilal Club, but reached a much wider audience through their weekly radio programme from the Baghdad Broadcasting House. Their forte was *maqam*, a unique musical form found only in Iraq. Their full band consisted of seven men, only one of whom, the percussionist Hussain Abdallah, was a Muslim. No live music was broadcast by BBH on the Jewish fast days of Yom Kippur and Tisha B'ab.

Another genre of women singers at the party were the Jewish *daqqaqa* (pl. *daqqaqat*), from *daqqa*, meaning 'beat'. *Daqqaqat* were a troupe of women, often related to one another, who sang and played drums at wedding parties for a modest fee, supplemented by tips from the guests. The troupe that came to this henna night consisted of five fairly elderly women, who sat on the floor with their drums and sang traditional wedding songs until the morning. They were eccentric, extrovert and humorous, and they generated a very jolly atmosphere. Their song 'Afaki' contained verses taunting the bride's mother for the ruses she employed to catch such a desirable groom. This song was not especially appropriate for this particular occasion, but no one raised objections.

People sat on the floor around the *daqqaqat* and joined in the singing and clapping. One of their most enthusiastic fans was the

American Consul General whose first name was William. He too sat
on the floor, having probably had a fair amount to drink, clapping and
cheering them. To show his appreciation, he even offered Saida the
highest prize he had to give – a visa to the United States. She asked
whether she would have servants, cooks and drivers over there. When
the answer was 'no', she politely declined the offer. The revelries went
on all night.

The wedding took place three days after the henna party, on
20 May 1942. Prior to the wedding, a marriage contract or *ketubah*
was signed by the groom in the presence of a Rabbi and two witnesses.
The ketubah outlined the rights and responsibilities of the groom in
relation to the bride and it also specified the amount of cash he would
owe her in case of divorce. The wedding party was held in the same
mansion as the henna party with the same décor, but it was a more
sedate and formal occasion with less music and more religious ritual.
Yet this too was a very glamorous affair. Saida, wearing a long, flowing
white dress, was led to the middle of the lawn by her brother Isaac – her
father was too ill to attend. Yusef wore a smart dinner jacket and white
gloves. He led Saida to the *chuppah*, a canopy held up by four poles.
The Rabbi conducted the marriage ceremony under the *chuppah* with
all the traditional prayers and blessings. He then handed the ketubah
to the bride. The next stage in the ceremony required the groom to
break a glass that was covered in paper and laid on the dais in front of
him. In what is an otherwise joyous occasion, the idea of this ritual is
to allow a moment of reflection. The groom recited in Hebrew Psalm
137, which translates as follows:

> If I forget thee, O Jerusalem,
> Let my right hand forget her cunning.
> Let my tongue cleave to the roof of my mouth,
> If I remember thee not;
> If I set not Jerusalem
> above my chiefest joy.

Loud cheering and clapping erupted the moment that the glass was broken. The guests kissed and embraced and kept repeating *mazal tov*, good luck! The ceremony was followed by a buffet dinner and more drinks. After dinner, the groom whisked his bride to his house in Bataween for their wedding night.

What transpired on the wedding night my mother shared with me for the first time on an outing to Bath in July 2019, when we were celebrating her ninety-fifth birthday. My elder sister Dalia, who lives in Tel Aviv, had come with her from Israel. My mother had some mobility problems and could not walk very far, but she refused the offer of a wheelchair because she considered it undignified. A cruise along the River Avon was ideal for her. After the cruise, my wife Gwyn and Dalia went on a tour of the Roman Baths while Aida and I went to have tea and cakes in the elegant Pump Room. A pianist playing Chopin and Strauss waltzes in the background added to the old-world ambience. In this unlikely setting my mother revealed in painful detail what I can now only think of as an assault, experienced nearly eighty years previously. I used to bombard my mother with questions throughout the time I worked on this memoir. On this occasion, however, without any prompting, she began the story of her wedding night, prefacing it by telling me that 'this is not for the book', meaning it was between us and not to be included in my memoir. She later lifted this prohibition.

On my mother's actual birthday, we cracked open a bottle of vintage champagne and sat down to a family dinner at our home in Oxford. Gwyn and I were joined by my younger sister, Vilma, who lives in London, and her daughter Amanda, as well as our daughter Tamar. After dinner, I invited my mother to repeat to the women the story she had told me in Bath. I was in two minds as to whether to retell the story in this book because it involved such intimate details and infringed my mother's privacy. Gwyn thought the story should perhaps be told for the light it sheds on the cruelty and insensitivity with which young women were treated in that society and the long-lasting effects of such treatment. As well as providing powerful

evidence of cultural practices that did not respect the autonomy or
the rights of women, it was interesting, she thought, because of the
effect on Aida of having her story heard by women who had a very
different perspective.

As was the custom, careful preparations were made for the deflower-
ing of the newly-wed bride in what was to be the marital home. Outside
the room stood Yusef's mother Lulu, his sister Rosa, and his niece Rachel.
Also present were Saida's venerable maternal grandmother, Habiba, and a
young female servant. Following the custom of the day, the bride's mother
was excluded. Again, following custom, a blood-stained handkerchief
was produced which was given to a driver whose task was to drive to
the Karrada and present it to the bride's mother as confirmation that the
honour of the family had stood the test. The driver expected a large tip
as he was the bearer of good news on an important occasion. Mouzli,
however, gave him a disappointingly small tip which Saida attributed
to her habitual stinginess. That night Saida's grandmother slept beside
her on the roof. The grandmother's task was to protect the girl in case
her husband tried to come to her for a second time.

My mother related this story in a calm and matter-of-fact manner,
but she did say that she was pushed into this sexual encounter suddenly
and without any anatomical or psychological preparation. She summed
up the whole experience in one word – 'terrible'. Her account gave rise
to an animated discussion, a kind of post-mortem between some of the
women present. My wife Gwyn, daughter Tamar, and niece Amanda took
part in the discussion. They were outraged by the brutal treatment to
which the teenage girl was subjected and called it rape. They questioned
the notion that the grandmother was there to protect Saida, arguing that
since the family had already forced her into the marriage and subjected
her to the ordeal, protection after the event was meaningless. Saida
herself did not say much during the discussion but the next morning,
at breakfast, having had time to reflect, she spontaneously opened the
subject up again, describing the experience which she had been forced
to undergo as a 'crime'. This was the strongest word she ever used about

this painful episode, stretching back almost eighty years. In a telephone conversation on 24 April 2021, two months before she died, she gave me permission to narrate this episode in my memoir, including more intimate details that I have opted to leave out.

Despite being forced into an arranged marriage, and despite the trauma of the wedding night, Saida quickly settled down to her new lifestyle as a lady of leisure. Pragmatism was her defining quality. In addition, there were ample material compensations in being married to a rich man. Marriage enabled Aida to leave behind the academic pressures of school and settle down to a new life as lady of the manor in her new home. Yusef, for his part, did everything in his power to smooth the transition and to pamper his young bride. By Saida's account, he was thereafter a perfect gentleman and a model husband: gentle, kind and considerate. He was also refined and had impeccable manners. So impressed was Saida with his good manners that she used to say to him: 'Where were you brought up – in Buckingham Palace?' Above all, Yusef was tremendously generous. One small example that Saida gave of his generosity is that he always kept cash in the right-hand pocket of his trousers as well as in his wallet. This meant that when they went out with friends to a café or restaurant, he was the quickest to produce money to pay the bill. And like Saida, Yusef was a gregarious social animal who enjoyed mixing with people, clubbing and dancing.

Yusef's family freed Saida from all the responsibilities that usually go with running a large establishment. His sister Rosa was in charge of the household, keeping a watchful eye on the motley crew of cooks, cleaners and gardeners. Social life consisted of a never-ending cycle of diplomatic receptions, official functions, parties, dinner parties, cards games with friends and visits to social clubs. A good deal of entertaining was done at our home. My father enjoyed having guests and he went to a great deal of trouble to make their visits as agreeable as possible. In this he was assisted by various members of his family. Around the side of the big house there was an outbuilding with three rooms and a bathroom

– two of his nephews, sons of his sister Ragina, lived there. One was the aforementioned Fouad, born in 1937, and the other was his elder brother Ezra, born in 1926. Both brothers moved to my father's house after the *farhud* because it was safer than staying in their poor Jewish neighbourhood. Their father, Liyahu (Eliyahu) Hamama, had a shop in the old market of Shorja, selling coffee, tea, nuts of all kinds, dried fruit and a vast array of spices. He regularly delivered these delicacies to the extended household.

Ezra was my father's favourite. He was a sensible, well-mannered and helpful young man who attended Shamash, the local Jewish high school. My father, who liked to lay on large quantities of food, nibbles and refreshments, could always count on Ezra to help with preparations and then attend to the guests throughout their visit. One day the guests arrived, but Ezra was on the roof with a friend, and did not go down to help. After the guests had left, my father scolded him and slapped him on the face. Ezra was hurt and deeply offended. He mumbled in self-defence that he had an exam in school the next day which he and his friend had been revising for. This incident happened in 1944 and soon after that Ezra left Iraq illegally and went to Palestine with the help of the Zionist underground. My mother speculated that the slap on the face prompted Ezra to approach Zionist emissaries. In fact, as I was later to learn from my cousin Fouad, Ezra was a committed Zionist and a longstanding member of its underground movement. He was entirely successful, however, in concealing his Zionist activities from his uncle. The slap on the face was unlikely to have been more than a minor factor in his decision to quit and start a new life in Palestine.

In any case, the story had an unhappy ending. On arrival in Palestine, Ezra changed his surname from Hamama to Zait, which means olive in Hebrew (and in Arabic). He joined Kibbutz Maoz Hayim where he drove a tractor, got married and volunteered to serve in the Haganah, the pre-independence paramilitary Jewish force. With the outbreak of the first Arab–Israeli war in May 1948, he joined the Givati Brigade and he died in action against the Egyptian army, defending Kibbutz

Nitzanim in the Negev. His wife Nehama was pregnant at the time. At their last meeting, Ezra told Nehama that if he did not come back from the front, and if she gave birth to a boy, to ask the boy when he grew up to avenge his blood. Nehama gave birth to a girl whom she named Tikva, the Hebrew word for hope. Nehama told Fouad about his brother's last wish. Fouad, who was renamed Herzl on arrival in Israel in 1949, told me that he felt he had fulfilled his elder brother's wish to be avenged by fighting with the IDF (Israel Defense Forces) against the Egyptian army in three wars: the Suez War of 1956, the June 1967 War and the October 1973 War.

One day in Israel, when I was my early teens, I was looking through an album of Israeli casualties from the 1948 war, which had been lent to me by our next-door neighbour, and came across the name of Ezra Zait (Hamama). There was a small headshot, the dates of birth and death, and one or two other details. I showed the picture to my father, who was visibly moved, even agitated. He was shaken by the picture of his dead nephew, but said nothing except asking me where I had found the album. Knowing what I know now about the circumstances of my cousin's departure from our home in Baghdad the year before I was born, I wonder whether my father may have been overwhelmed by a sense of guilt. But at the time he said nothing; he just looked stunned and upset. On this, as on many other occasions, he seemed unable to express his own feelings in words.

My mother was much more outgoing, more articulate and more talkative. One of the few things expected of her as a married woman was to bear children, and she gave birth to three in rapid succession. My sister Lydia was born on 14 February 1944, I was born on 31 October 1945 and my younger sister Vilma was born on 1 December 1948. My birth marked a generational change in the history of the family. My maternal grandfather Meir was languishing on his deathbed at home in Karrada, laid low by liver cancer. His daughter Saida was in the ninth month of her pregnancy, carrying his second grandchild. Mouzli and their eldest son, Isaac, were by his bedside in the last week of his life. They did not tell Saida about her father's terminal illness because they feared it might affect her health and imperil the baby.

A three-page letter written by Isaac to his brother Alfred, who lived in Tehran, gives many details about the circumstances surrounding their father's death. According to this letter, Meir started complaining of pain in his stomach two years before his death. The middle brother Salih took him to the Jewish hospital, Meir Elias. The doctor at this hospital thought that Meir had worms in his stomach and prescribed what he thought was the appropriate medicine. This turned out to be the wrong diagnosis and the treatment may have contributed to his death. When Meir's condition deteriorated, Isaac was summoned from Cairo. Seeing how weak and pale his father was, Isaac turned to the Army Medical Directorate in Baghdad for help. Dr Sinderman answered his call and accompanied him to Karrada to examine the patient. Dr Sinderman's diagnosis was that the patient was suffering from cancer of the liver and that nothing could be done to save him. As Meir was unable to eat, his carers dipped cotton wool in rose water and sugar to wet his lips. He passed away at 1600 hours on 6 November 1945, the day of my circumcision. Mouzli returned home post-haste from the circumcision ceremony and placed a piece of Turkish delight in her dying husband's mouth. Meir gave a faint smile, drew a deep breath and expired peacefully.

Avi in Baghdad at the age of four

SIX

MY BAGHDAD

I WAS TWO OR THREE YEARS OLD, IN THE CARE OF MY NANNY, sitting on a Persian rug on the roof of our house, surrounded by toys of various kinds, including a grotesquely large pair of plastic scissors. I chose to try out the scissors on my nanny's big toe. She seemed to enjoy the game hugely, roaring with laughter, and encouraged me to press harder and harder on the scissors. The harder I pressed, the louder were her giggles. This is one of the earliest and most vivid memories of my childhood. The episode is a miniature of my family life in Baghdad: we led a relaxed and comfortable lifestyle, surrounded by nannies and servants; I was privileged and pampered, and even seemingly naughty behaviour on my part was met with affectionate indulgence; the end result was a happy and care-free childhood.

I was born in Baghdad on 31 October 1945. As I drew my first breath, my grandfather Meir, in another part of Baghdad, was breathing his last. What was the city that contained so many generations of my family like? Our Baghdad had an illustrious past. It was founded in the eighth century and became the capital of the Abbasid Empire, the centre of the Arab caliphate during the 'Golden Age of Islam' in the ninth and tenth centuries. During this period, it evolved into a major commercial, cultural and intellectual centre of the Arab world. In 1534 Baghdad was captured by the Ottoman Empire and ceased to be a capital city of an empire, now overshadowed by Constantinople.

During the five centuries of Ottoman rule the city went into slow decline. With the dissolution of the Ottoman Empire, it fell under the British mandate and, in 1932, became the capital of the Hashemite Kingdom of Iraq. It regained some of its former prominence as a significant centre of Arab culture. The Baghdad of my childhood was thus a very different city to that of the Ottoman era. After the Second World War it developed rapidly and offered the upper middle classes modern forms of leisure and culture: cinemas, popular music, horse-riding, tennis and other forms of sport. Above all, it was a multi-ethnic metropolitan city, home to different minorities, littered with mosques, churches and synagogues. We had friendly relations with our Muslim and Christian neighbours, unencumbered by religious differences.

This is not to say that Judaism was not an important component of our collective identity. In fact, it was integral to the way we saw ourselves and to the way we conducted our daily life. We were decidedly secular, not orthodox Jews. But although we were not religious, we kept a kosher home. The chickens we consumed were slaughtered by a *shohet*, a slaughterer, in accordance with the Jewish ritual for the killing of animals. On Friday night we had a *kiddush*, a prayer and blessing recited by my father as the head of the household, with sweet wine in a silver goblet, at the traditional celebratory meal to usher in the Sabbath. The Meir Taweig synagogue was across the road from our house. My father did not go there to pray every Saturday; he attended services only on festivals and special occasions. On top of his dues as a member of the synagogue, he donated generously to a charity for the poor which was managed by the synagogue. Judaism for our family was more of a culture than a religion.

We were a well-to-do and comfortable upper middle-class family. We lived in a large house in 44 Alamein Street, in the prosperous neighbourhood of Bataween in the centre of the city, on the outskirts of Bab al-Sharji. Next to Bataween was Iliya and next to Iliya was Karrada, where my maternal grandmother lived. Most of the houses in Bataween were private villas surrounded by gardens and orchards. It was a mixed neighbourhood with a large proportion of Jewish residents. Ours was the house that my father had built for himself as a bachelor and, according to my mother, it was one of the finest in all Baghdad. As he himself was an importer and supplier of building materials, he had been well-placed to choose from the best contractors. On the ground floor was a hall; a sitting room with an American-made wood-burner, green velvet sofas and armchairs, precious Persian rugs; and a large dining room. A flight of stairs led to my parents' bedroom and a sumptuous bathroom with green tiles imported from England. On the next floor was another bathroom, two balconies and bedrooms for the children and a nanny. Another wing of the building housed my father's mother, sister, niece and other, more peripatetic members of his family. Altogether the house contained three bathrooms and seven toilets.

A flight of stairs led to a flat roof surrounded by a waist-high brick wall. In the summer, when it was unbearably hot, the servants would assemble special beds for us on the roof so we could sleep in the open air, cooled by the breeze coming off the Tigris. My parents had a double bed with a pole at each corner and a white net to give them privacy and protect them from mosquitos at night. My sisters and I had single beds with no nets. When it became too hot on the open roof, my parents would move to a roof terrace which was in the shade. My mother had a favourite duck-feather pillow which her paternal grandfather had brought back for her form one of his trips to China. Knowing how attached she was to this pillow, the servants would move it to the cool basement for her afternoon nap and back to the roof in the evening. Sleeping on the roof conveyed a curious feeling of solitude and communion with nature. One of my earliest memories as a child is lying in bed on the roof and gazing up at the moon and the stars. Looking back at this idyllic setup, I am more than a little embarrassed at how pampered and privileged I was as a little boy.

My father was the patriarch and the provider, always treated with great respect by everyone, as is the custom in Arab society. He was medium height, stocky, bald, and wore round, gold-rimmed glasses with very thick lenses. His wardrobe consisted of tailor-made three-piece suits of superior English fabric which he invariably wore with a white shirt and a matching tie. I remember him as a soft-spoken, kind, caring and generous man. Although I was never exposed to it, he apparently also had a violent streak. When he lost his temper, he was liable to hit people.

Most people called my father Abu Abi, the father of Abi, rather than Yusef. Mr Shlaim was too formal while Yusef was too familiar, so Abu Abi seemed to strike a happy medium, in accordance with Arab custom. Arab men are often called after their eldest son. In the past they were called after their eldest daughter only if there was no son. In recent years, however, a generational shift has taken place: men can be called after their daughter if she is the eldest even if there is a younger son. This was a small but telling example of discrimination against women in Arab-Jewish society in the last century, a theme I shall return to.

The range of names in my extended family was strikingly diverse, not to say confusing. Diversity stemmed from our hybrid status as Arab-Jews. Some names were Arab-Iraqi but not exclusively Muslim, like Mas'uda, Saida, Salih, Habiba, Mouzli and Fouad. Some names were distinctly Jewish like Meir, Menashe, Eliyahu, Ezra, Sha'ul and Haskell. Some names, like those of my sisters, Lydia and Vilma, and that of my uncle Alfred, were a typical mix of an Alliance-educated Iraqi-Jewish family.

My name was Abraham or Abi for short. I was named after my paternal grandfather, the one who had been killed by robbers. My civil registration document gives my name as Ibrahim – the Arabic version of Abraham. The date of birth is 31 October 1945. The father's name is Yusef and the mother's name is Mas'uda but there is no surname. Under religion the document says *musawi*, meaning a member of the religion of Moses. Why it did not simply say *yahudi*, the Arabic word for 'Jewish', is not clear to me. On the certificate there is a stamp bearing the portrait of the infant king, Faisal II, who would have been ten years old at the time.

I was the middle child, born between two sisters: Lydia, eighteen months older, and Vilma, three years younger. The atmosphere in our house was serene and relaxed, with toys scattered everywhere. My two favourites were a wooden horse I could ride and a train set with a wind-up locomotive that I learnt how to assemble and operate. My sisters and I got on well and we were well looked after by our parents, the relatives who lived with us, the nannies and the servants. Our father was not an absent dad. He used to come home every day for lunch and a siesta, so we saw a lot of him. Our mother was a lady of leisure: she had no work and no household chores so she could devote most of her time to pleasurable pursuits. By the age of twenty-four she had three little children, but she had as much help as she wanted in caring for them. She was a beautiful, lively and loving mum, and a lot of fun. The age gap between our parents was striking, but they were both good parents in their different ways and worked well as a team.

The other residents of the big house were all related to my father, and they occupied a separate wing. His mother Lulu, whom we called Yuma, did most of the cooking and was always on hand to help whenever needed. She spent most of the day in the kitchen, preparing breakfast, lunch and dinner. Her daughter Rosa, my father's older sister, was the one in charge of the household. She was short, thickset, with thick black hair and a parting in the middle, and she always dressed in black. I learnt of the tragedy that lay behind her sombre attire only when I grew up. Rosa was seventeen when she got married to a Jewish man and, a year later, she gave birth to a baby daughter. Following the outbreak of the First World War, her husband was drafted into military service by the Ottoman Empire. At that time present-day Iraq consisted of three Ottoman provinces: Kirkuk, Baghdad and Basra. The word drafted is perhaps a misnomer because the Turks did not have an orderly, bureaucratic process of recruitment, at least not in this part of their ramshackle empire. An empire at war needed cannon-fodder, so its recruiting sergeants would turn up unexpectedly and literally pick young men off the streets wherever they could find them. In the Ottoman army conditions were dire: food was in short supply and clothes were inadequate for harsh winter conditions. Rosa's husband had the misfortune to be picked up in one of these raids. He was never heard of again. His baby daughter, Rachel, hardly knew him. Rosa did not receive from the Turkish authorities any news of his fate, so she had no way of knowing whether he was alive or dead. Most probably, he died in the war, but there was no official notice to confirm it. This meant, according to Jewish law, that Rosa could not marry again. For the rest of her life, she wore black in mourning for the presumed death of her husband. She had to bring up her daughter as a single parent.

All the domestic servants reported to Rosa. She set high standards, she could be fierce and she had a reputation as a hard taskmaster. Any cleaner who did not live up to her exacting expectations was reprimanded and made to clean again. Rosa was a devoted mother to Rachel, her only child. Rachel lived with us, she went to school, but she was also called upon to help, especially as a waitress at dinners and parties. Like her mother, Rachel was not particularly attractive. Unfortunately for her, in those days a girl who was not pretty was expected to come with a higher-than-normal dowry in order to attract a husband. Matchmakers were usually involved. Relatives could play a major role in choosing a partner for their child, as my mother discovered to her cost. As Rachel had no father, my father acted in effect as her guardian, providing her with a dowry of 1,000 dinars. A dinar at that time was worth roughly the same as a pound sterling so it was not an insubstantial sum. Rachel might well have been able to find a husband without a dowry, but the dowry did her no harm.

My father's treatment of his younger brother Isaac was notably less generous than his treatment of his niece. Isaac's nickname was *S'hak al-aami* – blind Isaac – on account of his small eyes and short-sightedness; S'hak is the Iraqi-Jewish pronunciation of Isaac and *aami* in Arabic means blind. Isaac was not endowed with high intelligence, and my father regarded him as a liability. He often got angry with him and, on occasion, even slapped him. To avoid painful encounters, Isaac would come to the house only when my father was at work. Even then he would not come in through the main entrance but shuffle through the garage to the kitchen, where he was fed by his mother and his sister Rosa.

The division of labour among our various employees was less than precise. One man, Ruben, was my father's storeman and tasked with doing the shopping for the entire household. Although our family only had five mouths to feed, there was also the extended family and the staff. Rosa was in charge of the kitchen, so she was the one who instructed Ruben what to buy. At five or six o'clock every morning, Ruben would go to the Souk al-Shorja, Baghdad's oldest market, situated in the heart of the city. Fresh produce was in ample supply, including fruit and vegetables, eggs, poultry, meat, fish, and dairy products like milk, butter, sour cream, yoghurt, salty cheese and numerous other types of cheese. When the shopping was done, Ruben would load it on a horse-drawn cart, the local taxi, and head to our home in Bataween, about a kilometre from the market. Having delivered his shopping, he would then go to the store to start his day job. Everything was bought, cooked and consumed on the same day; leftovers were thrown away.

The gardener, a Muslim named Abed, reported not to Rosa but directly to the mistress of the house. Saturday was his only day off. The original plot on which our house had been built had a more than adequate garden and a cluster of mature trees. There was only one old palm tree by the house, but it produced a huge crop of exceptionally succulent dates. Family and friends who received parcels of those dates often remarked that they tasted better than chocolate. As a child I used to watch with a mixture of admiration and anxiety when Abed climbed up the palm tree to pick the legendary treats.

After my parents married, the possibility arose of buying an additional and even bigger plot of land next door. My father gave my mother the choice of a tennis court or a garden. She opted for a garden. A landscape gardener produced a plan for a harmonious space with a grass lawn, flower beds and an orchard with orange, fig, apricot and peach trees. The result was a very beautiful garden, lovingly tended by Abed. One of my random memories of Baghdad is waking up at night, walking to the balcony and seeing on the lawn down below a large number of guests sitting around long tables laden with food and drink, waiters running back and forth with trays and a band playing in the background.

The routine daily tasks of washing, dressing and feeding the children were entrusted to carefully chosen nannies. Marcelle, the main nanny, was the daughter of Ruben, the storeman. They were a poor Jewish-Kurdish family from Mosul in the north. Marcelle was a tall, blond and elegant young woman. Some of the wealthy Jewish families employed Armenian nannies, to whom a certain kudos was attached: they were professional, they commanded higher wages and they were marked out by their white uniforms. Armenian nannies enjoyed a good reputation among all communities, but they were Christian. Wealthy Jews who felt uneasy about employing Christians looked for Jewish nannies and these tended to come from Mosul or Kirkuk. My mother, who was acutely status conscious, wanted us to have an Armenian nanny. My father refused. He could easily afford to employ one Armenian nanny, but favoured Jewish nannies and Marcelle fitted the bill perfectly.

One day, on Marcelle's watch, I fell from my highchair and hit my head on the stone floor. I was meant to be eating but I had suddenly stood on the chair and toppled over. My parents heard the loud bang and my screams and rushed into the room in a panic. My father flew into a rage and slapped Marcelle hard on the face, yelling '*Amya*?' – are you blind? 'You were standing by him. How could you let this happen? Get out of here! We don't want you in this house!' When it became clear that the fall had not caused any serious damage, my father's rage subsided. My mother was very angry with him for striking the poor girl. In the end he agreed to let Marcelle stay but she walked on eggshells and the atmosphere in the house remained tense for some time after the accident.

My mother was an irrepressible optimist. Her gloss on the episode, many years later, was that the fall did not do any harm and it may have done some good by opening up and expanding my brain. Maybe, she mused, it was because of the fall that I turned out to be so clever! My mother loved plotting how to make me brainy. She theorised that vitamin-rich pistachio skins were vital for my intellectual development, so she plied me with pistachios. My sisters were spared this sort of nour-ishment – presumably as convention held that girls did not need brains.

This discrimination reflected a broader pattern of discrimination against women in contemporary Arab society. To put it at its crudest, boys were considered good news while girls were considered disadvan-tageous or even a curse. Boys would grow up into men, go to work, earn money and help to support the family. Girls, on the other hand, were considered a financial liability. They could also be a social liability, for example if they engaged in premarital sex, bringing dishonour on the family – boys, supposedly, could not. Consequently, it was not uncom-mon for parents to want to marry off their daughters at the earliest opportunity. The common expectation of girls was to finish school, get married and bring up children. None of this of course contradicts the fact that my family, like most others, contained very strong women in its midst. Some of them were, sadly, the most avid enforcers of gender discrimination.

Alongside these general customs came the specific circumstances of my family. I was the only boy in the family, and I received much more than my fair share of attention. It was not only my parents who gave me preferential treatment, but the grandmothers, aunts, servants and, to a lesser extent, nannies. I was doted on by many women who never stopped billing and cooing around me. My sisters received love and affection but never to the same degree as me. It would have been unnatural for them not to feel the occasional pang of jealousy at the preferential treatment that I received.

Some signs were not so subtle. Yuma used to say to Lydia and Vilma: '*Abi huwa al-assal wa-untum kshur al-basal*' – 'Abi is the honey, and you are the peels of the onion!' It was only as a grown-up that I began to appreciate the deeply detrimental effects such attitudes were bound to have for my sisters in terms of self-confidence and self-esteem. My only defence is that at the time I was simply unaware of the ways in which our family dynamics worked in my favour and to the long-term disadvantage of Lydia and Vilma.

An abiding sense of guilt towards my sisters impelled me, when I was writing this chapter, to press my mother on the issue of the favouritism back in Baghdad. She vehemently rejected the suggestion that my sisters had any reason to feel aggrieved. In the first place, she said, Vilma had been far too young to notice any of these things. Nor did Lydia feel at the time that she was not getting her due. On the contrary, she was pampered, and a great deal of fuss was made of her both before and after I was born. Yuma only called her the peels of the onion when she was naughty or when she hit me. Lydia's protests about the way she was treated only began after we moved to Israel, according to my mother. And the reason adduced for the change was that in Israel we had no servants and Lydia was expected to help with household chores.

My mother too was pampered in Baghdad. A typical day in her life began with a huge breakfast consisting of flat bread, hard-boiled eggs, fried aubergines, tahini, salad, cheese, and for dessert, cream with date-syrup. After breakfast a few of her women friends would come to our house to play cards while their husbands were at work. At about eleven o'clock they would have a coffee break which consisted of a lot more than just coffee. It was more like what English children colloquially call 'elevenses'. Here the ladies were served cheese-filled pastries, fried vegetables, chicken croquettes and cakes. Lunch to the whole family would be served around two o'clock, after my father returned from work. Lunch was a very substantial affair with a large selection of fish, meat and vegetable dishes but the staple diet was chicken and rice. There was usually one sweet-and-sour dish and some puddings. All the food was spread on the table before the start of the meal as is the Middle Eastern custom. After lunch, our parents would go down to the cool basement – *sirdab* in Arabic – for a siesta. The *sirdab* was equipped with a primitive kind of air conditioner: climbing plants on a thin wooden frame that had to be sprinkled with water from time to time. The plants transformed the incoming, warm wind into a cool and mildly fragrant breeze. Our parents would emerge from the basement after an hour or two for another round of tea, coffee and fresh fruit. My father did not go back to work in the afternoon: his employees ran the business for him.

In the summer we had frequent family outings on the River Tigris, ending on the beach of the large island, the Jazra, on a bend near the Karrada. Gauhouriyah, on the opposite bank of the river, was another popular spot for swimming and picnicking. Like many of our wealthy friends and relatives, we pitched a large tent in Gauhouriyah and kept it for the whole summer. Even Uncle Joseph, whose villa in the Karrada was on the riverbank, still pitched a large tent on the other side, in Gauhouriyah. He also had his own rowboat and employed an oarsman (*balamchi*), an elderly Muslim called Amer, who was always available to ferry any member of the extended family in any direction that took their fancy. We were usually joined on these jaunts by some of my mother's other uncles and their families, and occasionally by Haskell Shemtob, the head of the Jewish community whom I shall mention later in connection with the Jewish exodus from Iraq. The grown-ups would swim around the island and the more energetic among them, my mother included, would also swim all the way to the island alongside the boat. Covered with thick vegetation in the middle of the river, the island was an idyllic spot for recreation for people of all ages and all levels of fitness. We children were too young to swim in the river at that time, but we were allowed to paddle and play in the shallow waters.

The picnic was the star of the show. Iraqi-Jewish cuisine is renowned throughout the Middle East for its variety and exquisite-tasting dishes, and one of its most distinctive meals is *samak masguf*, barbecued fish. Our boatman would buy a big, live carp from the fishermen along the pier, tie it to the boat and trail it through the water to the island. He would make a fire, slit the fish with his sharp knife, add salt, aromatic curry, onions and tomatoes, and lay it on skewers alongside the embers of the fire. When the fish was ready, the picnickers would eat it with their bare hands, sitting on a blanket by the river. This primitive *samak masguf* was a culinary masterpiece and the pleasure of eating was enhanced by the scent of the wood fire.

For the grownups the picnic was sometimes followed by entertainment of another kind. After putting their children to bed, the adults would meet in one of their houses to play cards. Another meal awaited them which took the form of a midnight feast. Poker was the most popular game – it was not uncommon for them to carry on playing it until two or three in the morning. No thought was spared for the drivers who had to wait until their masters were ready to go home. After my mother died, I found in her papers a small pocket diary for 1947. In it there were short factual entries, all in French, in tiny letters and a very neat handwriting. It was striking to see how often card-games featured in my parents' crowded social calendar. In the diary my father is referred to not as Yusef but as Joseph and each entry records how many dinars he and she won or lost in the game.

Most of my parents' friends were Jewish but they also had close non-Jewish friends. One of them was Jamal Baban, the Kurdish lawyer and politician who served as minister of justice in a number of cabinets in the 1940s. He and his wife used to come to our house to play cards and they reciprocated by inviting my parents to their house. These card-playing sessions also lasted until the early hours. When hosting, Jamal Baban would insist on driving his guests to their homes as a sign of respect and implicit promise of protection. Rather ostentatiously, he got out his pistol and took it with him on the journey to demonstrate that he was ready for all eventualities. My parents thought the pistol was unnecessary and that Baban was carrying it for effect, but this did not detract from the respect and affection they felt for him. They say that a friend in need is a friend indeed and in their hour of need, Baban was to prove that he was a true friend. His wife struck up a friendship with my mother and would sometimes come to visit us with her children when the men were at work.

Another aspect of our social life involved clubs. There were seven or eight Jewish clubs in Baghdad. Jewish society was rather hierarchical and different clubs catered for different social classes. The most prestigious club was the al-Zawra; second was the al-Rashid. Wealth and social status were the most important criteria for membership. Being rich on its own was not enough; some rich men were rejected on account of being disagreeable. Each member of a club had a vote and could blackball an applicant he did not like. My parents made it to the top clubs and enjoyed going to them. Their favourite club was al-Zawra where the atmosphere was friendly and welcoming. Barbecued dinners were served on the lawn by waiters in smart uniforms. When they were not having a meal, the guests could play backgammon or card games or just lounge around and chat to friends. Little children were made very welcome in the club and a special area was set aside for them. The children were looked after by their nannies and the babies were pushed in their prams. Armenian nannies in their smart white uniforms were a common sight.

Once a week on average a band of Jewish musicians would be invited to entertain their co-religionists in the club. Many Jews distinguished themselves in Iraq as composers, songwriters, singers and players of traditional instruments. They were especially proficient in *maqam*, a modal system used in classical Arabic music; the word *maqam* in Arabic means place, location or position. *Maqam* was also part of Sephardic Jewish culture – Jews used it in their weekly prayer services and holy days in synagogues. Jews also distinguished themselves in traditional Arabic music and, as a result, they were in high demand both in Jewish and non-Jewish venues. Music acted as a bridge between Jews and Muslims, transcending their separate identities and emphasising common culture and humanity.[1]

My mother's two passions were popular Arabic music and travel. From a young age she nursed an ambition to travel abroad and explore the world. At school she and her classmates were once asked to write an essay outlining what they would like to do when they grew up and the reasons for their choice. Saida wrote that she wanted to be an air stewardess or alternatively to be a rich woman who could afford to travel under her own steam. Being married to a rich man gave her the money to travel and having nannies to look after her children gave her the freedom to do so.

Saida was accompanied by her mother on trips abroad. One trip took mother and daughter to Egypt, where they spent a few days in the famous Hotel Cecil in Alexandria. From there Saida sent a postcard to my father dated 12 August 1947. As the postcard is the only correspondence I have between my parents, it might be worth quoting in full. 'My dear Yusef,' she wrote.

We are now in Alexandria, enjoying ourselves very much. I cannot imagine a more beautiful or more fun place than this. We are staying at the Hotel Cecil, the one we always read about in the papers. All the ministers stay here. And they gave us a most beautiful room, especially the view. It is stunning: the sea on one side and Zaghlul Park on the other. I am contented and enjoying it very much. I swim in the sea and the beaches here are gorgeous. Last night we went to the Auberge Bleu and then to a show put on by Egyptian actors.

Saida was twenty-three years old and very beautiful. One evening she and her mother went to a prestigious nightclub called *Sans Souci*. To their great surprise, King Farouk was also there. Farouk had a reputation as a playboy with a long string of widely publicised affairs. (He would later be overthrown in the Free Officers revolution of 1952.) In *Sans Souci* Saida was approached by a member of the king's entourage who addressed her in French. He said that an important personality wanted to meet her but preferably not in the club. Would she like to go with them to the palace? Saida replied in French that she would but that her husband was about to come to collect them. She then turned to her mother and said that they had to leave the club right away. Having bought expensive tickets and having just settled down for an evening of entertainment, her mother questioned the need to hurry. Not wanting to tell her the real reason, that the lecherous king had his eyes on her, Saida invented on the spot the excuse that she had an acute stomach-ache. They got into a taxi and went back to the Hotel Cecil. The next day they went to Cairo and from there flew back to Baghdad. Saida had a narrow escape.

On the bigger geopolitical front, 1947 was an eventful year, the year in which the struggle for Palestine reached a crucial phase. The battle lines were clearly drawn between the Zionists and their international supporters on the one hand and the Palestinians and their Arab allies on the other. A much tougher kind of Zionism, 'fighting Zionism' as it was sometimes called, had been forged in the course of the Second World War, and the commitment to Jewish statehood grew deeper and more desperate in the shadow of the Holocaust. The prospect of minority status under Arab rule was considered little better than a death sentence for the Jewish community in Palestine and for the survivors of the Nazi 'Final Solution'. Zionist leaders were determined to proceed to statehood by diplomatic means if possible, but by military force if necessary. Having repeatedly failed to find a peaceful solution to the conflict between Jews and Arabs in Palestine, Britain tossed this political hot potato into the lap of the infant United Nations, the successor to the League of Nations. In February 1947 Britain gave formal notice of its intention to terminate the mandate on 15 May 1948, and on 29 November 1947, the General Assembly of the United Nations voted for the partition of mandatory Palestine into two states: one Arab, one Jewish.

The General Council of the Iraqi-Jewish community sent a telegram to the United Nations opposing the partition resolution and the creation of a Jewish state. Like my family, the majority of Iraqi Jews saw themselves as Iraqi first and Jewish second; they feared that the creation of a Jewish state would undermine their position in Iraq. Throughout the Arab and Muslim world, the partition plan was seen as a grave injustice to the Palestinians for which local Jewish communities were held partly responsible. The distinction between Jews and Zionists, so crucial to interfaith harmony in the Arab world, was rapidly breaking down.

The Jews of Palestine greeted the UN partition resolution with jubilation and rejoicing; the Arab states, loosely organised in the Arab League, rejected it as unfair, illegal and impractical and they went to war to frustrate it. The war for Palestine was divided into an unofficial phase and an official phase. The unofficial phase was between the two

communities in Palestine and lasted from 1 December 1947 until
14 May 1948. It ended with a Jewish victory and the proclamation of the
State of Israel at midnight. During this first phase of the war, Palestinian
society was decimated and the first wave of refugees set in motion. The
morning after the birth of Israel, the regular armies of seven Arab states
invaded Palestine with the aim of frustrating partition and keeping the
whole of Palestine in Arab hands. Fighting in this official phase of the
war continued in three rounds until 7 January 1949 and ended with a
Jewish victory and comprehensive Arab defeat.

In the course of the war the Jews extended the territory of their state
from the 55 per cent allocated to them by the UN cartographers to
78 per cent of mandatory Palestine. The West Bank was captured and
later annexed by Jordan; the Gaza Strip remained under Egyptian military government. Three quarters of a million Palestinians, more than
half the Arab population, became refugees and the name Palestine was
wiped off the map. For the Israelis this was 'The War of Independence';
for the Palestinians it was the 'Nakba' or catastrophe.

All the neighbouring Arab states – Syria, Lebanon, Jordan and Egypt
– signed armistice agreements with Israel when hostilities came to an
end. Iraq withdrew its army from the Palestine front without signing an
armistice agreement and, as a result, it has officially remained in a state
of war with Israel ever since. Refusal to sign an armistice agreement
with the 'gangster state' was something Iraq's leaders wore as a badge
of honour. By sending the Iraqi army to the rescue of the Palestinians,
the royal family had gained immeasurably in prestige. In the past it had
been viewed as a puppet of the British; now it was seen to be serving
the cause of Arab nationalism.

Another effect of Iraq's participation in the war for Palestine was to
fuel the tension between Muslims and Jews at home. Whether or not
they sympathised with Zionism, Iraqi Jews were widely suspected by the
general public of being secret supporters of the state of Israel. A powerful
popular wave of hostility towards both Israel and the Jews living in their
midst swept through the Arab world in the wake of the loss of Palestine,

and Iraq was no exception. Demonstrators marched through the streets of Baghdad, shouting 'Death to the Jews'. A campaign was launched to raise money 'to save Palestine from the Jews' and newspapers called for a boycott of Jewish shops to liberate Iraqis from the 'economic slavery and domination imposed by the Jewish minority'. The arrival in Iraq of eight thousand Palestinian refugees in the summer of 1948 brought home the human cost of failure on the battlefield.

Defeat in Palestine was a deeply felt national humiliation. To deflect attention from their own responsibility for Iraq's poor military performance, its leaders looked for a scapegoat and found in the Jews who dwelt among them a convenient target. The Iraqi government did not simply respond to public anger but actively whipped up popular hysteria and suspicion against the Jews. Using nationalism as a crude but powerful tool, the government led the campaign of incitement, denouncing the Jews as aliens, traitors and a dangerous fifth column. It was at this point that the official persecution of the Jews began. A law was passed in July 1948, making Zionism a criminal offence punishable by death or a minimum sentence of seven years in prison. Jewish officials were fired from their government jobs; Jewish employees dismissed from the railways, the post office and the telegraph department, ostensibly to prevent them from carrying out acts of 'sabotage and treason'. Jewish merchants were denied import and export licences, and restrictions were placed on the freedom of Jewish banks to trade in foreign currency.

The trial of Shafiq Ades in September 1948 stunned the Jewish community. Ades was the wealthiest Jew in Iraq with close ties to high-ranking Iraqi officials, including the Regent, Abd al-Ilah. After a show trial that lasted only three days, he was convicted on false charges of selling arms to Israel and supporting the Iraqi Communist Party. The presiding judge at the military court was Abdullah al-Naasni, a member of the nationalist, anti-Jewish, pro-Nazi Istiqlal (independence) Party. The court was presented with no credible evidence, no witnesses were allowed to appear and the defendant was denied the right to a proper defence. He was sentenced to death by hanging and ordered to pay a fine of five million dinars; the rest of his estate was appropriated by the ministry of defence. In the media, Ades was variously denounced as a serpent, a traitor, a spy, a Zionist and a Jew. To Moshe Gat, an Israeli scholar of Iraqi heritage, 'It was clear that the Ades trial was stage-managed, that he was a scapegoat of Iraq's defeat in the war with Israel; and that revenge was being taken against the Jewish community through this attack on one of its eminent members'.[2] The downfall of Ades set off alarm bells in the Jewish community, especially as he was an assimilated, non-Zionist Jew. If such a powerful man could be treated in such an arbitrary way, there was little hope of protection for less well-connected Jews. Some of them started escaping by secretly crossing the border into Iran and from there continuing the journey to Israel.

My family experienced directly the mounting anger against the Jews at both popular and official levels. The war for Palestine was a major turning point for the worse in Muslim–Jewish relations. My mother singles out the birth of Israel as the decisive point in the crisis of Iraqi Jewry. When Israel was created, to use her own words, 'everything was turned upside down. This is when the trouble started. There was harassment and persecution. We suffered a lot.' Martial law was proclaimed, severe censorship was imposed on the media and an alarming number of Jews were arrested. Letters written by Jews were opened by the military censor in search of incriminating evidence. Jews were summoned for interrogation by the police on the flimsiest evidence of links with Israel, and sometimes when there was no evidence at all. The police pressed charges in the military courts against Jews for supporting Zionism and they were not above fabricating evidence. In some cases, the threat of court action was used by policemen as a means of extorting money. In other cases that went to trial in the courts, Jews who were convicted were given prison sentences of varying lengths in accordance with the severity of their alleged offence. There was no appeal against the verdict of the military judges.

On one occasion, after their letters had been opened by the censor, Saida and her mother Mouzli were summoned to the local police station on suspicion of support for Zionism. In letters to Saida's elder brother Isaac, who lived in London, they had referred to Salim Sanduq, a codeword for the newly established state of Israel. (*Sanduq* in Arabic means a chest.) Salim Sanduq was a real person, a relative who had left Iraq illegally via Iran to go and live in Israel. At the police station Saida and Mouzli were separated. Saida was taken first to see a police officer. 'Who is Salim Sanduq?' he asked her. Saida improvised on the spot and replied that he was a fat man who always stayed hungry no matter how much he ate. As she left the room, Mouzli was ushered in and Saida just managed to whisper in her ear a word about Salim Sanduq. The officer asked Mouzli the same question to which she replied, with theatrical flourish, that this was an enormously fat man who ate like a hog but was never satisfied. Although the two accounts tallied, Saida was taken back to the office for further interrogation. This time she summoned her courage and said to the police officer: 'Look here, we are British. We have not done anything. So just leave us alone.' The implicit threat to involve the British authorities seemed to work.

In everyday life the Jews experienced minor pinpricks as well as more serious injuries. Individuals who harboured resentment against Jews were now less constrained in giving vent to their sentiments in public. Small incidents are indicative of a more general shift in the climate. Amid the changes she experienced all around her at this time, my mother recalled one incident in particular. Our driver had picked her up at home to take her to my father's khan. This was before the days of traffic lights – instead, a policeman with a whistle stood on a stand at the crossroads to direct the traffic. That day the policeman stopped our driver and asked him why he was speeding. Our driver replied that he was in a hurry to get to his master. On hearing this, the policeman loudly cursed the driver and his master. There was no doubt in my mother's mind that the policeman knew instantly from their dialect that they were Jewish and that he would not have dared speak to them so offensively in normal times.

My parents had no friends who were openly Zionist. In a context
where Zionism was punishable by death, this was hardly surprising. In
Israel my mother reminisced nostalgically about the wonderful Muslim
friends we had in Baghdad and the happy times we spent with them.
Among the qualities she singled out for praise were their many acts of
selfless kindness and their unswerving loyalty even when the popular
tide turned against the Jews. One day I asked her whether we had any
Zionist friends. My question took her by surprise. 'No!' she replied
emphatically. 'Zionism is an Ashkenazi thing. It had nothing to do with
us!' While insisting that the persecution of our community in Baghdad
was orchestrated by the authorities, my mother admitted that many Jews
greeted the Arab defeat in Palestine with barely concealed satisfaction
and even glee. Israel was called by the Arabs *al-dawla al-maz'uma*,
the so-called state. One Jewish song that made the rounds after the
Arab defeat in Palestine spoke of *saba' duwal mahzuma min al-dawla
al-maz'uma* – seven states ran away from the one so-called state.

Before the defeat, the mood in the Arab street was buoyant and it
was accompanied by blood-curdling rhetoric about throwing the Jews
into the sea. Cartoons depicted seven big Arab soldiers, representing
the seven regular Arab armies who took part in the invasion, with
bayonets at the end of their rifles, driving a little Jew with a hooked
nose from a diving board into the sea. These cartoons were crudely
racist in their imagery, but they reflected the prevalent conviction that
the infant Jewish state did not stand a chance against the combined
might of the Arab armies. Overconfidence was palpable not just in
the street but in the higher political and military echelons of Iraqi
society.

My grandmother Mouzli lived in a villa in the Karrada near the
Tigris River. Her neighbour and friend was a Muslim woman called
Umm Ahmad, the mother of Ahmad. Ahmad was a senior officer in the
Iraqi army. One day Mouzli went to pay a routine social call on Umm
Ahmad. Ahmad was in the house with a small group of fellow officers.
They stood around a table on which was spread a map of Palestine

and were engaged in a very animated debate. My guess, and it is only a guess, is that this was the map prepared by the military committee of the Arab League for the co-ordinated invasion of Palestine following the expiry of the British mandate. Umm Ahmad was not impressed with them. She elbowed them out of the way, got to the map and demanded to be told: 'Where is this so-called state?' The officers pointed on the map to the area that had been designated by the UN for the Jewish state. Umm Ahmad made no attempt to conceal her contempt for the officers who argued and agonised so much about alternative strategies for dealing with the embryonic state of Israel. 'Aren't you ashamed of yourselves?' she demanded to know and then quickly added: 'I, on my own, can pick up this so-called state and crush it between my teeth.' My grandmother listened to her friend in stunned silence. She did not doubt Umm Ahmad's assessment of the military balance and she was full of foreboding about the fate that awaited her younger sister Ghala and her other relatives in Palestine.

Years later, when we lived in Israel, my grandmother repeatedly recalled this scene with a triumphalism all her own. Every year on 15 May the Israeli army would put on an Independence Day parade. The parade was an awesome demonstration of military might. Infantry units marched through the streets, accompanied by tanks and artillery pieces, while air force pilots performed acrobatic exercises. My grand-mother used to watch this spectacle with evident admiration. To her way of thinking, this newly acquired Jewish military might offered some compensation for the impotence of the Jews in Iraq. 'Where are you, Umm Ahmad?' Mouzli would exclaim. 'Let us see you put this so-called state between your teeth and crush it.'

But this is to anticipate what came later. At the time we felt vulnerable because we were Jews. One day in October 1948 a letter came through the letterbox addressed to my father. On the envelope was a skull with crossbones underneath. My mother decided to open it. It contained the threat that unless my father paid a ransom of 10,000 dinars, a gang would kidnap my sister Lydia, followed by a warning: the house was being watched and if anyone tried to inform the police, they would be killed. It was Saturday and my father was sitting in a café by the river with some of my mother's maternal uncles. My mother left the house through a back door, taking the letter with her, and walked on foot all the way to the café. Having told her husband the story, and having shown him the letter, she urged him to pay the ransom money.

My father's instant reaction was to refuse to give in to blackmail. He pointed out that in the past he had done many favours to various ministers, including the current minister of the police; now he needed their help and it was their turn to do him a favour. From the café he went to the home of the minister of the police, told him what had happened and got his immediate promise to take charge of the case. Uncle Jacob accompanied my mother back to the house and they went in through the back door. Soon after they got back, the phone rang. At the other end of the phone was a man with a very loud, booming voice. It later transpired that this man was the leader of the gang and that he worked in the telephone exchange. Uncle Jacob answered the phone and pretended to be the servant. The voice which reverberated throughout the house said: 'Tell your master that if my demands are not met, I'll blow up his house.' In Arabic 'to blow up' and 'to sweep' sound rather similar and Uncle Jacob, deliberately confusing the two verbs, replied: 'You don't have to sweep the house, I have just swept it.' The blackmailer angrily repeated the threat and slammed the phone down.

Later in the day the gang leader phoned again and this time my father answered. The gangster warned my father not to tell anyone, to go to the bank to withdraw 10,000 dinars, put the money in a parcel, and wait for a man who would come to the door at a specified time to ask for the *amana*, the parcel or deposit. He was to hand over the parcel to the man without saying a word. By this time the chief of the Baghdad police, on the instructions of the minister of the police, was on the case. He sent a team of several policemen to intercept the caller: two inside the house, two disguised as beggars in the street, and one hidden at the top of a tree at the entrance to the house. My father had prepared a parcel with some real high-denomination dinar notes but mostly newspaper cuttings to inflate the parcel. At the appointed hour, a man came to the door, rang the bell and asked for the parcel. No sooner had my father handed the parcel over than all the policemen pounced on the caller. At first the caller protested his innocence, claiming that another man had given him five dinars and asked him to collect the parcel and that was all he knew. When my father gave him two hard slaps on the face, the man raised his hands to signal surrender and said he would confess. He was taken to the police station where he confessed that he was a member of the gang and he gave the names of the other members. All of them were then rounded up by the police.

The name of the gang was *isabat al-leil wa al-hawa* – 'the gang of the night and the wind'. Newspapers relished the drama, likening them to 'Ali Baba and the Forty Thieves'. The gang included some common criminals, but the leaders included the nephew of a minister and an official in a key position in the telephone exchange. The gang targeted Jewish merchants both because they were rich and because they were a softer target than rich Muslims. Newspapers published sensational reports of the trial on a daily basis, with pictures of the judges and the accused and a running commentary. At that time Iraq was under martial law because of the war in Palestine. The judges were army officers in uniform. They handed down severe sentences to all the members of the gang: two to five years in prison, all with hard labour. My mother grew extremely worried that these blackmailers would seek revenge after leaving prison. She was terrified that they would make good their threat to blow up the house, but her biggest fear was that they would kidnap or kill one of her children. The possibility of this nightmare coming true made her start thinking about leaving Iraq for good.

Haskell Shemtob (right) and Tawfiq al-Suwaydi (left)

SEVEN

BAGHDAD BOMBSHELL

THE YEARS 1950–51 MARKED A CATACLYSM FOR IRAQI JEWS. In the space of just over a year, nearly the entire community left behind their ancient homeland and made their way to the young and impoverished state of Israel. My family was among them. Our comfortable lifestyle collapsed around us – a change I could not even dimly comprehend as a child. Ever since, I have been trying to make sense of what happened and why.

My family was part of what was called the 'Big Aliyah'. Between June 1950 and June 1951 around 110,000 Jews emigrated from Iraq to Israel. The number of emigrants from the establishment of the State of Israel in 1948 to the end of 1953 reached nearly 125,000 out of a total of around 135,000 Iraqi Jews. Several thousand left Iraq for other countries and only about 6,000 Jews stayed in Iraq. A Jewish presence that went back two and a half millennia, to the destruction of the First Temple and the Babylonian exile, came to a sudden and painful end. A Diaspora that had been the living embodiment of Muslim–Jewish co-existence was no more. Jewish property left behind in Iraq was valued at 200 million dinars, roughly 200 million pounds at that time. Apart from private property, the Jewish community collectively owned about 200 buildings, including 50 synagogues, 20 schools, hospitals, office blocks, community centres, clubs and cinemas. But this was just one aspect of the tragedy.

Much more serious and more lasting were the emotional and psychological scars caused by being violently uprooted from our natural environment and catapulted to a new country with a different culture, a different ethos and a foreign language. A number of authors have described the painful ordeal of displacement. Itzhak Bar-Moshe, a distant relative of mine, remarks bitterly in his memoirs *Exodus from Iraq*: 'We left Iraq as Jews and arrived in Israel as Iraqis.'[1]

The circumstances surrounding the Jewish exodus from Baghdad are the subject of a heated and ongoing controversy. There are conflicting narratives about the causes. My own family narrative contains added layers of idiosyncratic experience. The standard Zionist narrative portrays the exodus as a voluntary act caused by local enmity, framing it in the context of primordial Islamic antisemitism and of the harassment to which the Jews were allegedly subjected by all Arab regimes throughout history. According to this narrative, the *farhud* in Baghdad in 1941 was only one link in a never-ending chain of persecution and mistreatment; following the first Arab–Israeli war the Jews of Iraq faced an imminent threat of annihilation; and the Zionist movement came to the rescue, giving them a refuge in the newly born state of Israel to lead the rest of their lives in freedom and dignity. This altruistic-heroic version, which casts the Zionist movement as the saviour of Iraqi Jewry, is reflected in the official name given to the airlift: Operation Ezra and Nehemiah, after the men celebrated in the Hebrew Bible for leading the Jews out of exile.

An alternative account, which may be termed the post-Zionist narrative, maintains that the great majority of the emigrants did not want to leave Iraq; that they had no ideological affinity with Zionism; and that they were the victims of Zionist actions designed to intimidate them into abandoning their homeland. The most serious charge levelled against the Zionist movement and Israel in this connection is that they actually instigated the bombing of Jewish targets in Baghdad in a bid to spark a mass flight of Iraqi Jews to Israel. In this understanding, Zionism, which emerged as an answer to antisemitism in Europe in the late nineteenth century, resorted to violence against the Jews of the Arab lands in order to achieve one of its other objectives, 'the ingathering of the exiles', or the bringing of as many Jews as possible from all corners of the earth to Zion. Although some Iraqi Jews believed in Zionism and saw Israel as their true homeland, they were a tiny minority. One estimate is that out of a total of 130,000 Iraqi Jews, no more than 2,000 belonged to the Zionist movement, that is to say 1.53 per cent.[2]

Some writers on this subject place the terrorist attacks in Baghdad under the heading of 'Cruel Zionism'.[3] Others have suggested that the Zionist movement began to play a role in undermining the relations between Muslims and Jews in the Arab countries long before the emergence of the state of Israel. Marion Woolfson, for example, in her book *Prophets in Babylon*, makes the point with a telling quote from Sir Francis Humphrys, the British ambassador to Baghdad. Towards the end of 1934 Sir Francis wrote that while before the First World War the Jews had enjoyed a more favourable position than any other minority in the country, 'Zionism has sown dissension between Jews and Arabs, and a bitterness has grown up between the two peoples which did not previously exist.' Sir Francis remained of the opinion that 'there is no natural antagonism between Jew and Arab in Iraq.'[4]

Attacks on five Jewish targets in Baghdad in 1950–51 provided a dramatic illustration of how far relations between Muslims and Jews had deteriorated since the 1930s. The most famous and the only fatal incident occurred on 14 January 1951 when a hand grenade was lobbed into the forecourt of the Mas'uda Shemtob synagogue, killing four Jews and wounding twenty others. The question of who was behind the bombs is of crucial importance for understanding the real origins of the exodus. Zionist spokesmen have consistently denied any involvement in the bombings. They ascribed the attacks either to the Iraqi government in search of a scapegoat for the Arab defeat in the war for Palestine and for the country's domestic problems, or to extreme right-wing Iraqi elements who wanted to drive the Jews out of the country. The finger of blame was commonly pointed at the xenophobic, fiercely anti-Jewish, pan-Arab Istiqlal Party.

Two commissions of inquiry were appointed by the Israeli government to look into the matter, one in 1952 and one in 1960, and
both concluded categorically that there had been no Israeli involvement whatsoever. A number of Iraqi Jews and Iraqi-born scholars in
Israel have argued, to the contrary, that the Zionist underground was
responsible.[5] To support their claim they relied on various testimonies, circumstantial evidence and fragmentary pieces of information,
but they were unable to produce a smoking gun. All my relatives in
Israel were utterly convinced, evidence or no evidence, that the Zionist
underground engineered our departure from Iraq.

Ever since my early teens, I was fascinated by the story of the
bombs. Later, after I became a historian of the Arab–Israeli conflict,
my curiosity deepened. And in the course of writing this book it has
deepened further. In 1981–82 I was on a sabbatical year in Israel,
doing research for what became my first book on the Middle East:
*Collusion across the Jordan: King Abdullah, the Zionist Movement,
and the Partition of Palestine*. I spent most of the year in the Israel
State Archives in Jerusalem, ordering file after file of newly released
official documents. One day I ordered a file I had seen in the catalogue
entitled 'Iraq, 1950'. I was told that this file had not been declassified
so I could not see it. 'Aha,' I thought to myself – this file must contain
incriminating evidence and possibly even a smoking gun. Israel had
copied from Britain the thirty-year rule for the review and declassi-
fication of official documents, and so I pleaded with the archivist to
apply the general rule to this particular file. He promised to check but
the following day he came back with the disappointing news that this
file could not be released because it contained some documents of the
Mossad, Israel's external intelligence agency.

The archivist's explanation only heightened my suspicions. I asked
him to go through the file document by document, keep back the documents of the Mossad and release those of the Foreign Ministry. Once
again, he promised to check, and after consulting with his superiors, he
informed me that this could not be done; the entire file had to remain

classified. The archivist assured me, however, that he himself had read the file and that it did not contain any incriminating evidence. I had no choice but to accept this. I am a historian, not a conspiracy theorist, so I cannot fling allegations without credible evidence to substantiate them. On the other hand, I also know that not every official act leaves behind a paper trail. I suspended judgement about the identity of the culprits but retained a burning interest in this saga.

One day, during a visit to Israel in 2017, almost by accident, I came across potentially credible evidence that the *Mossad l'Aliyah Bet* (the Yishuv's unit that handled illegal immigration to Palestine), and the Zionist underground in Iraq were behind the Baghdad bombings. This enabled me to see the story of my family as part of the much bigger story of the exodus of the Jewish community from Iraq. The decision to leave Iraq was extraordinarily agonising for us, as it was for many other Jewish families. We had lived in Iraq for generations, we had deep roots in the country, we were well integrated socially, my father's business was thriving and we had no desire to change either our identity, our nationality or our lifestyle. Going to Israel involved a leap in the dark for which we were utterly unprepared. On the other hand, the political situation in Iraq was deteriorating very rapidly with no prospect of improvement in sight. In some ways the outlook in 1948–49 was more depressing than it had been after the *farhud* in 1941. The *farhud* was a one-off event, whereas now the persecutions were more prolonged and many-sided. In 1941 it was the mob that had turned against the Jews; now it was the government.

In this climate of fear several thousand Jews took the risk of leaving Iraq illegally. Some were encouraged and assisted by the Zionist underground. In 1942, in the aftermath of the *farhud*, Zionist emissaries began arriving in Iraq from Palestine to make contact with local Jews, to teach them Hebrew and to spread the Zionist message. Their other tasks were to organise the illegal escape of Jews from Iraq to Palestine through Iran and to plan for local self-defence in the event of another pogrom. Small arms were smuggled into the country and the local recruits trained to use them. The underground was called Hatenua or 'the Movement' and its military wing was called Hashura or 'the Column'. Most of the recruits were young Jews from poor families. In secret meetings they would pass from hand to hand a pistol and the Jewish Bible. This is how they swore loyalty to the Movement. Zionists had no desire to ameliorate the conditions of Jews in Iraq – they wanted only to hasten their departure. The real aim was to prepare the recruits for Aliyah, for emigration to Palestine, and as this was not permitted by the authorities, it had to be done clandestinely. Iran offered a convenient, though risky and hazardous, route of escape for those Jews who wanted to leave Iraq, whether under the auspices of the Movement or under their own steam. Iran was the second Muslim-majority state to recognise Israel as a sovereign state after Turkey. The Shah of Iran was on bad terms with Iraq, while maintaining close covert ties with Israel. Consequently, the Jewish Agency was allowed to have an office in Tehran and to open a transit camp from which Jews could be airlifted to Israel.

Two of my cousins, Avraham and Fouad Hamama, made the clandestine journey to Israel via the Iran route. They were the sons of my father's sister Ragina, who had two other sons and four daughters. Ragina's husband Liyahu (Eliyahu) had a shop in the Shorja market in Baghdad. Ragina and Elias were illiterate. They were a poor family, unlike my mother's uncles who were all prosperous middle-class merchants. Life in the Hamamas' neighbourhood was considered unsafe after the *farhud* so Ezra, the eldest son, and Fouad, the youngest son, moved into my father's house which, as related in Chapter 3, enjoyed police protection. In 1944 when Ezra left the country illegally to go to Palestine, Avraham, the second son, took his place. Avraham was a quiet teenager, courteous and well-behaved but rather withdrawn. Unbeknown to my father, as far as I can tell, all three of his nephews were active in the Zionist underground.

Avraham was born in Baghdad in 1928; he attended the Shamash School, a Jewish high school with a good academic reputation supported by the Anglo-Jewish Association. While still at school, Avraham was recruited by the Zionist underground and, after thorough indoctrination, promoted to Hashura, its military wing. His job was to find suitable places to hide weapons, to maintain them, to repair them and to distribute them to the other activists as necessary. Training in the use of weapons was undertaken by Zionist emissaries in remote spots outside Baghdad. Avraham's task was to fetch the weapons from various caches in town and to return them when the training session was over. Whether he ever hid weapons in our house is an intriguing question to which I have no answer.

A female member of the movement who was equally fired by its ideals was Tsipora. Being a member of a secret society and handling weapons is empowering for a young man. For a young Jewish woman, given the conservative social customs of the times, it was even more liberating. One of the tenets of the movement was complete equality between women and men. Tsipora was an activist in her own right: she and Avraham worked as a team. The two teenagers fell in love and later married in Israel.

Fouad was too young to understand what was going on, but he too was of some help to the movement. When Avraham and his colleagues transferred weapons from one secret location to another, they would sometimes take Fouad with them to give the impression of an innocent family outing. In the autumn of 1949, facing an imminent threat of arrest by the police, Avraham and other members of his group crossed the border illegally and made their way to Tehran. After a year during which he assisted the Zionist officials in the transit camp, they arranged his flight to Israel. The Iranian government had agreed to treat any Iraqi Jew who came into its territory as a refugee and to facilitate their onward journey to Israel. Bribes on a large scale to senior Iranian officials were rumoured to have paved the way to this agreement.

In October 1949, Fouad followed in his brother's footsteps but his exodus, as he told me in Israel in 2019, was more eventful. He was only twelve years old when he embarked on the hazardous journey to Israel with a guide from the movement and about twenty other Jews. He was the only child. They made their way to Amara, a city in south-eastern Iraq about fifty kilometres from the border with Iran. In Amara they were arrested and sent back where they had come from in a police car, accompanied by a policeman who was meant to take them to jail. A bribe induced the policeman to set them free. Once freed, they did not go back to their homes in case the police came looking for them.

After a few days in hiding, the group set off again, this time with a Muslim guide, more smuggler than guide. The smuggler got them to the border, pointed to a border post and told them to complete the journey on foot. In fact, there were two border posts, one Iraqi, one Iranian. The smuggler, having received his fee, deliberately pointed them towards the Iraqi post because he wanted them to be arrested and sent back. Luckily, an Iranian officer ran towards them and steered them to his side of the border. An Iraqi officer came over immediately and demanded that the men be handed over to him. The Iranian refused, and the Iraqi threatened to come back with reinforcements to recover the criminals. The Jews reminded the Iranian officer that the Shah had issued instructions that any refugee from Iraq should be made welcome in his country. He in turn assured them that they had nothing to worry about. But they were still anxious and demanded to know what would happen if the Iraqi officer came back to claim them. The Iranian replied that he would shoot him, and this allayed some of their fears.

It took the group three months to get from the border to Tehran. The journey was rough, and food was hard to come by. It was a bitterly cold winter with rain and snowstorms. They made their way slowly, sometimes on foot, sometimes on donkeys, staying in poor villages where the standard breakfast consisted of pittas and dates. In Tehran they went to the transit camp of the Jewish Agency. Facilities in the camp were pretty elementary but here the newly arrived inmates could at least rest and enjoy regular meals. An Iranian official would come to the camp to do the paperwork before issuing the necessary exit permits. It was a slow process as individual forms had to be completed before issuing each exit permit. On one occasion, when the official was drinking and socialising with the older members of the group, young Fouad picked up his stamp and liberally dispensed exit permits. Once all the formalities had been completed, the Jews were put on a plane which took them to Lydda airport near Tel Aviv. The Shah's Iran played a pivotal part in facilitating the illegal immigration of Iraqi Jews to Israel.

Another relative who left Iraq illegally in 1949 was Jacob Saltoun, the brother of my grandmother Mouzli. This was a very different story. Uncle Jacob was a comfortable middle-class businessman with no links to and no sympathy for the Zionist movement. It was not the lure of Zion but the dire situation of the Jews in Iraq in the aftermath of the first Arab–Israeli war that drove him to flee; he felt that there was no future for himself and his family in Iraq because they were Jews. The decision to leave was agonising for him as it entailed the loss of most of his assets. But the danger of staying, as he saw it, outweighed the material benefits. He made up his mind, got some of his money out of the country through irregular channels, and left behind his house, his business and his car. Smugglers took Uncle Jacob, his family, and their faithful maid Sabiha, across the border into Iran. My grandmother called it 'on the black market' because leaving the country without an exit visa was an offence. In Tehran the family was helped by my mother's brother Alfred, who lived there, and from Tehran they completed the journey to Israel by air.

Policing its border with Iran was just one of the many concerns of the Iraqi government at that time. The fundamental question for Iraqis was whether to 'develop' and 'Westernise' in the way their former colonial masters had expected them to, or to chart an independent Arab course and pay the price. More immediately, the government had to cope with all the problems connected with colonialism and neo-colonialism. Although Iraq had gained formal independence in 1932, Britain continued to exercise indirect but decisive power through the royal family and a loyalist political elite headed by Nuri al-Said. The British, however, were unpopular in the country at large and their local friends were widely seen as collaborators.

The main opposition was the Istiqlal, a right-wing nationalist party which called for the assertion of complete Iraqi independence from British colonialism. It was formed in 1945; many of its members had shared Rashid Ali al-Gaylani's pro-Nazi sympathies and supported his anti-British coup in 1941. The party had a strong base of popular support and it offered vigorous opposition to the conservative ruling party. It was hostile to the Jews both because of its right-wing ideology and because the Jews were perceived as the allies of the British. Its newspaper, *Liwa al-Iraq* (the Flag of Iraq), which repeatedly described the Jewish minority as the lackeys of British colonialism and as a fifth column, called for the expulsion of all Jews from the country and the confiscation of their property. Iraq, it was argued, should treat the Jews as Israel treated the Palestinians.

The government had no intention of expelling the Jews, but it did need to regain control of the situation by acting to stem the illegal flight of Jewish people and Jewish money out of the country and to curb the subversive activities of the Zionist underground, which included the payment of bribes to politicians, civil servants, the police and the border police. Once it realised that the illegal flight of people could not be stopped, it decided to regain control by passing a law legalising it. Before enacting the law, the Iraqi cabinet asked Salih Jabr, the minister of the interior, to seek the advice of the British government. Jabr went to see the British ambassador in Baghdad and was informed that the British not only agreed that Iraq's Jews should be permitted to move to Israel but that they had already drafted a law to make it possible.

On 9 March 1950, the Iraqi Parliament passed the Denaturalisation Law, empowering the government to issue an exit visa to any Jew who wished 'of his own free will and choice' to leave the country for good. In addition to giving up their Iraqi nationality, those who left under the law had to waive their right to return to Iraq ever again. Those who chose to remain were assured of equal rights to those enjoyed by any Muslim. The law was to remain in force for one year. Nothing was said about the property rights of those who chose to leave. With the promulgation of this law, opening the gates to legal Jewish emigration to Israel, the illegal flight of Jews from Iraq declined dramatically. The official justification given for the law was the rising rate of illegal Jewish emigration, which was causing the country considerable economic damage. The driving force behind it was prime minister Tawfiq al-Suwaydi (1892–1968).

Suwaydi was a progressive Iraqi politician, a lawyer by profession, a Sunni Muslim whose family claimed the status of *sadah* (plural of *sayyid*), descendants of the Prophet Mohammad. Suwaydi had enjoyed an unusually cosmopolitan upbringing. As a child he had been sent to the Alliance elementary school in Baghdad, where most of his friends had been Jewish. This was generally recognised as the best school in Iraq at the turn of the twentieth century. Several other *sadah* families also sent their boys to this Jewish school because of the superior quality of its education. After school Suwaydi studied law in a college in Istanbul and at the Sorbonne in Paris, becoming fluent in Turkish and French in addition to English.[6]

Following the creation of Israel, the Arab League imposed a total boycott of the Jewish state. Iraq, like all other members of the league, observed this boycott. Iraqi Jews were only allowed to leave the country by depositing a large sum of money, forfeited if they failed to return within three months. This rule was intended to discourage Iraqi Jews from migrating to Israel. As leader of the Iraqi delegation to the United Nations in 1949, Tawfiq al-Suwaydi was well aware of the international pressure, orchestrated by Israel and its friends in America, to allow free movement to the Jews of Iraq. Zionist propaganda was ramped up against the Iraqi government, portraying the Jews as a community on the verge of annihilation, with Israel offering the only possible refuge. In Iraq Suwaydi had a reputation for being extremely well-disposed towards the Jews. He had many Jewish friends from his days at the Alliance school. Haskell Shemtob, the head of the Jewish community in Baghdad, was his neighbour and very close friend. Shemtob came from a prominent Jewish family. He was a businessman, an intellectual and former honorary consul of

Czechoslovakia. He was the epitome of the hard-working, successful, law-abiding and patriotic Iraqi Jew.

Shemtob sympathised with the general aims of the Zionist movement, but he deplored the illegal activities of its agents in Iraq and feared they would backfire against his community. Of high-handed Zionist methods Shemtob had first-hand experience. Back in 1943 Zionist emissaries had spirited away eighteen young Jews from well-to-do families out of the country without getting the permission of their families. Among them was Yosef, Shemtob's eighteen-year-old son. Shemtob was incensed and intervened forcefully with the Jewish Agency in Palestine, demanding the return of the youngsters. As it turned out, after a few months on an austere kibbutz, Yosef wanted to go back home anyway. By this time, however, he had no passport. He went to the Iraqi Consul in Jerusalem, who by chance was a friend of his father, and told him that he had lost his passport. The Consul issued him with a new one and urged him, with a wink, not to lose it again. [7] This was just one example of the growing tension between the leaders of the Baghdadi Jewish community and the intrusive Zionist emissaries.

Shemtob developed a particularly intense dislike for Mordechai Ben-Porat, the senior Mossad l'Aliyah Bet emissary to Iraq. Ben-Porat was in charge of all the other emissaries, controlled the budget, had the secret transmitter for communicating with his superiors back home and acted in the interest of the state of Israel, not in the interest of the local Jewish community. Shemtob accused Ben-Porat of acting irresponsibly, of impinging on the prerogatives of the elected local leadership and of jeopardising the position of the Jewish community. My mother recalled that Shemtob spoke with bitterness about Ben-Porat, calling him a liar and a low-class person. In Shemtob's eyes, Ben-Porat had no saving graces; he combined rudeness and recklessness in roughly equal proportions. On one occasion Shemtob was so angry with Ben-Porat that he took off his hat and flung it on the floor. Tawfiq al-Suwaydi agreed with Shemtob that emigration was a matter for the local Jewish community and its leaders, not for the agents of an enemy country. This agreement paved the way to the Denaturalisation Law. It also led the Iraqi government to delegate to the Jewish community the tasks of registering and arranging transport for those of its members who opted to leave.

My mother had some observations to make on both the law and on its principal architects. According to her, many of the Jews who registered under the law had not finally made up their mind to surrender their Iraqi citizenship; they simply wanted to give themselves a way out should the situation became intolerable. In other words, it was an option rather than an irrevocable decision. Moreover, they assumed, reasonably enough, that even in the event of leaving, their property rights would not be affected. Consequently, when another law was passed a year later, freezing the assets of those who had registered, they felt deceived.

For the two architects of the 1950 law my mother had nothing but praise. Haskell Shemtob was our close family friend. In the summer, he and his family often joined us for picnics by the Tigris River and shared the world-famous *masguf*, barbecued fish. Other picnics were held on the mainland. My mother, a young socialite, was good at spotting attractive venues for picnics such as private estates with lakes, gardens and parks. She would tell Shemtob of a suitable spot and he would contact the owner to obtain permission to use the grounds. On one occasion Shemtob turned to my mother, who was young enough to be his daughter, and said to her, 'Mama, where are you going to take us next time?' He and his wife used to come to our house to play cards and my parents used to go to theirs. They played poker for moderate sums of money. It was at social gatherings at their house that my parents met Tawfiq al-Suwaydi and his wife Fakhriya. Mr Suwaydi did not play cards, but his wife did. Like her husband, Fakhriya came from an upper-class Iraqi family. She had attended the Alliance Française school in Basra where she had been taught by French nuns.[8] Mrs Shemtob, Mrs Suwaydi and my mother became good friends and sometimes met to play cards in the morning when their husbands were at work. While most Jews of my parents' social class mixed freely in Muslim high society, Haskell Shemtob was especially well-connected and well-integrated.

He was one of a handful of Jews who belonged to an exclusive social club in Baghdad.

My mother's maternal uncle, S'hak-Moshi Saltoun, also belonged to this club. He was the butt of friendly banter between the two branches of the Semitic family. On one occasion Muslim friends asked S'hak-Moshi whether it was true that the Jews believed that when the Messiah arrives, the Muslims will become donkeys and the Jews will ride them. S'hak-Moshi did not deny the story. He was further pressed on this: would they choose Sunni or Shi'i donkeys? S'hak-Moshi dodged the question by saying that when the Messiah came, there would be utter pandemonium and the Jews would jump on the first donkey that came their way without checking out its sect!

My mother believed that Haskell Shemtob bribed Tawfiq al-Suwaydi to allow the Jews leave the country. When I asked her what made her think that Suwaydi received a bribe, she responded typically with a question: 'Why else would he do it?' She went on to observe that in Iraq in those days if you wanted anything done, you had to bribe the policeman, official or minister concerned. A bribe was nothing unusual: it was part of the prevailing political culture. A bribe, however, may be too strong a word for what transpired in this particular case. As well as being prime minister, Tawfiq al-Suwaydi served as chairman of the board of Iraq Tours, a well-established travel company based in Baghdad. The franchise for arranging the airlift of the Jews out of Iraq was given to an American company called Near East Air Transport which was in fact a front organisation for Israel, a partner of the national carrier El Al. At first the planes had to stop in Nicosia airport in Cyprus but later the pretence was dropped, and the planes were allowed to fly directly to Lod airport, near Tel Aviv. Iraq Tours was to receive a share of the revenue from the airlift based on the number of passengers. The sums involved were considerable: ten pounds per head multiplied by 100,000 passengers would have yielded a profit of a million pounds.[9] In this sense, the prime minister could be said to have profited indirectly from the deal.

The attitude of the Jewish community to the law was ambivalent. Some suspected that it was a ploy to unmask and arrest Zionists intent on leaving and taking their money with them. Some who were undecided were put off by the serious bureaucratic hurdles involved. In order to obtain a one-way exit visa an applicant needed a raft of permits – from the tax authorities, the ministry of justice, the local council and the police – to certify that he or she did not owe the authorities any money. Some families were deeply divided between leavers and remainers; when one member reached a firm decision to leave, the rest of the family usually followed. But the great majority of Iraq's Jews simply had no desire to abandon the land in which they had such deep roots. Consequently, in the early days after the passing of the Denaturalisation Law, very few Jews registered to relinquish their Iraqi nationality. In the following year, a series of explosions in Jewish buildings accelerated the pace of registration. The effect of the bombs was to generate fear, panic and disorientation in the Jewish community and to induce the great majority of the remainers to change their minds. The bombs were only one factor in a steadily deteriorating situation. Their effect, however, was not negligible. There was a direct correlation between the bombings and the rise in the number of applicants to emigrate from Iraq.[10]

An office was opened in the Meir Taweig synagogue for those who wished to register for *tasqit al-jinsiyya*, cancellation of citizenship. This was a condition for a one-way exit visa. Officials of the Jewish community were meant to be in charge of the formalities, but the Zionist militants elbowed them out of the way and usurped their place. Shlomo Hillel was in overall charge of arranging the charter flights to Israel. The exodus became known as *sant al-tasqit*, the year of the *tasqit*.[11] But it was very slow to get going. On the first day only three Jews came to the office in the synagogue to register. On 19 March 1950, a bomb went off in the American Cultural Center and Library in Baghdad, a centre frequented by many Jews. The bomb damaged the building and injured several people, but the psychological impact was limited because Jews were not the specific target. By 7 April the number of would-be emigrants had risen to 126.

The first attack on a Jewish target occurred on 8 April at 9.15 p.m. when a hand grenade was tossed from a moving car on the pavement outside the Dar al-Beyda, a Jewish-owned coffee shop in Abu Nuwas Street on the bank of the Tigris. No one was killed but four Jews were injured in the explosion. Although the damage was minimal, this incident shook the Jewish community. The following day, 3,400 Jews turned up at the emigration office to register. Most of them were poor, with very little to lose. By the end of the month, the number had reached 25,300.[12] This unexpectedly large number of applicants forced the authorities to open new emigration offices in Jewish schools and synagogues. In the middle of 1950, however, the pace of registration slowed down. Jews who had made it to Israel had reported on the dire conditions in the transit camps and warned their relatives against following in their footsteps. The warning had some effect, especially on the wealthier Jews. By this time, however, a vicious circle had been created and the waverers found it harder to remain. Zionists exploited the bombing incidents, issuing warning to the Jews to hurry up and leave the country before it was too late. By the end of the year, over ninety thousand Jews had registered to surrender their Iraqi citizenship. Then came the big bomb.

On 14 January 1951, at 7.00 p.m., a hand grenade was hurled into the outer courtyard of the Mas'uda Shemtob synagogue, which served as an assembly point for those who had been cleared by the authorities for departure. The grenade was a British-made Mills, used by the Iraqi army and police. Eyewitnesses reported that the grenade was thrown by an Arab-looking man. The grenade hit a high-voltage cable and exploded, killing four Jews and injuring twenty others. As the grenade was thrown at an almost empty courtyard, it may have been intended to scare rather than to kill; it was the accidental encounter with the cable that caused the fatalities. Whatever the intentions behind it, this deadly attack caused real panic and an instant spike in the number of people who opted to leave.

As soon as the dust had settled, rumours began to circulate about the identity and the motives of the attacker. People that Itzhak Bar-Moshe talked to assumed that the perpetrators had to be Nazis, Istiqlalis or some other extremist group of Jew-haters. Others suspected that this was the work of the Zionist underground. One man told Bar-Moshe that only the men of the movement could have done the terrible deed. 'Why would they do that?' asked Bar-Moshe. Because they were no less interested in accelerating the departure of the Jews from Iraq than the government or the police was the answer. Whatever its provenance, concluded Bar-Moshe, the bomb fulfilled its function: 'A new fear attacked the Jews… They felt that the earth was shifting beneath their feet, and they were assailed by apprehension of what was to come… The throwing of the bomb is a new chapter in our recent period in Iraq, an abyss has opened up in front of us.'[13]

Taken together with the earlier attacks, this one seemed to indicate that there was a malevolent organisation plotting against the Jews. Little doubt remained in the minds of most Jews that Iraq was no longer a safe place for them. Even wealthy upper middle-class Jews were compelled to review their options. By the beginning of March 1951, 105,400 had registered to leave, 70,000 of whom were still in the country – in a state of limbo.

At this point came another body blow to the Jewish community, this time from the Iraqi government. The offer of voluntary denaturalisation was valid for one year and was thus due to expire on 9 March 1951. By this time Nuri al-Said had replaced Tawfiq al-Suwaydi as prime minister. Nuri had not displayed any anti-Jewish sentiments in the past. On the contrary, he was associated with Faisal I's policy of befriending the Jews, a policy that Gertrude Bell had strongly recommended to both of them. But the large number of Jews who had participated in the Communist demonstrations against the Portsmouth Treaty in January 1948 was said to have incensed Nuri. This treaty was supposed to revise the 1930 Anglo-Iraqi Treaty, but effectively kept Iraq as a British protectorate. Popular protests forced Nuri to repudiate the new treaty, but they also turned him against the rebellious Jews. It was even rumoured that he swore to reduce the Jews to pauperism, to the selling of chickpeas in the streets of Baghdad.[14] Over the next couple of years Nuri canvassed and then shelved the idea of deporting the Jews of Iraq to Israel or alternatively of exchanging them for an equal number of Palestinian refugees.

This was Nuri's eleventh government. He now feared that the Iraqi economy could not survive the transfer of Jewish capital to an enemy Jewish state that had expelled more than half of Palestine's Arab population. On assuming office, he abruptly reversed Suwaydi's accommodating policy towards the Jewish community. On 10 March 1951, Nuri called the Chamber of Deputies into a special session and passed Law No. 5: Control and Administration of the Property of Denaturalised Jews. This law froze all the assets of the Jews who had renounced their citizenship: houses, businesses, shops, merchandise, securities and bank accounts. The law took immediate effect and it was implemented in a merciless manner. Banks were ordered to close their gates for two days, Jewish companies were impounded and Jewish shops were closed and sealed by the police, denying access to their owners.

By passing this law Nuri sought to punish both Iraq's Jews and the state of Israel. Jewish-Iraqi wealth, a potential asset to build the fledgling Jewish state, was diverted into the coffers of the Iraqi treasury. For the departing Jews this law was nothing short of a catastrophe. It caught them stateless, jobless and in many cases homeless. Those who had not yet sold their homes, as well as those who had sold their homes and deposited the proceeds in the bank, lost everything. Some assets were spirited out of the country by illicit means, but most of the 70,000 Jews who had registered to leave but had not yet left were made paupers overnight. Each adult, waiting for a seat on a plane to leave the country, was allowed to take only 50 dinars in cash and one suitcase.

During the rest of the year two more bombing incidents occurred. On 10 May 1951, at 3 a.m., a hand grenade was hurled at the display window of Jewish-owned Beit Lawee car dealership in Rashid Street. The company was the agent for importing American cars. Part of the building was destroyed but no one was hurt as the place was empty at the time of the explosion. On 9 June, an explosive device was set off at the entrance to a building owned by a Jew named Stanley Sha'shua, another agent for importing American cars. The explosion caused some damage to the building but no casualties. In the meantime, the government had extended the deadline for registration from March until the end of July. By the end of 1951, over 120,000 Jews had registered and by the beginning of 1952 nearly all had left for Israel. Israel was the only destination of Operation Ezra and Nehemiah. The planes were flown by Jewish pilots equipped with foreign passports. For Israel the operation yielded, apart from its human cargo, hundreds of thousands of pounds in hard currency.

That the five bombs played some part in persuading the Jews of Iraq to emigrate to Israel is beyond dispute. The big question is who planted the bombs? The evidence I have unearthed provides a partial answer to this question: three of the five bombs were the work of the Zionist underground in Baghdad. But before presenting the evidence for my version of events, I would like to dispose of the conventional Zionist version about the mass exodus from Iraq. This version categorically denies any Zionist role in the planting of the bombs. The two most prominent exponents of this version are Shlomo Hillel and Mordechai Ben-Porat. Shlomo Hillel was born in Baghdad in 1923 and emigrated to Palestine in 1934. After the Second World War, he played a key role in organising the illegal and then the legal immigration of the Iraqi Jews to Israel. His biggest success was a meeting with prime minister Tawfiq al-Suwaydi, at which he posed as an official of an American charter company, Near East Air Transport, and obtained the franchise for transporting the Jews out of the country. Hillel went on to have a distinguished public career as a diplomat, a minister and as the Speaker of the Knesset, the Israeli parliament. Hillel published a personal account of what he presented as a heroic Zionist effort to rescue the Jews of Iraq. In this book he dismisses the claim that the hand grenades had been thrown by Jewish agents to frighten the Jews into fleeing Iraq as 'patently absurd', a cynical fabrication peddled by Arab parties with their own axe to grind.[15]

Mordechai Ben-Porat was born in Baghdad in 1923 as Murad Kissas, was active in the Zionist underground, and left Iraq illegally for mandatory Palestine in 1945. He was sent back to Baghdad in 1949 by the Mossad l'Aliyah Bet, the organisation in charge of clandestine emigration, to prepare the ground for the exodus. He was in overall charge of Operation Ezra and Nehemiah and thus a key figure in the story. Ben-Porat was an abrasive and domineering personality who antagonised the leaders of the Baghdadi Jewish community by his brashness, by acting without consultation, by encroaching on their prerogatives and by endangering the lives of the Jews who preferred to stay in Iraq. During his four terms as Member of the Knesset, he represented five different political parties. He strenuously denied any involvement in the Baghdad bombs, but the rumours persisted. Disaffected Iraqi Jews in Israel called him Murad Abu al-Knabel, Murad of the Bombs.[16]

Ben-Porat published his own account under the title *To Baghdad and Back*. The book is boastful and self-congratulatory. Nevertheless, it is a valuable record of an eventful period in the history of the Jews of Iraq. Chapter 12 is entitled 'Bombs in the Streets of Baghdad'. Here the author states bluntly, as someone who headed the operation, that the claim that it was Israel's envoys who threw the bombs in the heart of Baghdad to frighten the Jews to make Aliyah was both base and utterly baseless. Indeed, he goes as far as to call this claim a blood libel.[17] As an appendix to his book, Ben-Porat includes the 1960 report of the commission of inquiry into the affair. The report stated that the commission did not find any factual evidence that the attacks were carried out by a Jewish organisation or Jewish individuals. Nor could the commission think of any logical reason that might have led a Jewish organisation to instigate such attacks. The commission was equally convinced that no Israeli organisation gave the order for these attacks.[18] In 1977 an Israeli journalist called Baruch Nadel accused Ben-Porat directly of planting the bombs. Ben-Porat sued the journalist for libel and won an unqualified apology.[19]

For Ben-Porat this was the end of the matter. But it is not for me. I can now say with full confidence that Ben-Porat did not throw any of the bombs that exploded in the streets of Baghdad in 1950–51. Whether he was complicit, and indeed whether he had any advance knowledge at all, is a separate question. Given his central position as the top Israeli emissary to Iraq, it is difficult to believe that he had no inkling of what his colleagues in the Zionist underground were up to. But we have no definite answers yet.

The person who was responsible for three of the bombs was Yusef Ibrahim Basri, a 28-year-old Baghdadi Jew, a lawyer by profession, a socialist, an ardent Jewish nationalist and a member of Hashura, the military wing of Hatenua, the Movement. In December 1949, as the persecution of the Jewish minority intensified, Basri left Iraq illegally and proceeded through Tehran on his way to Israel. In Israel he was recruited to the Mossad and sent back to Baghdad as a spy and security agent. Basri was not responsible for the fatal incident in the Mas'uda Shemtob synagogue; but he was responsible for three of the other explosions. His purpose was not to kill but to frighten hesitant Jews and to prod them to register to cancel their Iraqi citizenship. At least this is the impression I gained from talking to another Baghdadi Jew who belonged to the same close-knit Zionist circle and who, sixty-seven years later, gave me the untold story behind the exodus.

The name of my source is Yaacov Karkoukli, an Iraqi Jew who was born in Baghdad in 1928, served several prison sentences for Zionist activities and eventually escaped from Iraq to Israel in 1973. He was a neighbour and friend of my mother's in Ramat Gan and I met him through her on a visit in March 2017. My mother had a circle of friends, elderly Iraqi Jews, who regularly met every Monday evening over coffee and cakes in the lounge of the hotel in Kfar Ha-Maccabiya, in a leafy suburb of Ramat Gan. One Monday, Yaacov and his wife Dalia came to pick us up and drove us to the hotel. Both in the car and later in the hotel I sat next to him. He is a bespectacled man, of medium height, thin as a rake, with sunken cheeks and snow-white hair, eyebrows and moustache. He is hard of hearing, speaks slowly and deliberately, and his Hebrew is inflected with a distinct Arabic accent. In our group there

were four or five couples and the conversation was conducted in a mixture of Hebrew and Arabic. Most of those present, like Karkoukli, were
right-wing, Arab-spurning, Likud voters and much of the talk was about
current affairs. I tried to steer my private conversation with Karkoukli
away from the present and towards the distant past.

In the course of the evening, and in several subsequent conversations, I learnt a great deal about Karkoukli's background. His story is
worth retelling for the light it throws on the close links between Israel
and the Zionists among Iraq's Jews and on the manner in which Israel's
security services operated behind enemy lines. Unusually for a Jewish
boy, Yaacov went to a Muslim secondary school. In his early thirties
he acquired a deep knowledge of Muslim history and theology, of the
Qur'an and of Sharia or Islamic law. This was after the military coup
of 14 July 1958 which overthrew the monarchy. The leader of the coup
was Brigadier Abd al-Karim Qasim who happened to be Karkoukli's
neighbour. Qasim was an Iraqi nationalist, a genuine social reformer
and an anti-imperialist. His experience as a young officer in the 1948 war
for Palestine turned him against Britain and its Zionist protégées but
not against Iraq's Jewish minority – he displayed a remarkably liberal
and generous attitude towards Iraq's Jews until he was overthrown by
a Ba'ath coup in 1963. Karkoukli remembered Qasim as a decent and
upright man who gave half his salary to his parents and continued his
modest lifestyle after his rise to power. The two men became friends.
Qasim helped him to gain admission to the Faculty of Islamic Studies in
Baghdad to which non-Muslims were not eligible. Karkoukli completed
his studies with distinction in 1961. He received a sumptuous Qur'an
from the dean to which was attached a letter of congratulations from
the prime minister. The letter noted with pride that it was the first time
that a son of a minority had won that prestigious prize.

In July 1968, a dark age was inaugurated in Iraq by another Ba'ath
party coup which elevated Saddam Hussein to the position of vice-presi-
dent. Saddam put in place harsh measures against all of Iraq's minorities
and especially against the Jews. In this generally hostile environment,

Karkoukli was arrested and taken for interrogation first to Basra and from there to Qasr al-Nihaya in Baghdad, a former Ottoman royal palace turned by the Ba'ath regime into a notorious prison popularly known as the Palace of No Return. It was called the Palace of No Return because the prisoners, who were said to be enemies of the regime, were tortured and killed there. There was a special wing for Communists. Karkoukli spent five years in this prison, some of it in solitary confinement. He was subjected to the most excruciating forms of torture and his physical and mental health deteriorated to the point that he begged his guards to shoot him. No formal charges were ever pressed against him and no official trial was held. In January 1973 he was suddenly released with no explanation and allowed to leave Iraq with his family to go to live in Israel.[20]

From a very young age Yaacov had been attracted to the Zionist movement. The same was true of his sister Ruth and younger brother Avraham. The whole family had been traumatised by the *farhud* and pinned their hopes for a better future on the Zionist ideal of an independent Jewish state in Palestine. When Yaacov was seven or eight years old, his elder brother Shlomo impressed on him that their real home was not Iraq but Palestine. In 1944, when he was sixteen years old, Yaacov visited Palestine for the first time to stay with his sister Ruth. During his visit someone took him to see Isser Harel, the head of the internal security service of the state in the making. Harel remarked that Yaacov could be an asset and asked whether he would be prepared to help them. Without hesitating, Yaacov said 'Yes'. He was given the codename Gideon. His first task was to help an expert replicate the various stamps and permits on his Iraqi passport. These forged documents had been used by the movement repeatedly to get its members out of Iraq through Iran and into Palestine. In Baghdad Yaacov continued to serve the Zionist cause by collecting information and by helping its secret envoys in countless practical ways. He claims to have supplied Israel with a full list of Iraqi arms acquisitions in 1948, the year of the first Arab–Israeli war.

Yaacov Karkoukli stressed to me that he became a Zionist activist purely out of ideological conviction. He was trained as an account-ant, earned a good living and did not need any financial support. Indeed, he was prepared to pay a high price for his services to the Zionist cause, including arrest and torture. Although he survived the ordeal, it left deep physical and emotional scars. Yet he had no regrets. Looking back on his life, he was proud of what he had done and frankly amazed by the courage he had displayed as a young man in the face of adversity. If he had his way again, he would do it all over again, he said. His commitment to the state of Israel was unconditional and he even justified the violent methods it had used to liquidate the Jewish Diaspora in Iraq. A few individuals had paid with their lives and many lost their assets but the gains for the fledgling Jewish state had been incalculable. Although he himself is a life-long supporter of the right-wing Likud, Karkoukli thought that David Ben-Gurion, the leader of the Labour Party and Israel's first prime minister, had possessed the foresight and the wisdom in 1950 to look fifty years ahead. If he had not acted as he had, a unique opportunity would have been missed: less than a fifth of Iraq's Jews would have made Aliyah and Israel would have ended up in poorer shape demographically, economically, and in terms of security. The uprooting of the Jewish community from Iraq was fully justified.

In other words, he thought the end justified the means. But he had something more interesting to say about the Baghdad bombings and the Zionist underground. When I got home, I hurriedly jotted down everything I could remember. In short: Yaacov Karkoukli belonged to a small group which had made the practical arrangements for those Jews who had opted to leave following the passage of the Denaturalisation Law; the group included Yusef Basri, a lawyer and a member of Hashura; Basri carried out terrorist attacks on his own without ever telling the others what he was up to; Basri's controller was an Israeli intelligence officer, Max Binnet, who was based in Iran; Binnet supplied Basri with hand grenades and TNT; Basri had carried out three of the attacks on Jewish sites but definitely not the one on the Mas'uda Shemtob synagogue.

Karkoukli was most insistent that Basri had had nothing to do with the attack on the synagogue. This invited the obvious question: who was the real perpetrator? Karkoukli replied, a touch self-importantly, that he was the only person in the world who knew the answer to this question. After a bit of prompting, he divulged the identity of the perpetrator. It was Salih al-Haidari, a Sunni Muslim of Syrian origins. Haidari, according to Karkoukli, was an unsavoury character and a crook who lived off fraud and the immoral earnings of his five sisters. He had some Jewish acquaintances, but had made the mistake of trying to defraud them. They had reported him to the police, he had been arrested and convicted, and had served a prison sentence. Haidari had lobbed the hand grenade into the courtyard of the synagogue as an act of revenge against the Jews who had reported him to the authorities.

These revelations were intriguing and whetted my appetite for more. I was due to fly back to the UK the following day in the late afternoon. I asked Karkoukli whether I could visit him at his home in the morning with a notepad to take notes. He replied that a few hours would not be enough. He knew the whole story, he had documents to validate it, but I would need two or three whole days with him to get the full story. I had no choice but to leave it at that. The tally so far was three bombs by a Jew, one by a Muslim criminal and one bomb of uncertain provenance. There were still many unanswered questions in my mind as I boarded the British Airways flight from Ben Gurion Airport to Heathrow.

My next trip to Israel was in late October 2017. This time I went armed with a tape recorder. The main purpose of the trip was to give the keynote speech at a Palestinian conference in East Jerusalem on the hundredth anniversary of the Balfour Declaration. As well as attending the conference, I spent a week with my mother in Ramat Gan. On 28 October, Yaacov Karkoukli and his wife Dalia came in the evening to my mother's flat. The interview, which I recorded, was entirely in Hebrew and lasted an hour and a half. It was punctuated by interventions from my mother, in a mixture of Hebrew and Arabic, to answer some of the questions I put to our guest or to offer us coffee, tea, Arak, nuts, dates, dried apricots, chocolates and other refreshments.

I now propose to report in detail the substance of the interview although it involves some overlap with what I have already written in this chapter. Following the passage of the Denaturalisation Law, a small group, consisting of Israeli envoys and local Zionists, was formed to speed up the process of registration and emigration. The group included Mordechai Ben-Porat, the senior Israeli emissary, Yusef Basri, Yusef Khabaza, Sasson Sadiq, Yaacov Karkoukli himself and a few others. They used to meet in the house of Sasson Sadiq to play cards, but this was just a cover for their real activities.

The response of the Jewish community to the law was slow and hesitant. Only hundreds came forward in the initial phase. The Israeli authorities were seriously disappointed by this response. Consultations took place and a decision was reached to take action to encourage Jews to give up their Iraqi citizenship. Israel needed the manpower both to build the country and to boost numbers in the army. At that time Israel's population was tiny, only 600,000 people, while surrounded by Arab countries with a combined population of tens of millions. There was an urgent need to increase numbers on the Jewish side of the demographic equation.

Karkoukli could not remember specific dates and locations of the bombing incidents. But he did recall the names of the Dar al-Beyda, Beit Lawee and Stanley Sha'shua, and he had noticed that on one occasion Yusef Basri was absent for several days without giving any explanation and that the absence had coincided with an explosion. On another occasion Basri had left a meeting for a couple of hours and when he returned, he was silent and visibly stressed. On a third occasion Karkoukli saw Basri in the street in his car, a small black Austin. Basri arrived at the meeting about five minutes after Karkoukli, looking slightly dishevelled, a bit anxious and rather confused. He was reluctant to talk and just sat quietly in a corner in an effort to regain his composure. Karkoukli thought, but could not be sure, that this may have been the day of the explosion in the Dar al-Beyda café in which one Jew had been injured in the eye. In any case, he did not disclose his suspicions to Basri, nor did he discuss them with any other member of their group.

Karkoukli said that Basri's controller was an Israeli intelligence officer named Max Binnet, based in Tehran. His full name was Meir Max Binnet and he was a major in the intelligence branch of the IDF. In Tehran Binnet enjoyed considerable freedom of action within the framework of the covert collaboration between the two countries. Binnet provided Basri with maps, intelligence, instructions, hand grenades and TNT. The grenades, the explosives and the instructions were all carefully calibrated to terrorise and not to kill. Basri would leave his car in Khanaqin, about eight kilometres from the border with Iran, on the Alwand tributary of the Diyyala River, and then cross the border illegally to meet with his controller. This was not too risky as the border was not closely guarded. After Basri was arrested, traces of TNT identical to those from the bomb site were found in his car.

Basri was arrested on 10 June 1951 due to an error he had made. After four bombs had gone off in the streets of Baghdad, the Criminal Investigation Department (CID) had come under tremendous pressure to find the culprits. Detectives noticed that a group of Jews congregated in Sasson Sadiq's house under suspicious circumstances, so they took him to the police station for interrogation. Sadiq maintained that his friends came to his house to play cards. He could not tell them anything about the bombs because he knew nothing. Basri was Sadiq's cousin and legal representative.

One morning Basri called on Sadiq's wife, Simha, to help her arrange a visit to her husband in the police station. There was a knock on the door. Basri peeped out of the window and saw a CID car. He should have stayed put and told the detectives that he was Sasson Sadiq's legal representative and that he was there to try to secure his release. But he panicked and hid inside a wardrobe. The detectives asked Simha whether she knew Yusef Khabaza. She said she knew him but had no idea where he was. In fact, Khabaza had just managed to escape from Iraq with forged documents and was on his way to Israel. The detectives began to search the house and found Basri hiding in the wardrobe. 'Who are you?' they demanded. Basri told them his name, that he was a lawyer, and Sasson Sadiq's cousin. But it was now too late for Basri to feign innocence. If he was innocent, why was he hiding? Basri was unable to provide a plausible explanation. He was arrested on the spot, taken into custody, subjected to protracted torture and tried to commit suicide. After nearly a month of horrific torture, he broke down and confessed that he was responsible for three of the bombs but not for the one in the Mas'uda Shemtob synagogue.[21]

Karkoukli had already told me at our first meeting that the perpetrator of the bomb in the synagogue was a disreputable Syrian character called Salih al-Haidari. He had also told me that this was an act of revenge against the Jews, who he claimed had wronged him. But now he surprised me by saying that Haidari was put up to it by a police officer of the Bataween district. This did not make much sense and I said so. Why should an Iraqi police officer do the dirty job for the Zionist underground by putting pressure on the Jews to emigrate to Israel? On hearing Karkoukli's explanation, I nearly fell off my chair: the man in question was a collaborator who had received a bribe from the Zionist underground. The movement wanted to frighten the Jews who still hoped to stay in Iraq, so they had bribed the police officer, who had hired Haidari to do the dirty deed.

I asked in disbelief if that meant that Zionist activists had deliberately set off bombs in Jewish premises. Yes, was the calm answer. Were Israel's emissaries directly involved in the payment of the bribes to the corrupt Iraqi policeman, I wondered. Karkoukli did not know the answer. He thought the movement paid the bribes. But he compared the Mossad to an octopus. He did not know the word in Hebrew so he used the Arabic words – akhtaboot and ogdobus.[22] Did Basri know that the police officer was in the pay of the Zionists? Karkoukli was inclined to think that he did but he could not be sure. What he did know was that the police officer was arrested, tried and convicted of collaboration with the enemy. Little publicity, however, was given to his trial. The movement, naturally enough, kept as low a profile as possible in this affair. It desperately tried to minimise the publicity given to its bribing of officials and false flag operations. The authorities, for their part, were embarrassed by the discovery of a traitor in their midst. They therefore did their best to keep this particular case out of the limelight. By contrast, they proudly proclaimed their success in uncovering and bringing to justice the ring of Zionist spies and saboteurs.

Another Zionist activist caught by the CID was Basri's assistant, Shalom Salih Shalom. Shalom was a rather naïve nineteen-year-old cobbler who was recruited into the ranks of Hashura and trained as a weapons expert. Israeli emissaries, as noted earlier, smuggled weapons to Baghdad and secretly trained young Iraqi Jews in their use for the purpose of self-defence in the event of another *farhud*. Shalom's job was to hide the weapons in various synagogues and private homes. He was also detailed by the Zionist underground to help with registering Jews who decided to give up their Iraqi citizenship. The main registration venue was in the Meir Taweig synagogue but as the numbers increased, an additional venue was opened in the Mas'uda Shemtob synagogue. Shalom was arrested in this synagogue, which served as a major storehouse for illicit weapons. Under interrogation, which was accompanied by the most horrific forms of CID torture, Shalom broke down. He confessed that he, Yusef Basri, and Yusef Khabaza had carried out three out of the five attacks. He took the police from synagogue to synagogue and from house to house, showing them where the weapons were hidden.

At the house of Yusef Khabaza, who managed to escape in the nick of time, they found weapons, explosives, a map marked with the location of the other caches and a list of the members of the movement. This enabled the police to round up the entire ring. They arrested twenty-one activists, including some women, and put them all on trial. The prosecution charged the suspects with membership of the underground Zionist organisation. The suspects' primary aim was said to be to frighten the Jews into emigrating as soon as possible and the most serious charges were pressed against those involved in the planting of bombs to achieve this aim. Some of the defendants were released and the rest were sentenced to various terms in prison, ranging from five months to five years. Yusef Khabaza was sentenced to death *in absentia*.

The trial of Yusef Basri and Shalom Salih Shalom began on 15 October 1951. They were charged with carrying out three terrorist attacks: on 19 March 1950 on the American Cultural Center; on 10 May 1951 on the Beit Lawee company building; and on 9 June 1951 on the Stanley Sha'shua car dealership. A sample of the TNT found in Basri's car was one of the pieces of incriminating evidence submitted to the court to prove his guilt. Basri and Shalom were sentenced to death by hanging. According to Shlomo Hillel, Basri's last words before going to the gallows were 'Long live the State of Israel!'

All in all, twelve caches were uncovered by the CID, yielding a substantial haul. The sentences passed against those convicted cited 425 grenades, 33 submachineguns, 186 revolvers, 24,647 bullets, 79 magazines for submachineguns and 32 daggers.[23]

I have not been able to identify who was responsible for the fourth bomb. Yusef Khabaza, Yusef Basri and Shalom Salih Shalom perpetrated three of the terrorist attacks on their co-religionists. The Israeli government categorically denied any Jewish or Israeli involvement in any of the explosions. Mordechai Ben-Porat and Shlomo Hillel attributed all the attacks to right-wing Muslim extremists from the Istiqlal Party. Yaacov Karkoukli was sure that Basri did not lob the hand grenade into the Mas'uda Shemtob synagogue but unsure whether he was responsible for three or four of the other explosions. I am inclined to believe that Basri was involved in three of the remaining explosions while the Istiqlal Party was implicated in the other one. I reached this conclusion not in the spirit of compromise but, tentatively, on the basis of one flimsy piece of evidence.

In 2013 an Iraqi journalist named Shamil Abdul Qadir published a book entitled *History of the Zionist Movement in Iraq and its Role in the*

Emigration of the Jews in 1950–1951. The author reports that an Istiqlal Party member, whom he only identifies by his initials as M.Sh.A., confessed to him that he and another party member (T.B.) carried out the attack on Dar al-Beyda in April 1950 under the direction of Adnan al-Rawi, a poet and one of the leaders of the party. In the alleged confession,

> Al-Rawi told us that the hesitation of the Jews to leave Iraq requires action to force them to leave Iraq, and we in the party are hoping for the expulsion of all Jews from Iraq. Actually, a decision was taken to blow up Casino al-Beyda, which was frequented by Jewish youth. Al-Rawi told us that he would supply us with the bombs to throw on the casino to put terror in the heart of the Jews. After a few days, al-Rawi came and I and (T.B.) were tasked with throwing the bombs on the casino, and on the designated day in April 1950 we threw the bombs on the Jews sitting there and we escaped and hid in a house rented near the entry of Abu Nuwas Street near the casino and we disappeared.[24]

On the basis of this confession, I have concluded that the Istiqlal Party, not the Zionist underground, was probably responsible for the grenade attack on Dar al-Beyda on 8 April 1950.

Shamil Abdul Qadir is a friend of Haifa Jajjawi, an Iraqi woman who works in the Middle East Centre Library in my college, St Antony's College, Oxford. Through her he donated the above-mentioned title and his other books, none of which have been translated into English, to our library. With the help of Haifa I contacted Shamil Abdul Qadir and corresponded with him by email in April and May 2022. He was extremely well informed and very helpful. He informed me that the man who received the bribe from the Zionist underground to organise the bombing of the Mas'uda Shemtob synagogue was Salem al-Quraishi, a captain in the Special Division of the Baghdad City Police Directorate. Al-Quraishi later participated in the raids on the synagogues and the schools in search of the hidden weapons. He was transferred from service in the Special Division to a regular police

station. After the 14 July 1958 coup, he was arrested and sentenced by the
revolutionary court to prison with hard labour.

Karkoukli was inaccurate on the back story of the bribe and the
bombing of the synagogue. In most other respects, however, what he
told me tallies with the rest of the evidence that I have been able to
gather from other sources. For one of his claims I have not been able to
find any supporting evidence. This concerns the policy of the state of
Israel towards the property of the Jews who left Iraq. One of the reasons
for the Iraqi government's refusal to allow free exit to the Jews before
March 1950 was the fear of the economic consequences for the country.
The Jews were a major pillar of the national economy and the banking
system and if they were to leave *en masse* with all their assets, the consequences could have been serious. Some writers have claimed that the
Israeli government was so desperate for people that it indicated that it
would welcome the Jews even without their property. One, Avraham
Shama, claims that 'sometime in the spring of 1950, the Iraqi authorities
reached an agreement with Jewish Agency representatives to allow Iraqi
Jews to leave Iraq on a one-way visa to Israel, provided that they give up
their Iraqi citizenship and leave their assets to the Iraqi government.'[25]

Karkoukli did not go that far. But he did claim that from the beginning, the Israeli government regarded Iraqi-Jewish wealth as a bargaining
chip in future peace negotiations with the Arabs. Israel came under
strong international pressure to allow the 750,000 Palestinians who
became refugees in 1948 either to return to their homes or to receive
compensation. Israel flatly rejected the right of return. This left the
alternative of compensation but this too Israel was extremely reluctant
to concede. In this context the idea arose of offsetting the property left
behind by the Palestinian refugees against the property of Iraqi Jews.

Karkoukli maintains that all along this idea was in the back of the
minds of the Israeli policymakers and that it was for this reason that
they did not defend as robustly as they should have done the property
rights of the Iraqi-Jewish community. More specifically, he maintains
that Shlomo Hillel and Haskell Shemtob reached a tacit understanding

with Tawfiq al-Suwaydi that if the Jews were allowed to leave for Israel, their property could remain behind. This claim cannot be reconciled with the fact that Hillel met Suwaydi on 28 April 1950, seven weeks after the Denaturalisation bill became law. Moreover, Hillel went to see the prime minister masquerading as the representative of an American charter company to do business, to arrange a transport deal. He could not possibly have made any such offer on behalf of the Israeli government. Shemtob was the head of the Jewish community so it is highly improbable that he would have agreed to such a cynical deal at its expense either.

The only person who actively sought such a deal was Mordechai Ben-Porat. By his own account, he wrote to the Mossad on 19 March 1950 stating that there was a chance of moving things forward by bribing the prime minister and the minister of the interior. He suggested giving these two men part of the property that remained in Iraq and compensating the Jewish owners with the property left by the Palestinian refugees in Israel. Ben-Porat requested permission to go ahead but, as he records in his book, he received no reply of any kind.[26]

Israel did take a position on Iraqi-Jewish property but only after the passage of the property-freezing law. On 19 March 1951, Moshe Sharett, Israel's foreign minister, denounced the law from the podium of the Knesset as 'an act of robbery' and linked it for the first time to the property that the Palestinian refugees had left behind in Israel. Sharett announced that his government had decided that the value of the Jewish property frozen in Iraq would be taken into account in calculating the sum of compensation that may be paid to the Arabs who had abandoned their property in Israel.[27] This statement is significant for the linkage it makes between the two sets of property. I have found no evidence, however, of an agreement between the Israeli and Iraqi governments regarding the property of Iraq's Jews before the Denaturalisation Law came into force. This does not mean that there was no agreement. What it does mean is that the available evidence does not permit any final judgement on this critical issue at this stage.

During one of my visits to Israel I tried to check the story about the alleged Israeli-Iraqi deal with Shlomo Hillel himself by calling him at his home in Ra'anana. On 30 July 2018, we spoke over the phone for an hour and a half. He was ninety-five years old, but his mind was sharp, his voice was strong, he radiated self-confidence and he welcomed the opportunity to put forward once again the heroic version of Operation Ezra and Nehemiah. At the very beginning of our conversation, he dismissed categorically as utterly preposterous the claim of an Israeli agreement with Tawfiq al-Suwaydi that his government could keep the assets of Jews who left for Israel. Hillel reminded me that, as he wrote in his book, he went to the meeting with Suwaydi on 28 April 1950 not as Shlomo Hillel but with a false identity as Richard Armstrong, a representative of the American charter company, Near East Air Transport, and that the sole purpose of the meeting was to discuss the cost and logistics of the airlift of the Jews who had opted to avail themselves of the Denaturalisation Law.

Hillel added that Suwaydi had expected only a small number of Jews to take up the offer. His evidence for this is that Sir Henry Mack, the British ambassador to Baghdad, reported to the Foreign Office that he had asked the prime minister how many Jews he estimated would leave following the passage of his bill in parliament and that the answer had been 6,000 or 7,000. Hillel also rejected as baseless Karkoukli's suggestion that Israel may have given the Iraqis its tacit consent to their keeping the property of Iraq's departing Jews in the expectation that this could be used to offset the demand for compensation from the Palestinian refugees. There were no direct or indirect negotiations between the Israeli and the Iraqi governments on the property of Iraqi Jews, Hillel insisted.

Hillel went on to reject most emphatically the suggestion of Israeli or Zionist involvement in setting off the bombs. The main thrust of his argument was that in 1950 Israel was in no position to absorb a large number of Iraqi Jews. In the first and second year of its existence Israel was flooded with immigrants from different countries and the Jewish Agency was forced to allocate national quotas to keep within its limited resources. Immigrants from Poland and Romania were given priority. Romania defied Moscow's orders and opened its gates to Jewish emigration to

Israel. The Jewish Agency had to pay a sum of money to the Romanian government for each emigrant. Fear that the gates would shut again led the Jewish Agency to put Romanian Jews at the head of the queue. This was very frustrating for Shlomo Hillel, who had been sent to organise the legal Aliyah from Iraq after the gates were opened.

In March 1950 Hillel went to see Levi Eshkol, the treasurer of the Jewish Agency, to press the case of Iraq's Jews. Eshkol reportedly said to him, 'Tell them they'll be welcome but not now. We have no houses, no tents, no schools, no employment, and no food.' Two days later Hillel went to see prime minister David Ben-Gurion. Ben-Gurion reportedly said to him, 'Eshkol is right. We don't have anything. But there is a risk that the Iraqi government will change its mind. So, go and bring over Iraq's Jews as soon as possible!' Hillel argued that under the circumstances it made no sense for Israel's leaders to give the order to plant bombs in order to accelerate the pace of Aliyah from Iraq.[28] But I do not claim that the order, if there was an order at all, came from the top Israeli leadership.

With the exception of the property deal, Karkoukli impressed me as a reliable source on the part played by the Zionist movement in the climactic events of 1950–51. Unlike some of the other, better known participants in the drama who later went into public life in Israel, he had no axe to grind. By the time we met, the majority of his generation had passed away. Karkoukli was eighty-nine years old and he was anxious to leave behind a record of the momentous events in which, as he was well aware, he had played only a very minor part. Yet, as he repeatedly pointed out to me, he was one of only a handful of survivors who knew the backstory. And he was keen to tell the story rather than to take it with him to his grave. At one point he even suggested that he and I write up the story together. I replied that I was no expert on Iraq's history, that I was only writing a personal memoir and that he would be better off writing his story in collaboration with an Israeli journalist.

There remains the matter of the supporting documents, most notably the Baghdad police report on the affair, which at our first meeting Karkoukli had told me he had in his possession. As a diplomatic

historian I am deeply interested, not to say obsessed, with documentary evidence. At our second meeting, the one at which I recorded the
interview, I reminded Karkoukli of his promise, but he was evasive.
He said that his personal archive was in Kiryat Ono, in a flat he had
shared with his first wife until she died. After he had met Dalia and
moved to her flat in Ramat Gan, he had rented the flat in Kiryat Ono
to an old couple. I offered to go with him to Kiryat Ono to retrieve
the police report. He politely declined my offer. I began to suspect
that the document did not exist and that Karkoukli was just stringing
me along. I kept badgering him for the report and he kept procrasti-
nating. My mother also stayed on the case and her persistence paid
off. One day she called me to say that she had the report and that she
would mail it to me in Oxford. This report was well worth waiting for.

The police report is not on headed notepaper. It is on plain paper, one
page long, in Arabic of course, with no date, no signature, no subject
line and no indication of who it was intended for. I had to ask Karkoukli
where this report came from, and how he got his hands on it. His reply
was that many years after the event he felt he needed to know the whole
truth, so he had conducted his own inquiries. As it happened, he had
a Muslim friend, a retired senior police officer, who he turned to for
help. Karkoukli claimed that he had succeeded in convincing the friend
that his interest was of a historical rather than a political nature and the
friend had obliged by procuring for him a copy of the report from the
Baghdad police archive. Here is what it says:

> The confidential records of the special police division revealed the
> misinformation techniques by which (a cadre of) the secret Zionist
> movement in Iraq resorted to trick the Jewish sect and convince them
> to leave Iraq, as those coming from Israel utilized and clung to immoral
> ways to (facilitate) their mission such as the payment of large bribes and
> the forging of official documents.
>
> Kurgi Sabih Laoui recalls: Israeli agents used the doctor (Abdulnabi),
> an Iraqi Jew, in forging the signature of Iraqi minister of interior Salih

Jabr and that one of those close to that minister requests 200 dinars for each permit (to migrate) an Iraqi Jew and that the travel department refused all transactions that carried the signature of Salih Jabr due to their discovery of them being forged!

Moreover, Jewish employees at the airport were used (to smuggle) many bags, and the police arrested a Lebanese citizen named (Adel) who was attempting to smuggle twenty-six bags for individuals belonging to the secret Zionist organisation.

On 21 June 1951, the orders were issued for the arrest of 149 members of the secret Zionist organisation, and after a week the police caught in the Mas'uda Shemtob Synagogue two military transmission devices carrying the code D-5 which were used by some members of the emigration committee to send telegrams to Tel Aviv.

A few days before that, more precisely on the 16 June, Shalom Salih Shalom confessed in detail his role and that of Yusef Basri and Yusef Murad [Yusef Murad Khabaza] in the case of throwing bombs and explosives on Jewish shops; and with that the police were able to crack the big puzzle which engulfed Baghdad due to the disappearance of the real culprits of these crimes which targeted Iraqi Jews.

Shalom told the investigator: On this day I found myself in a dilemma, whether to reply with an untruthful confession regarding the facts that you have faced me with, but as I have confessed some of the issues such as pointing to the weapons hideouts, I decided to disclose all the facts that I have.

Yusef Basri also confessed his role and added: after a law was promulgated for revoking citizenship, orders were given from Israel to recall all the members of the secret Zionist movement and indeed we were able to move out many of them while Yusef Murad [Khabaza] and Habib [Mordechai Ben-Porat] remained.

Investigator: Do you know anything about Habib?

Yusef Basri: I thought that he came from Israel and that he converted our activities to a terrorist activity such as throwing bombs and he depended on known sources in spying on Iraq such as Ezra Hindy,

Shamoun Ballas, Salim Sadiq, Eliyahu Binmoor, Dad Basha, Lateef Fraem, Zilkha, and the two doctors Salim al-Shukurjy and Edwar Marwan.

Yusef Murad [Khabaza] was known by the name Johnny, and he was enthusiastic about migrating Jews and he frequented their shops and markets urging them to relinquish their citizenship and he was paid by Habib. Habib was not at that time in Baghdad as he had escaped to Israel and appeared with the name Mourdkhay bin Furat [Mordechai Ben-Porat]. With his escape the number of Iraqi Jews who relinquished their citizenship under the influence of the secret Zionist movement reached 108,154, and the number of Jews that had emigrated was 99,546, and 8,608 remained in waiting until 20 June 1951!

This report constitutes undeniable proof of Zionist involvement in the terrorist attacks that helped to terminate two and a half millennia of Jewish presence in Babylon. I hesitate to call it a 'smoking gun' because it does not carry any of the usual marks of an official document. On the other hand, it is evidently based on inside knowledge. It could not have been compiled without access to the police records. The minute details contained in the report, and the naming of names, enhance its credibility.

Any lingering doubts I may have had were finally laid to rest by the testimony of the Iraqi journalist and leading expert on the subject, Shamil Abdul Qadir. Abdul Qadir had a friend, a retired police officer, Colonel Abdul Rahman al-Samarrai. In 1950–51, al-Samarrai commanded the unit of the Special Division of the Baghdad City Police Directorate that investigated the illegal Zionist activities. He acted on orders from the Director General of the Baghdad police, Abdul Jabbar Fahmy, and took part alongside Salem al-Quraishi in the arrest and interrogation of activists and in the raids into Jewish buildings in search of weapons. Al-Samarrai gave Abdul Qadir a copy of the entire file of the investigations of the Zionist activists. The file is 258 pages long. I sent the one-page report in my possession to Abdul Qadir and he confirmed that it was part of the larger file.[29]

There are two aspects to the saga of the bombs: the personal and the professional. The story I heard from my family and relatives when I was a boy affected me emotionally and raised many unanswered questions. It was distressing and disempowering to think that fellow Jews might have played a part in uprooting us from our homeland. I became obsessed with this story. Later came my engagement with the story as a professional historian. It was tempting to adopt a conspiracy theory but as a historian I needed hard evidence to confirm or refute it. This was the source of my lifelong search for the truth of the matter. If I failed to get to the bottom of it, it was not for lack of trying. What I hope I have achieved is to put together the best available evidence, including the new evidence I have unearthed, and to use this evidence to unpick the Zionist version of this sorry saga. My correspondence with Shamil Abdul Qadir was the last stage in my quest for the truth. He left no room for doubt that the police report given to me by Yaacov Karkoukli was genuine. Just the extract I have from this longer report is a serious indictment of the Zionist activists and of the methods they employed to achieve their ends, such as the payment of bribes and the forging of documents. But the most serious charge contained in the report is that Israel's emissaries turned their local Jewish followers into terrorists.

Yusef Basri and Shalom Salih Shalom were hanged in Baghdad in January 1952, about half a year after the official conclusion of Operation Ezra and Nehemiah. As the Israeli sociologist Yehouda Shenhav observed:

It would have been only natural for Iraqi Jews in Israel to have reacted with outrage to news of the hanging. But on the contrary, the mourning assemblies organized by leaders of the community in various Israeli cities failed to arouse widespread solidarity with the two Iraqi Zionists. Just the opposite: a classified document from Moshe Sasson, of the Foreign Ministry's Middle East Division, to Foreign Minister Moshe Sharett maintained that many Iraqi immigrants, residents of the transit camps, greeted the hanging with the attitude: "That is God's revenge on the movement that brought us to such depths." The bitterness of that

reaction attests to an acute degree of discontent among the newly arrived
Iraqi Jews. It suggests that a good number of them did not view their
immigration as the joyous return to Zion depicted by the community's
Zionist activists. Rather, in addition to blaming the Iraqi government,
they blamed the Zionist movement for bringing them to Israel for reasons
that did not include the best interests of the immigrant.[30]

Controversy surrounding the responsibility for the Baghdad bombshell
continues to reverberate in Israel to this day. In 1954 this infamous episode received renewed attention because of the so-called 'Unfortunate
Business', otherwise known as 'Operation Susannah' or 'the Lavon
Affair'. A number of Egyptian Jews were arrested for planting bombs
in public places and in the US Information Service offices in Cairo and
Alexandria. This was an Israeli false flag operation designed to create bad
blood between the revolutionary regime headed by Gamal Abdel Nasser
and the Western powers. Israel's military intelligence had recruited,
trained and equipped the Jewish spy and sabotage ring. The arrest of one
member led to the collapse of the whole ring, a well-publicised trial of
its nine members, the execution of two of them and the capture of the
Israeli officer in charge: Meir Max Binnet, the same Max Binnet who
had directed the false flag operations in Baghdad a few years earlier. In
1954 he was a lieutenant-colonel in the military intelligence branch of the
IDF. He committed suicide in the Cairo prison by cutting his veins with
a razor blade after being tortured and hearing that the Iraqi authorities
had requested his extradition.

The intention behind Operation Susannah was to sour relations
between Egypt and the West; its effect was to sour relations between
the Egyptian people and the Jews who dwelt in their midst. The terrorist attacks seemed to confirm the suspicions of Egyptian Muslims
that their Jewish compatriots owed allegiance to a foreign country
and posed a threat to national security. As Stanford professor Joel
Beinin put it, 'The involvement of Egyptian Jews in acts of espionage
and sabotage against Egypt organized and directed by Israeli military

intelligence raised fundamental questions about their identities and loyalties.'[31]

The whole affair backfired disastrously on Israel. Pinhas Lavon was the minister of defence at the time and strenuously denied ever giving the order to military intelligence to activate the ring. He denounced the type of action in the affair that bore his name as stupid and inhuman and added that it had all started in Iraq.[32] Lavon was forced to resign; 'Cruel Zionism', however, continued to characterise Israel's conduct long after the 'Lavon Affair' had died down. The 'Unfortunate Business' may have started with the bombs that went off in central Baghdad back in 1950 but it probably had much deeper roots. In any case, it is one of the most shocking examples of 'Cruel Zionism' that I have encountered in my fifty years of scholarly meandering around the highways and byways of the Arab–Israeli conflict.

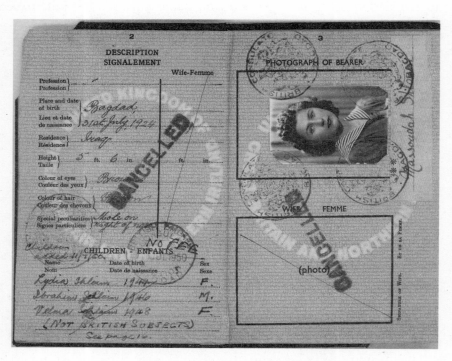

Mas'uda Shlaim's British passport with the
names of her three children added

EIGHT

FAREWELL BAGHDAD

ON 21 JULY 1950, MY MATERNAL GRANDMOTHER, MY MOTHER, my two sisters and I left Baghdad for good. We left legally with Iraqi exit visas stamped on the adults' passports. My mother Saida was a British subject by birth because her father Meir had been born in Bombay in 1882 when India was under the Raj. My grandmother Mouzli, born in Baghdad in 1888, had acquired British nationality when she married my grandfather. My sisters and I were added to my mother's British passport ten days before our departure. We left on a regular flight to Cyprus with a stopover in Beirut airport. From Cyprus, after a stay of about two months in a hotel in Nicosia, we continued the journey by boat to the port of Haifa in Israel. My father, who had Iraqi nationality, stayed behind. He joined us in Israel about a year and a half later, having left Iraq illegally across the border into Iran with the help of Kurdish smugglers.

Our separate departures from our homeland were not entirely of our own free will: we felt pressurised, if not compelled, to leave by circumstances beyond our control. For us, as for the majority of Iraq's Jews, despite the *farhud* and the 1948–50 persecutions, leaving a country in which we had such deep roots was not an easy choice. Tearing up these roots caused profound grief, accentuated by the knowledge that there was no going back to our homeland and beloved hometown.

On the precise reasons for our departure, my only source was my mother and her account was not entirely consistent. One motive she cited a very long time ago was concern over my health. I was born with flat feet, which apparently is not at all uncommon among Jews. For some obscure reason, however, my parents suspected that I might have contracted polio. They therefore took me to a leading paediatrician. Part of the examination consisted of pricking the palms of my feet with a pin. My lack of response only deepened my parents' suspicion that something was wrong. When we got home my mother asked me whether I had felt any pain as a result of the pin pricks. 'Of course,' was my terse reply. So why had I not shown any sign of the pain? To this question I purportedly replied: 'Isn't the doctor ashamed of himself? He is a grown up! So why did he hurt me with a pin? I was angry with him and that's why I pretended that it didn't hurt.' Another claim made by my mother, which sounds equally implausible, is that the Muslim paediatrician told them that there was a doctor in Tel Aviv, an internationally renowned specialist, and advised them to take me to see him. I have no recollection of this episode, but it always struck me as an unlikely cause for the momentous decision to leave Iraq. On closer interrogation, my mother admitted that the suspected polio story was not the real reason but merely a *hijja*, an excuse, she deployed in her efforts to persuade my father to leave.

The real reason for leaving, according to my mother's later account, was that life in Iraq had become too dangerous by 1950, for the Jews in general and for our family in particular. Persecution of the Jews was intensifying, and it assumed many different forms. The government, the judiciary and the public became overtly hostile. Restrictions were placed on Jewish trade and commerce. Jews in the civil service were dismissed and the entire community was placed under surveillance. Young Jews were barred from admission to colleges of further education. The police arrested, tortured, imposed arbitrary fines and extracted money from innocent Jews in what looked like a government-sanctioned campaign of harassment. On top of all of that came the series of bombs, described in the last chapter, that provoked real panic in the Jewish community and compounded the sense of insecurity. By the end of April 1950, over 25,000 Jews had registered to relinquish their citizenship and leave Iraq on a one-way visa. My mother did not remember the dates or the details, but she vividly recalled the general atmosphere of fear and foreboding following the explosions.

In addition to the general insecurity, my family faced a more specific threat: the release from prison of the members of *isabat al-leil wa al-hawa* – 'the gang of the night and the wind' – that had tried and failed to blackmail us back in 1948. The gang's original threat, to kidnap my sister Lydia, still resounded powerfully in my parents' ears. During the trial and after, members of the gang had continually promised to exact revenge, sending us death threats. Now those who had received shorter sentences were about to be released from prison with unpredictable consequences for us. Other Jews faced uncertainty; we had to contend with deadly threats from convicted criminals. Despite the risks, my father wanted to stay. My mother, on the other hand, thought the risks were too high, especially for her children, and she made up her mind to leave. My father did not try to dissuade her or to stop her. Once she had made the decision to leave, he gave her his full support in all the many practical tasks that had to be accomplished prior to departure.

My father preferred to stay in Iraq because he was an Iraqi. He had not lived abroad, he had not travelled abroad and he did not speak any foreign languages. He could read Hebrew but solely for the purpose of reciting Jewish prayers that he had learnt by rote. Nor did he have any ideological affinity with Zionism. His identity as a Jew was ethnic-cultural, not Zionist-nationalist. If there was such a thing as 'diaspora nationalism', a primeval yearning to return to an ethnic homeland, he did not feel it. Israel for him was a foreign country, more foreign than any other Arabic-speaking country would have been. Moreover, he had weighty material reasons that tied him to the country of his birth. He had a magnificent house which was his pride and joy, a thriving business and a warehouse full of expensive merchandise. Last but not least, he had four Jewish employees who depended on him for their livelihoods. A sense of moral responsibility obliged him to keep going at least until they had made up their minds whether to leave or stay. At the very least, he needed time to sell his assets, to wind down his business and to discharge his duty towards his employees.

Even had my father wanted to leave the country at this point, with us or soon after us, he would not have been able to do so, at least not legally. Like any other Iraqi Jew, he had been given a year in which to register for a one-way exit visa under the March 1950 law. But in order to obtain such a visa, he would have needed to prove that he did not have any outstanding debts of any kind to the authorities. My father was not in a position to do so because he had been let down by a friend. As mentioned in Chapter 2, in the interwar period my father had a business partner and a close friend named Shouwa' Obaid. The business partnership ended due to misconduct by Obaid's son, but the friendship endured. In 1949 Obaid asked my father for a favour: he needed to borrow money which involved signing 'I Owe You' documents, and he wanted my father to underwrite them. My father agreed. This meant that if Obaid defaulted on the debt, my father would be liable. Obaid then asked my father for another favour: to underwrite his trip abroad – in 1946 the Iraqi government had decreed that a Jew who wanted to go abroad had to commit a deposit of 2,000 dinars which would be forfeited in the event of failure to return. On 15 May 1948, the deposit was increased to 3,000 dinars, and in 1949 it was increased again to 5,000 dinars. With the help of my father's bond, Obaid secured a permit to leave Iraq for a limited period. He went to Israel and did not return. Once again, my father was left in the lurch.

One advantage of not registering to leave was that my father was able to keep all the rights that went with his Iraqi citizenship. His property was not confiscated, and his bank account was not frozen. House prices dropped dramatically as a result of the mass exodus of the Jews from Iraq. It was very much a buyer's market. Eventually, my father succeeded in selling our house for 10,000 dinars. This was a substantial amount but only a fraction of what the house might have fetched in normal times. The same was true of the merchandise in the warehouse. Having realised some of his assets, my father needed to get the proceeds out of the country. He could not do so legally due to the government's currency restrictions. To do so illegally involved the risk of losing the money and of heavy penalties in the event of discovery.

Moving money out of the country was difficult but not impossible. For Jewish bankers who retained their Iraqi citizenship it was more or less business as usual. Fortunately for my father, he had a trustworthy Jewish friend named Yusef Masri. Masri was the nephew of Haskell Shemtob. Shemtob came to my parents in their hour of need and offered his help, but they did not wish to trouble him. Masri was a banker who had moved from Baghdad to London when the situation for the Jews had deteriorated. He had worked out an elaborate scheme for getting Jewish money illicitly out of Iraq. My father would hand over the money to a trusted person in Baghdad, from there it was moved to London, and from London to Israel. This is how we survived in Israel financially until my father caught up with us.

My father used his status as an Iraqi citizen to help other members of the family who were in an even worse predicament than he. One of them was Uncle Sha'ul, the younger brother of my grandmother Mouzli. Sha'ul was a wealthy merchant and a happily married man. Fear for the safety of their family had induced Sha'ul to register for exit in case the situation deteriorated further. He had not made up his mind to leave; he had merely sought the reassurance of an exit strategy. Law No. 5 of 10 March 1951 caught him by complete surprise. Like the 100,000 other Iraqi Jews who had put their names down in the register but had not left the country, he suddenly had all his assets frozen, including his bank account. Like them, he was now in a state of limbo. Sha'ul had in a bank a safe deposit box full of money, gold and jewellery to which he was now denied access. My father got himself a safe deposit box in the same bank and by bribing a bank employee he was able to scoop up the contents of Sha'ul's box and deliver it to him.

Sha'ul and his family left Iraq with proper one-way exit visas, one suitcase each and 50 dinars for each adult. He gave his valuables to a man who smuggled them out of the country and delivered them safely in Israel. Other Jews were not so lucky. They had the option, before getting on the outbound plane, to entrust their valuables to Zionist activists who gave them a receipt and promised to deliver the valuables in Israel. Some of these activists were honest, and some were not. My mother knew of one official who received valuables for safekeeping in Baghdad but failed to return them to their owner in Israel, claiming they had been confiscated from him in the airport. But the owner later spotted his wife's diamond ring on the hand of the official's wife. There were many similar stories of Zionist activists who exploited the plight of Iraqi Jewry for personal gain.

My father wanted to repeat the same trick with Uncle Joseph, my grandfather Meir's brother. Joseph had a wife and four children. Success in business had enabled him to buy a beautiful villa with a large garden in the Karrada district in southern Baghdad, right on the bank of the Tigris River. My grandparents also had a villa in the Karrada, but it was inland, not on the water front. Joseph owned a number of houses and after registering to leave Iraq, started to cash his assets. Every time he sold a house, he bought a gold bar and stashed it in his deposit box at his bank, or so the story goes. Eventually, he sold the family home to a Muslim at a knock-down price. They closed the deal and signed the papers. But instead of delivering the money, the man hit Joseph on the head with a blunt instrument and injured him. The injury was not fatal, but it was enough to shake Joseph to the core. He decided to abandon the safe deposit box with the gold bars. He did not want to take any more chances himself or to expose my father to the risk of being caught. When his number came up, Joseph gathered his family and got on the charter plane that took them to Israel via Cyprus. It was the same deal for all the passengers: one suitcase each and 50 dinars for every adult.

As in post-independence Algeria in 1962, the choice for Uncle Joseph was the same as that for Algerian Jews: *'la valise ou le cercueil'* – the suitcase or the coffin.

Our predicament was rather different from that of Uncle Joseph. He opted to go to Israel with his whole family, using the officially sanctioned route. In our case the decision was for my mother to leave with the children and for my father to stay for the time being, to dispose of his assets as best he could, and then to figure out an exit strategy. The problem was that my sisters and I were Iraqi nationals by virtue of the fact that we had an Iraqi father. We could therefore not leave the country with our mother on her own because she was a foreigner. Being a determined and resourceful woman, she found a solution to this problem. There is an Arabic concept called *wasta*, that may be loosely translated as nepotism, 'clout' or 'who you know'. It refers to using one's connections to get things done, including getting civil servants to bend the rules. My mother was a great believer in *wasta*. For her, *wasta* was a way of life. In her hour of need, she rustled up every possible connection to facilitate our departure.

My mother's first port of call was the British consulate in Baghdad. She explained the problem and asked them to add her three children to her British passport so she could take them out of the country with her. The straightforward, bureaucratic answer she received was that this was against the rules and there was no way they could help her. Disappointed but unbowed, my mother turned to Ali Ghaleb, our closest Muslim friend, a senior civil servant in the Ministry of the Interior with the authority to issue exit visas. Ghaleb did not play cards so he was not a regular visitor. He used to come with his family to our house for dinner and reciprocate with invitations to dinner at their place. He was a genuine friend and an enlightened individual who rose above sectarian divisions and tribal loyalties.

Ali Ghaleb showed special empathy towards the Jews and strongly disapproved of the measures taken by his government to harm them. During the crisis of the Jewish community in 1950, he was transferred

by the Ministry of the Interior from Baghdad to Basra. Rumour had it
that the reason for the transfer was the discreet help he was giving the
Jews in circumventing the official rules. At first Ghaleb told my mother
that he could not help her: he had authority to stamp exit visas on Iraqi
passports but not on British ones. On his last day in his post, however,
he sent one of his assistants to tell my mother to come quickly to his
office with her British passport. She went and handed over her passport.
He wrote on page 14 in Arabic that the bearer of the passport was permitted to leave the country with her three children: Lydia, Ibrahim and
Vilma. He affixed the official stamp, added his signature, and turned to
my mother and said: 'This is the very last exit permit that I have issued.'
The date was 9 July 1950.

Two days later, my mother turned up again at the British consulate
and presented her passport with the Iraqi exit visa. She was worried that
they would deny the validity of the exit visa and possibly even lodge an
official complaint with Ali Ghaleb's superiors. To her great relief, they
readily accepted the Iraqi exit visa and even used it as a basis for revers-
ing their own earlier decision. If the Iraqi government had no objection
to Iraqi children leaving the county with their foreign mother, nor did
they. Accordingly, they added to my mother's passport the names, years
of birth and genders of her three children. Just to remove any doubt,
the entry stated in capital letters: '(NOT BRITISH SUBJECTS). See
page 16'. On page 16, the vice-consul wrote: 'The entry of the children's
names in their mother's passport is <u>not</u> to be accepted as evidence of
their nationality.'

A major bureaucratic hurdle had been cleared but many practical
problems remained. Some of them were related to the strict limits
imposed by the government on taking gold, silver, jewellery, antiques and
Oriental rugs out of the country. Leaving my mother's jewellery aside,
our family possessed a substantial treasure trove of valuable items. It was
a Jewish custom when a child was born to give him or her gold chains or
bracelets, silver mugs, talismans and other gifts. Every birthday was an
occasion for more expensive presents. There were three of us and most

of our family friends were well off, so the hoard was quite substantial. However, because of the sudden Jewish exodus from Iraq, the market value of precious metals and stones had dropped dramatically. As with houses and cars, this was a buyer's market.

To get anything out of the country above the basic quota, one needed a special permit. The head of the committee that issued the permits was Munthar al-Azali, scion of a Shi'i Muslim family who had been sent to the Alliance school where he became a close friend of my uncle Salih. In this particular instance, however, *wasta* was of no avail. Azali recognised my mother as Salih Obadiah's younger sister but he rejected her application. She thought that his decision was unfair; that he had discriminated against her because she was British. It is more likely, however, that, as an honest civil servant, Azali was simply applying the rules without fear or favour. In any case, my mother was forced to sell the valuables to a jeweller who came to our house with a pair of weighing scales and offered what she considered to be about a tenth of their actual value. The scales, she remarked bitterly, were for weighing fruit and vegetables, not for weighing precious metals.

You win some, you lose some. My mother had better luck in using *wasta* to procure a special permit to take Persian rugs out of the country. Here again there were strict rules and regulations. In our house in Baghdad we had no wall-to-wall carpets because these were not suitable for the hot weather, especially in the summer. The floors in our house were covered with Persian rugs, especially Kashan. Kashan rugs are very tightly woven and therefore hard-wearing; they hardly deteriorate with normal use and tend to keep their value.

Playing by the book meant giving our precious rugs away or selling them for a fraction of what they were worth. *Wasta* in the shape of Jamal Baban enabled us to bypass the rules. Baban was a famous Kurdish politician and many times minister of justice. He also headed a top-class law firm which counted a large number of prominent Jews among its clients. He and his wife were friends of my parents; they used to come to our house to play cards. My parents, following the common Jewish

practice of the day, contrived to lose as a way of cementing the friendship with their distinguished guest. Baban was not offended when my
mother sought his advice in the trivial matter of the Persian rugs. On
the contrary, he was only too happy to help. He gave her the name of
the Kurdish official in charge of the customs and excise office.

The next day my mother went and joined the queue to see the manager. She told him that Jamal Baban had sent her to speak to him and
that he sent his regards. After chatting about their mutual friend, my
mother came to the real purpose of the visit: to seek a permit to take
six Persian rugs out of the county. She explained that at home her three
little children slept on one rug and covered themselves with another;
that they were going to London where it would be very cold; and that
the children would not be able to cope without the rugs. The man then
wrote on headed notepaper with an official stamp 'Permission to leave
Iraq with six Persian carpets' and handed it over to her.

There remained the question of what to do with my mother's
diamonds, the jewel in the crown of the collection as it were. Once
again, Ali Ghaleb came to the rescue. He told my mother not to worry,
suggested she give him the diamonds in a small pouch, and he'd do
his best to give them back to her on the plane after she had cleared
passport control and customs, just before take-off. She had no hesitation in doing as he suggested, because she trusted him completely.
Her only concern was that he might be caught and end up paying a
high price for his kindness in doing her a favour.

Shortly before our departure, Ali Ghaleb, his wife and children came
to visit us to say goodbye. They too were about to relocate to Basra. The
atmosphere in the country was tense and gloomy and no one could tell
what the future held in store. But the friendship was deep and solid.
It was a warm summer evening and we sat in the garden for what was
going to be the last supper *en famille*. Ali confessed to my parents that
he had not slept all night after inserting the exit permit for the three
children in my mother's British passport. The mood around the table
was melancholy and the conversation did not flow as easily as it had

once done in normal times. All the adults probably knew deep inside that they would never see their friends again. The Ghalebs were only moving to Basra, whereas we were going to live in an enemy country that had recently fought against the Iraqi army in the War for Palestine and was officially still at war with Iraq. Despite the surrounding gloom and doom, or possibly because of it, the adults kept a brave face and made an effort to sound optimistic. We children played as usual, cheerfully and rumbustiously, and in blissful ignorance of the existential worries weighing so heavily on our parents.

The last few days before departure were extremely hectic: saying good-bye to friends and relatives, disposing of household goods, last-minute errands and packing. Although we were going on a regular flight to Cyprus, we took a staggering amount of luggage with us. This included large suitcases bulging with clothes for all seasons, children's books, toys, tea chests full of household goods, a posh dinner service and a big bundle with the aforementioned six rolled-up Persian carpets. Grandmother Mouzli, sixty-two, was coming with us on the long journey. As she had a British passport, she did not need an exit visa. The passport also meant she could also retain ownership of her house in the Karrada.

My father took us to the airport on 21 July 1950. If he felt fear and anxiety, he kept it to himself. My mother must have wondered whether she would ever see him again. We kissed goodbye, cleared passport control and customs and got on the plane. Ali Ghaleb had not said whether he himself would come to the plane. All he told my mother was not to worry. My mother, however, could not stop fretting about what might happen to her friend if he were caught red-handed, helping a Jew to smuggle diamonds out of the country in flagrant violation of Iraqi law. In the event, Ghaleb did not come himself; he sent one of his assistants who had a security pass and was therefore not subject to inspection. The assistant came up to the plane, ostensibly to say goodbye. He went up to my mother to shake her hand. As he did so, he also slipped the pouch with the diamonds into the palm of her hand. For my mother, as she pointed out to me, the diamonds represented much more than a valuable material possession: they were a testimony to the sincerity and integrity of a Muslim friend, the tangible proof that human decency had not been completely obliterated by the political pressures of the Zionist-Arab conflict.

The flight took us to Nicosia airport in Cyprus, though our final destination was Israel. At that time Cyprus was a British colony. Having approved the Iraqi government's plan to allow the Jews to leave the country, Britain now offered Cyprus as a stopping point between Baghdad and Tel Aviv. There were, of course, no regular commercial flights from Iraq to Israel. On the morrow of the War for Palestine, the Arab League had decreed a diplomatic and economic boycott of the newly born Jewish state, and this excluded any contact by land, sea or air. Nor could we go from any of the neighbouring Arab countries because all were bound by the Arab League's resolution. The nearest non-Arab country to Israel was Cyprus, which made it the obvious destination for the first leg of the journey.

A scheduled stop-over in Beirut airport gave rise to the first complication since leaving our homeland. As the porters were unloading the luggage of the passengers who left the plane in Beirut, my mother noticed her big bundle with her six Persian carpets. She immediately started shouting that this was her luggage and insisted they put it back on the plane. At first, she was told that she was mistaken and as proof was shown that the label with her name was now attached to an insignificant-looking parcel. The switching of the labels was evidently part of the scam, but my mother was not fooled by it. She insisted that the label be reattached to the bundle and the bundle be put back on the plane. My mother's vigilance foiled the plot to steal our precious rugs. And I remain the proud owner of one of the six – my sole family heirloom from our time in Baghdad.

My father's journey to Israel was much longer and infinitely more hazardous than ours. About eighteen months elapsed between saying goodbye in Baghdad airport in July 1950 and his arrival in Israel. This was undoubtedly the most stressful period in his life, but he never spoke

Left: The Shlaim family home in Bataween neighbourhood, Baghdad.
Right: The Balfour Declaration, 1917.

Below: Jewish musicians of the Baghdad Broadcasting House, 1938.

Above: Hotel Cecil, Alexandria, Egypt.

Left: Saida Shlaim, Grosvenor House, London, 1947.

The coronation of Faisal I, Baghdad, 23 August 1921.

Haj Amin al-Husseini (*left*) and Rashid Ali al-Gaylani, Berlin, 1943.

Sir Kinahan Cornwallis (*left*), British ambassador to Iraq.

Prince Abd al-Ilah (*left*) and Nuri al-Said.

Wedding party of Yusef and Saida Shlaim, Baghdad, 1942.

Yusef Basri, Zionist activist in Baghdad.

יוֹסֵף בַּצְרִי
Josef Basri

Mordechai Ben-Porat, Mossad emissary to Iraq.

محاضر التحقيقات السرية لشرطة الشعبة الخاصة كشفت عن أساليب التضليل التي لجأ اليها (كادر) الحركة الصهيونية السرية في العراق لخداع الطائفة اليهودية واقناعهم بترك العراق كما ان هؤلاء القادمين من اسرائيل استعانوا وتشبثوا بالطرق اللا أخلاقية لـ(تسهيل) مهماتهم كدفع الرشاوى الضخمة او تزوير الوثائق الرسمية.

ويذكر كرجي صبيح لاوي: ان عملاء اسرائيل استخدموا الدكتور (عبد النبي) وهو يهودي عراقي في تزوير توقيع وزير الداخلية صالح جبر وان احد المقربين من هذا الوزير يطلب (200) دينار عن كل موافقة (تهجير) يهودي عراقي وان دائرة السفر رفضت جميع المعاملات التي تحمل توقيع صالح جبر لاكتشافها بانها مزورة!؟

كما استخدموا الموظفين اليهود في المطار (لتمرير) حقائب كثيرة وان الشرطة القت القبض على مواطن لبناني الجنسية اسمه (عادل) وهو يحاول تهريب (26) حقيبة لافراد المنظمة الصهيونية السرية.. في 21 حزيران عام 1951 صدرت الاوامر بالقاء القبض على 149 عضواً في الحركة الصهيونية السرية وبعد أسبوع ضبطت الشرطة في كنيس مسعودة شنطوب جهازي ارسال عسكريين يحملان الرمز د ـ 5 استخدما من قبل بعض اعضاء لجنة التسفير لارسال البرقيات الى تل ابيب، قبل ذلك بايام قلائل وبالتحديد في يوم السادس عشر من حزيران اعترف شالوم صالح شالوم بالتفصيل عن دوره ودوري يوسف بصري ويوسف مراد في قضية القاء القنابل والمتفجرات على المحلات اليهودية وبذلك تمكنت الشرطة من فك اللغز الكبير الذي لف بغداد من جراء اختفاء الفاعلين الحقيقيين لهذه الجرائم التي استهدفت اليهود العراقيين. قال شالوم للمحقق: في هذا اليوم وجدت نفسي محتارا اذا اجيبكم باقوال غير حقيقية نظرا لما جابهتموني به من الحقائق ومادمت قد اعترفت ببعض الامور كالاشارة الى مخابئ الاسلحة فقد قررت ان ادلي بجميع ما لدي من الحقائق، واعترف يوسف بصري ايضاً بدوره واضاف: بعد صدور قانون اسقاط الجنسية صدرت الاوامر من اسرائيل بتهجير جميع ملاك الحركة الصهيونية السرية وفعلا تمكنا من تسفير الكثير منهم وبقي يوسف مراد وحبيب ، المحقق : هل تعرف شيئا عن حبيب؟ يوسف بصري اعتقد انه قدم من اسرائيل وقد حول نشاطنا الى نشاط ارهابي كالقاء القنابل وكان يعتمد على مصادر معروفة في التجسس على العراق مثل عزرا هندي وشمعون بلاص وسليم صديق والياهو بينمور وداد باشا ولطيف فرايم وزلخا والطيبيين سليم الشكرجي وادور مروان، ان يوسف مراد يعرف باسم جوني، وكان متحمسا لتهجير اليهود ويدور في محلاتهم واسواقهم يحثهم على تسقيط جنسياتهم وهو مدفوع من حبيب، لم يكن حبيب وقتذاك في بغداد فقد هرب الى اسرائيل وظهر موردخاي بن فرات وبهربه كان عدد اليهود العراقيين الذين اسقطوا جنسياتهم بتاثير الحركة الصهيونية السرية قد بلغ 154 و 108 وبلغ عدد اليهود الذين تم تهجيرهم 546 و 99 وبقي 608 و 8 بالانتظار حتى يوم العشرين من حزيران عام 1951!؟..

Extract from Baghdad police report on the interrogation of Zionist activists, 1951.

Transit camp for Iraqi emigrants in Pardes-Hanna, Israel.

Shlomo Hillel, Israeli emissary to Iraq.

Uncle Isaac Obadiah and his wife Doris on holiday in Israel, 1963.

Menachem Begin, leader of right-wing Herut party, 1948.

Theodor Herzl, the Viennese
visionary of the Jewish state.

David Ben-Gurion, Israel's
first prime minister, widely mocked
for doing headstands on the advice
of his doctor.

about it. During this period, he was able to send us money, but he could not communicate by phone or by post. The few details I have about his ordeal come from my mother. In her rendition, her husband was basically a prisoner in Iraq: he could not leave on a regular flight or on the Zionist-organised airlift because he did not have and could not get an exit visa. The only way to escape was by crossing the border illegally into Iran. This involved a huge risk: some Jews who took this route died on the way, some were robbed and some were killed. But my father had no other choice, so this was the route he eventually took. Kurdish smugglers helped him and a few other Jews who shared his predicament to a northern point of the border with Iran. The journey was extremely tough, with meagre rations, makeshift sleeping arrangements and the ever-present fear of being detected. To avoid being seen, the group made its way at night, partly on foot, partly on the back of a donkey. On more than one occasion, my father thought he was not going to make it. But once they reached the Iranian side of the border, the stress level dramatically declined. Iran welcomed Iraqi-Jewish refugees and there were procedures in place to enable them to proceed to their ultimate destination. The passage from the border to Tehran was relatively easy. In Tehran my father stayed with his brother-in-law, Alfred, for about a month. He badly needed a period of rest and recuperation. From Tehran he made his way to Israel.

My grandmother, my mother, my two sisters and I spent two months in Nicosia, staying in a big hotel. I was four years old and I retain only dim memories of this period. One vivid recollection is of a waiter named Angelie who was extremely attentive and indulgent towards my sisters and me. This encouraged us to start taking liberties. There was a gong in the dining room: we picked it up from its stand and marched around the hotel, banging on it and shouting again and again '*Hatha Angelie!*' – 'This is Angelie!' Another memory is of a trip to visit friends in Famagusta, another Cypriot city. It is not so much the trip I remember as the loud prelude to it. We found the name Famagusta hilarious, so once again we picked up the gong and announced repeatedly in Arabic at the top of our voices 'We are going to Famagusta, we are going to Famagusta!'

The people we went to visit were Iraqi friends who had bought a villa in Famagusta and settled down there. The villa had a large garden with a well. My mother had some English gold coins in her purse. Lydia got hold of one of the coins and threatened to throw it into the well. She looked very determined but in the end my mother succeeded in retrieving the coin. According to my mother this was an early example of how stubborn and difficult Lydia could be. But it could have been an illustration of my mother's own intolerance at any sign of defiance, or even just independence, on Lydia's part. The episode also exposed the double standards, based on gender, that my mother applied to me and to my elder sister: I was a boy and I could do no wrong as far as my mother was concerned, whereas Lydia was a girl and therefore subject to a different set of rules. She was expected to be demure and submissive, to follow orders and not to act on her own initiative.

For my mother, Cyprus was not without its stresses and strains. It was the first time she had to attend to her three young children without the help of nannies and servants. Her mother was a help but not a proper substitute for a professional, full-time nanny. Another source of stress was the additional cargo sent to her in Cyprus by her Uncle Sha'ul. The wily uncle had bribed the porter to give him back the permit that the Kurdish head of customs had given my mother. Sha'ul then used this permit to send six Persian carpets of his own and informed my mother of the plan by phone. He then repeated the trick and sent *another* lot of six rugs before my mother warned him over the phone that, if he sent any more rugs, she would throw them in the sea. The threat apparently worked because that was the end of the consignments.

From Nicosia we sailed to Haifa by boat. With us we had our suitcases, tea chests, our six Persian rugs, as well as Uncle Sha'ul's twelve. One turbulent chapter in the history of our family had come to an end.

Another was about to begin. Our mode of departure from Iraq was unlike that of the majority of the 120,000 Jews who left at the same time. We had left independently and under our own steam; the majority had been transported from Iraq to Israel in Operation Ezra and Nehemiah. Yet we were all part of a bigger story: the tragic end of Babylonian Jewry. We were leaving a country in which we had enjoyed, on the whole, a good life, and going to a new and poor state whose future seemed uncertain at best.

My distant relative Itzhak Bar-Moshe experienced this moment more poignantly than most. In his autobiographical book *Exodus from Iraq* he reflected on the melancholy of the Jewish exodus from Iraq:

> Relations that were shaped over hundreds of years were erased in a few hours. A whole community detaches itself from the past and quickly moves to the future that stands at the gate. A history of more than two thousand years is liquidated in less than two thousand hours... Here everything is crumbling... The past is shaking and collapsing... There is no poet in the world who can express our experience... Jews walk like sleepwalkers.

Bar-Moshe wondered: did the leather suitcases know that inside them they were carrying not just everyday objects but the history of our ancient community?[1]

Avi in Ramat Gan in first form (top row, second from the left)

NINE

PROMISED LAND

IN SEPTEMBER 1950 MY GRANDMOTHER ('NANA'), MY MOTHER, Lydia, Vilma and I arrived by boat at the port of Haifa. Israel was only two years old when we landed on its shore. What sort of a country was it? One obvious answer is that it was a country of new immigrants, of Jews from different parts of the world, dissimilar cultures and multiple languages. At the end of the 1948 war the population of the infant state was only 650,000 of whom 150,000 were Arabs. Aliyah was therefore a top priority for Israel's leaders. For David Ben-Gurion, the first prime minister, it was a question of survival. By the middle of 1951, the population had nearly doubled. First had come the Jews from Europe, some of them Holocaust survivors. They received preferential treatment, at least as far as housing was concerned: they were given the houses of Arabs who had fled or were expelled during the war and were not allowed back. In defiance of UN resolution 194 of December 1948, Israel refused to give the 750,000 Palestinian refugees either the right of return or compensation. But by 1950 there were no more Arab houses to allocate.

For my family Aliyah was a painful process. In the first place, our Aliyah was involuntary. The interaction of two forces – Zionism and Arab nationalism – forced us to leave our homeland and transformed our lives beyond recognition. Aliyah literally means going up or ascent. But migration involved descent for us, *yerida* in Hebrew. Not only did we descend down the social and economic ladder, we also lost our self-confidence, our social status and our proud sense of identity as Iraqi Jews. Zionist historiography portrays Aliyah from Arab states as a move from East to West. For my mother it was a move from the Anglophone and Francophone Baghdadi milieu to a socialist Ashkenazi world whose rules and codes she did not understand. Admittedly, we suffered much less than the majority of Iraqi immigrants who ended up in tents and shacks. Nevertheless, the move entailed dislocation, displacement, emotional distress and psychological disorientation for the whole family. My mother, my two sisters and I adapted to the new environment as best we could. For my two grandmothers it was too late to adapt. For my father the obstacles to assimilation were insurmountable. He never recovered from the displacement and dispossession and remained a broken man for the rest of his life. In Israel he was a shadow of the man he had been in Iraq. He and the grown-ups in the family, alongside the rest of the Iraqi Jews, held on to the images and echoes of their Iraqi past in Ramat Gan.

For the State of Israel too, the task of absorbing all the new immigrants was not an easy one. After the Jews of Europe came the Jews of the Middle East and North Africa: Iraq – 120,000; Yemen – 45,000; Turkey – 31,000; Iran – 21,000; Egypt – 16,000; Morocco – 30,000; Tunisia – 13,000; Libya – 31,000; Algeria – 1,500. They were not called refugees but *olim*, immigrants. In the official Zionist rendition, this was 'rescue Aliyah': the new state had saved the Jews of the Middle East and North Africa from an implacably hostile environment, welcomed them with open arms and performed a heroic task of immigrant absorption under exceptionally difficult conditions. All this was said to be part of fulfilling the Zionist dream of the 'ingathering of the exiles'. Israel, in this dominant Zionist narrative, was still 'the Promised Land' despite its early teething problems.

The actual experience of the overwhelming majority of the Iraqi immigrants fell a long way short of the Zionist myth. In the first place, they suspected that Israel had actively worked to uproot them from their Arab homeland and this fed their resentment from the start. Second, these newcomers were the victims of the widely held perception that Israel was doing them a favour by taking them in from the cold. Israeli propaganda over the previous two years had portrayed the Jews of Iraq as facing the threat of physical annihilation at the hands of a fascist regime. This framing was intended to serve Israel's campaign against Iraq in the international arena. But at the same time, it led the Israeli public to believe that while the gates of the country had to be kept open for these hapless outcasts, the price of absorbing them would be heavy. Consequently, the Iraqis were not received as proud olim but as refugees who owed a heavy debt of gratitude to their saviours. This image was in line with the condescending attitude that the Zionist movement had all along displayed towards the Jews of Iraq.[1] Third, the Jews who in Iraq had had their own leadership and institutions arrived at the gates of the Promised Land as penniless, powerless and leaderless individuals who were at the mercy of the absorption authorities.

Most decisive, however, was the actual experience of the Iraqis on arrival in Israel. At the airport, they were sprayed with DDT pesticides to disinfect them as if they were animals. This was a deeply humiliating experience. From the airport they were taken to *ma'abarot*, transit camps. Housing in the ma'abarot consisted of tents or corrugated iron shacks, with primitive washing and cooking facilities. The living conditions were squalid and unsanitary. Water was in short supply. Employment opportunities were largely limited to one or two days a week of kitchen duty, construction and other menial tasks like digging up weeds along public paths. Bankers, lawyers, doctors and other professionals were reduced to begging for such casual work in order to feed their families. The freedom of the inmates of the transit camps was severely limited. Some camps were surrounded by barbed wire and guarded by policemen. The bitter irony of Jews behind barbed wire could hardly be missed.

Olim who had no professional qualifications and no financial means of their own, i.e. the majority, were allocated housing by the absorption authorities in agricultural settlements and development towns in the periphery. They were rarely consulted, and they were often lied to about the location of their new houses. Most olim wanted to be in or near the big cities in the centre of the country but often ended up in remote rural places in the arid Negev and in the border areas. Some physically resisted being dumped in the new destination that was decreed for them. Avi Gil, a former director-general of the Israeli foreign ministry, told me that his father, a bus driver, sometimes came home late at night in the early 1950s with bloodstains on his shirt following scuffles with immigrants who refused to get off the bus. In general, 'The adoption of Israeli citizenship', in the words of Orit Bashkin, 'was a painful, violent, and traumatic transformation'.[2]

The attitude of the immigration and settlement authorities towards the newcomers overshadowed everything else. They simply had no understanding of the customs, culture or aspirations of Iraqi Jews. They thought of them as backward and primitive and expected them to take their place at the bottom of the social hierarchy and be grateful for whatever they were given. The olim came from nine different Arab countries but for the transit camp managers they were all the same. Tensions between Ashkenazi and Sephardi Jews were exacerbated by a cultural gulf between East and West. Jewish-Arab culture was looked down upon as decidedly inferior.

Furthermore, the Israeli establishment was bent on suppressing the Arab culture and erasing the identity of the Oriental Jews by forcing them into a European-Ashkenazi melting pot. David Ben-Gurion referred to the immigrants from the east as 'savage hordes'. Another purveyor of this arrogance was foreign minister Abba Eban, who stated that 'The goal must be to instil in them a Western spirit, and not let them drag us into an unnatural Orient'. The lens through which the new immigrants were viewed was the same colonialist lens through which the Ashkenazi establishment viewed the Palestinians. The goal was not to promote a multicultural society in Israel but to delegitimise the cultural roots of the Orientals, to emphasise the European character of Israel and to preserve an Ashkenazi monopoly over the cultural as well as political centres of power.

The problem of adjusting to the new society is a central theme that runs through the novels of Iraqi immigrants to Israel. Prominent among them was my friend Sami Michael. Born in Baghdad in 1926, he joined the Communist Party when he was seventeen, helped to distribute its underground publications critical of Nazi influence in Iraq, was sentenced to death in 1948 and fled to Iran. In Iran he made contact with the Tudeh, the local Communist party, and renewed his activities against Iraq's rulers. Iraq demanded his extradition, so he was forced to go underground a second time. He intended to go to the Soviet Union but ended up in Israel 'by accident'. In Haifa he joined the Communist Party, wrote for its Arabic-language newspaper *al-Ittihad* (Unity), and became involved in peace movements with Palestinians. He gained a national reputation as an uncompromising critic of the Ashkenazi establishment and of its racist attitudes towards the Arabs, the Palestinian citizens of Israel and the Jews of the Arab world. He was among the first Israelis to call for the creation of an independent Palestinian state alongside Israel. In 2001 he was elected President of the Association of Civil Rights in Israel.

I got to know Sami Michael in 2000–01 when he spent time at the Oxford Centre for Hebrew and Jewish Studies under their 'Visiting Hebrew Writers Fellowship' programme. He and his wife Rachel, a journalist of Iraqi origin, lived in the Orangery at Yarnton Manor, a seventeenth-century stately home in the village of Yarnton, ten kilometres northwest of Oxford. In this quintessentially rural English setting, they enjoyed the respite from the raucous political arguments in which they were perpetually caught up in Israel. I spent many evenings in their company. The spicy Iraqi dinners they prepared, like meatballs with okra on a bed of rice, reminded me of the food we used to eat at home. Most of our conversations were about Israeli society, politics and culture, all of which Sami knew a great deal more about than I did. He was riled by the injustice, inequality and blatant racism of Israeli society and he illustrated his points with some telling personal anecdotes. Sami is dark-skinned. In his early days in Israel he walked into a bookshop and started browsing. The fair-skinned shop owner shouted at him in front of the other customers, 'We don't carry illustrated books!' The insult burnt deep but it also clinched Sami's determination to prove himself as a Hebrew writer. What Sami, Rachel and I shared was the feeling of being outsiders. Although Sami eventually achieved fame as a writer and political activist in Israel, he was never part of the establishment. Apart from his radical political views, there was the problem of language: it took him a quarter of a century to find his voice in Hebrew.

Sami was nearly fifty when he published his first novel in Hebrew *All Men Are Equal – But Some Are More*, recalling the famous line in George Orwell's *Animal Farm*. Sami's book exposed the hypocrisy of the Israeli authorities and the degrading treatment to which they subjected the new immigrants in the transit camps. The book established the motif of the DDT pesticide spray as a symbol of their humiliation and *All Men Are Equal – But Some Are More* became a familiar phrase for referring to the struggle for equality of the Jews from Arab countries. It sparked a lively debate on the socio-economic gaps in Israeli society and by doing so it helped to bring the ethnic question onto the national agenda. In his other novels and plays Michael dealt with the aspirations and struggles of both Jews and Arabs, always from a progressive, egalitarian and humanistic perspective.

Michael's 1995 novel *Victoria*, however, was not about Israeli society: it was the saga of a working-class Jewish family in Baghdad at the beginning of the twentieth century – it was aptly described as an Arabic novel written in Hebrew. In Chapter 6, 'My Baghdad', I dwelt on the lavish lifestyle of my family. My main source was my mother for whom Baghdad, with the passage of time, looked more and more like a 'Lost Eden'. We were not, however, a typical Jewish family: we were an affluent and privileged upper middle-class family. As a boy, I had no idea what life was like for poor working-class Jews. I gained that much-needed insight from reading *Victoria*.

The novel describes in searing detail the harsh reality of a Jewish neighbourhood: the dirty alleyways, crowded housing, power struggles

and intrigues, poverty and starvation, seductions and betrayals, incest
and prostitution. It portrays a backward patriarchal society in which
women were utterly dependent, regarded as inferior, humiliated and left
without hope. Women's main role in this society was to serve the men
and produce male offspring. Until *Victoria*, all of Michael's novels had
dealt either with the conflict between Jews and Arabs or the cleavage
between European and Middle Eastern Jews. In *Victoria* he goes farther
back in history to draw on his own experience as a child to illuminate the
dynamics of a working-class Jewish-Iraqi community. Although this is
a work of fiction, Michael insists on its historical accuracy. What lends
complexity and credibility to all his novels is that he himself is a blend
of all the different identities he writes about: an Arab-Jew, an Iraqi, a
Communist and an Israeli.

Victoria is a literary masterpiece about a woman, written by a man,
about a gallery of lesser characters around her, and about a unique society
that had long since ceased to exist. With extraordinary sensitivity the
author gets into the skin, the mind and the soul of his central character.
With sober realism, and without a trace of nostalgia, he reconstructs
the no less complex story of the life of working-class Jews in Baghdad.
It is difficult to imagine a more honest or authentic portrait. Yet the
publication of *Victoria* faced a vociferously hostile reaction from affluent
Iraqis in Israel, who complained that the book painted a false picture of
the life of the Jewish minority in Iraq and in doing so brought shame
upon the entire community. My mother joined in the chorus of criticism. *Behdalna*, she said to me with some vehemence – 'he disgraced
us'. To my question whether she had read the book, she replied that she
had read the first ten pages and then put it down. 'Why?' I inquired, to
which she replied, 'It is not true!' That was the end of the conversation.

Literary critics showered praise on *Victoria* and it quickly became a
bestseller, translated into many different languages, including Arabic. In
1995, it was published in English. The Arabic edition was published in
Cairo with an introduction which presented Michael as a Jewish author
of Iraqi descent and dwelt on his transition from writing in Arabic to

writing in Hebrew. It stressed that even though Michael lived in Israel and wrote in Hebrew, he showed deep consciousness of his Arab cultural roots. The novel itself was held out as a major contribution to the cause of cultural normalisation between Arabs and Jews.

Later in life, long after I had settled down in England, and added a British identity to my collection, I came to share some of Sami Michael's radical views. Belatedly, I also came to share his attachment to his original identity, that of an Arab-Jew. These views, however, were not rooted in my personal experience or the experience of my family at the time.

Our first encounter with 'the Promised Land' was not as traumatic as that of the bulk of Iraqi immigrants. We were not sprayed with DDT on arrival and we were not sent to a *ma'abara*. Although we lost most of our assets due the move, we had enough to live on in Israel, at least for the first few years. Moreover, we had a family network that gave us much-needed support. When we disembarked from the boat at the port in Haifa, Uncle Jacob, Nana's brother, was there to welcome us. He had come from Ramat Gan with a driver and a roofless lorry. We loaded all our belongings – suitcases, trunks, tea chests and bundles of Persian rugs – on the back. On the drive south along the coastal road, my sisters and I sat in the cabin next to the driver; my mother and Uncle Jacob sat on top of the luggage at the back. My mother was in an elated mood: we had arrived at 'the Promised Land' and her favourite uncle was there to greet us.

Uncle Jacob lived in Ramat Gan, the largest satellite city in the Tel Aviv-Yafo metropolitan area. It was established in 1921 as a *moshava*, a communal farming settlement, but it gradually shifted from agriculture to light industry. In the 1940s it became a battleground in the country's language war: a Yiddish language printing press was blown up by Hebrew-language fanatics. In 1950 it became a city and by 1955 its population had reached 58,000. Ramat Gan had some fine residential areas, parks and gardens, including a national park, a zoo and the country's largest football stadium. But my principal recollection is of a dull and drab urban space with so many apartment blocks going up at bewildering speed everywhere as to make it look like a sprawling building site.

A great many immigrants from Iraq settled in Ramat Gan. It absorbed the Jews from Khayriya, Saqiya and Kafar Ana, the transit camps around it. Because of the large number of Iraqi Jews who came to live there, Ramat Gan was sometimes referred to as Ramat Baghdad. This gave the city something of an Eastern flavour: numerous shops, restaurants and cafés had Iraqi owners and clienteles who mostly spoke Arabic. More importantly, it made it possible to develop like-minded support networks. With the money Uncle Jacob managed to get illicitly out of Iraq, he bought a substantial villa with a large sitting room, half a dozen bedrooms, a balcony, a garden and a vegetable garden. He also owned a grocery store next door to his house. For a merchant of his standing, to run a grocery store was a considerable comedown in the world but it had the advantage of providing a steady income for the family. At home with him lived his wife Violet, his daughter Esperance, and his four boys: Meir, Albert, Dudi and Eli. They also had the lively and energetic maid, Sabiha, who had come with them from Baghdad. Having to accommodate all of us certainly cramped their style but they did not complain. Nor could they be prevailed upon to accept any rent from us or any contribution towards the running costs of the household.

The standard of meals was well below that of our home in Baghdad and the hotel in Nicosia, but the older ones among us were far too polite to say so. Vilma, however, who was barely two years old, was less inhibited. One dinner, served by Sabiha soon after our arrival, consisted of thick slices of black bread with tinned sardines mashed on top. The sardines were oily and smelly. Vilma pushed the plate at Sabiha and said accusingly, '*Hatha akl? Hatha khara!*' – 'Is this food? This is shit!' Rather than take offence, Sabiha roared with laughter, repeating Vilma's words again and again.

The early 1950s in Israel was a period of austerity, with high unemployment, all sorts of foreign currency and other restrictions and food rationing. People were issued coupons for basic necessities like sugar, milk, butter, eggs and meat. Uncle Jacob and his family were citizens, so they got regular rations. We had the status of temporary residents and were accordingly entitled to double rations: the five of us received ten books of coupons. This enabled us to make a modest contribution towards raising the culinary standards for the whole extended family. I particularly remember the slabs of butter that came with a wrapping which announced in red letters 'Imported butter from the United States of America'; America sold surplus agricultural products like butter to Israel and was paid in local currency, which helped boost the Israeli currency as well as eventually end rationing. This was a gift from Uncle Sam to the struggling people of the young state, an early sign of the preferential treatment accorded by the USA to Israel.

We arrived in Israel with British passports, but with no clear plan to settle down there. At that time there was strong pressure on all immigrants, from Europe as well as the Arab lands, to become citizens of Israel. Most Iraqi immigrants arrived in Israel without a passport, with only a *laissez-passer*, a one-way visa. They were immediately issued with a *te'udat oleh*, an immigrant's certificate, and an identity card. There was no test of citizenship such as knowing Hebrew or elementary civics; Israel prided itself on being a melting pot with a mission to forge a new national identity for all immigrants whatever their origin.

Pressure was brought to bear on the newcomers to change their Jewish names from the Diaspora into Hebrew names. Zionist leaders set an example. David Green from Plonsk in Poland became David Ben-Gurion; Moshe Shertok from Russia became Moshe Sharett; Goldie Myerson, who came from Russia via America, became Golda Meir; and Goldberg became Har-Zahav, literally a gold mountain. Acquiring Hebrew names was part of a systematic process intended to erase all traces of the Diaspora. Fairly soon after our arrival, some members of my family yielded to this pressure. My mother was called Mas'uda or Saida for short. In Israel, of her own accord, she changed her name to Aida. Lydia became Dalia. Vilma's name remained unchanged: although it was a foreign name, it was not an Arab name and therefore allowed to stand. I became Avraham instead of Abraham and Avi instead of Abi for short.

Although my mother changed her name to a non-Arab name, she refused to apply for an Israeli passport. This was very unusual in the early years of statehood. New immigrants automatically received Israeli citizenship or, in some cases, had dual nationality. My mother arrived with a British passport and firmly rejected the offer of an Israeli one. As a matter of policy, the authorities made it easy for Jews to come and settle in Israel but difficult to leave. My mother arrived in Israel as a tourist but because she was Jewish, she was given an identity card and the status of a temporary resident. Interestingly, under 'Nationality', her ID says 'Jewish' – there was no such thing as Israeli nationality. It did not take long for my mother's initial optimism to evaporate and for disillusion to set in. She toyed with the idea of going to England with a view to settling down there. To use her own words, she was afraid of being 'stuck' in Israel. A year or so later, when my father arrived in Israel, the matter was finally settled: we were staying.

We stayed with Uncle Jacob for about six months while looking for a more permanent place to live. It so happened that Nana owned a plot of land in Ramat Gan. After her husband Meir, my maternal grandfather, died in 1945, Nana needed a change of atmosphere, so she travelled to visit her younger sister Ghala in mandate Palestine. Ghala lived in Ramat Gan, which was home to the early Iraqi emigrants as well as those of the 'Big Aliyah' of the early 1950s. In the central square of the city there was an Iraqi-owned café where the wealthier Iraqis tended to congregate. One of them was an estate agent who persuaded Nana to buy a plot of land as an investment. Unless she was very far-sighted, at that time she could not have guessed that one day she might build a house on this plot of land. But that is precisely what happened when we arrived in Israel.

Ghala and her husband Salim had been the first members of our family to move to Palestine. Their two older children, Reuven and Matok, were born in Baghdad; the younger two, Shula and Amnon, were born in Israel. The whole family integrated well into Israeli society and, as is often the case with new immigrants, they became ardent nationalists. My uncle Isaac, Nana's eldest son, had been a captain in the intelligence corps of the British Army. He had been based in Cairo in the Second World War and made occasional visits to Palestine, travelling in military uniform. This did not endear him to his militant teenage cousins. Under the League of Nations mandate, Palestine was governed until 1948 by Britain and a High Commissioner was based in Jerusalem. British policemen, notorious for their severity, patrolled the streets, and British soldiers were a familiar sight. Britain was perceived by some Jews not as a protector but as a colonial power and British Army uniform was the symbol of foreign rule. Isaac recalled that Ghala's boys were very cheeky, that they gave him a hard time for serving with the British Army and that they assured him that they were going to kick all the Brits out of their county. On the whole, members of our family were not very interested in politics. This was one of the rare instances in which politics cut across family loyalties.

In 1945–46 the economic conditions in Palestine were bad and food was in short supply. On the trip to Palestine, Nana therefore took with her a big basket, *chinbil* in Arabic, with two cooked chickens on a bed of rice and a dozen brown hard-boiled eggs on top. When stopped by customs officers, she said in Arabic that her son Isaac was a captain in the British Army and proudly placed three fingers on her shoulder to indicate his rank. They were not impressed. They demanded to know why she was carrying all that food with her. She replied with a straight face that this was her breakfast. They waved her through, joking that they had no choice – if they refused, she might eat them for her lunch.

Nana's plot of land came in handy when we arrived in Ramat Gan. During our stay with Uncle Jacob, a contractor had given us the idea of building on Nana's plot a small bungalow with one big room, a kitchen, a bathroom and a balcony. We accepted his offer and he began to build. What he did not tell us was that first we needed to apply for planning permission from the town hall. At an early stage, an inspector from the town hall came and knocked down the half-finished structure. An Iraqi friend called Alfred Bashi, a lawyer by profession, took Aida to see the mayor, Mr Avraham Krinitzi, to complain about the demolition. Krinitzi was the first mayor of Ramat Gan and remained in office for forty-three years. He explained that our modest structure was not a good use of space: a very small house on a large plot of land. But in the end, he gave permission for the small house to be built on condition that it would be only a temporary structure, to be replaced eventually by an apartment block. The builder resumed work on the little bungalow and, when it was ready, we moved in there. It was pretty cramped, with only one room and a dramatic drop from the villa we had left behind in Baghdad. When my father arrived, Nana moved back to Uncle Jacob's house to make room for him. With the money he had received for our house in Baghdad, my parents bought a two-bedroom flat on the fourth floor of a large building in 5 Yahalom Street, which was renamed Krinitzi Street after the mayor was killed in a car accident.

Auntie Ghala was an important part of the family network that helped us find our feet in the new and unfamiliar environment. She was a short and stocky woman with a warm heart, a smiley face and a very friendly manner. She spoke Hebrew fluently and without the guttural sounds that distinguished the recent Iraqi immigrants. Although it was a time of austerity and they were relatively poor, she invited us to dinner at her home every Friday night and served a traditional Iraqi-Jewish meal of chicken and rice. She also helped us fill in forms and battle with the notoriously arbitrary and nepotism-riddled local bureaucracy. This particular aspect of life in Israel did not come as such a shock to my mother. In Iraq she had been a great believer and a polished practitioner of the art of *wasta*, of using connections to get things done. The Israeli equivalent of *wasta* is Vitamin P. P stands for *protektzia*, which may be loosely translated as preferential treatment or exerting influence through connections. Here my mother was a fast learner. Getting the mayor of Ramat Gan to reverse the decision to demolish our bungalow marked her first success in a new setting.

One of the first things that Auntie Ghala did was find a kindergarten
for me and register Dalia for the first grade of a state primary school
called *Ha-Givah*, the hill. In the kindergarten I had my first encounter
with the Hebrew language. At home in Baghdad and in Uncle Jacob's
house we spoke Arabic only. Children at this age pick up languages
easily and I was no exception. My mother thought that I had set myself
unusually high standards of linguistic proficiency for a four-and-a-half-
year-old child. According to her, I hardly spoke at all during our first
year in Israel and the family began to worry about me. It was only after
I started going to school and felt confident in my ability to speak the
language properly that I reportedly overcame my inhibition to speak
the language.

In nursery, there was the usual range of activities – toys, painting,
books with illustrations, games, singing and dancing. There was also an
outing for which the fee was ten Liras. My mother gave me the money
but I did not hand it over to the teacher. Eventually the teacher sent my
mother a note with a reminder. My mother turned to me and asked why
I had not given the money. I replied that the other children who gave
the money to the teacher only got back a piece of paper and it was not
worth it. My mother explained that the piece of paper was a receipt;
only then did I hand over the money.

Dalia used to pick me up from the kindergarten after her school
day had finished and we would go home together. It was reassuring
to have an elder sister as a companion, especially as the way home
involved crossing a six-lane inter-city road called Jabotinsky Way,
popularly known as *ha-kvish ha-shahor*, the black road, on account of
the frequent lethal accidents that happened there. The name Jabotinsky
meant nothing to me, but it was to feature prominently in my later
work: Ze'ev Jabotinsky was the spiritual father of the Israeli Right. He
was the architect of a hard-line strategy for dealing with the Palestine
Arabs – 'the iron wall'.

The following year Dalia moved up to the second grade in *Ha-Givah*
school and I entered the first grade in the same school. A little certificate

from the kindergarten, the size of a postcard, confirmed that I was qualified to move on to a primary school. During breaks I often spotted Dalia playing with her classmates as I played with mine. I looked up to her as she was older and more confident than me and hers felt like a reassuring presence. After school we usually walked home together to our bungalow which was nearby and did not involve crossing the dreaded Jabotinsky Way. On the way home we occasionally bought broken pieces of chocolate waffles with our pocket money because they were cheaper than the ones with proper wrappings. More bang for our buck.

The school consisted of a row of separate, simple wooden structures, all on the ground floor. My memory of the teaching is very hazy, but I remember with affection my first form teacher, Hannah Oppenheimer. She was young, probably straight out of teacher training college, pretty and very sympathetic. My report for the first term, signed by her, stated that while my behaviour was 'good', my academic achievements were just 'average'. The report for the second term was the same. The report for the third term allowed me to move up to the second grade but noted that I needed to make more progress with my reading.

By the end of the first year, we had moved to our new flat and Dalia and I transferred to a much bigger state school called Yahalom. Once again, my memories of the early years in Yahalom School are rather hazy, but the end of term reports that survived suggest that I was struggling. Struggling may be the wrong word because it implies an effort on my part. In fact, I hardly made any effort at all: I showed no interest in any of the subjects taught at school and turned in the bare minimum of homework. In class I paid little attention to what the teachers were saying and spent most of the time daydreaming. The teachers had a habit of asking questions and we pupils were expected to raise our hands to answer. I cannot remember a single occasion when I raised my hand. Whether by design or by coincidence, I always sat at the back of the classroom, farthest from the teacher, and minded my own business. I was not disruptive, far from it, but not constructive either. This sullen, self-isolating attitude did not endear me to the teachers.

The extant end of term reports all testify to poor performance. First term of the second grade: my homework was inadequate, my progress was not satisfactory, I was especially weak in Hebrew and Maths, and I needed 'fundamental help with all subjects'. First and second terms in third grade: I was not trying hard enough; my homework required monitoring; and I needed to increase my knowledge and make progress in my studies across the board.

While my lack of interest in schoolwork persisted, I developed a keen interest in reading books that had nothing to do with school. My mother recalls that I became a voracious reader of children's books and adventure stories: whenever we visited Nana, I would sit in the garden with a book in my lap. My mother contrasted my love of reading with my resolute lack of interest in doing homework or in anything to do with school. Nana's house occupied just a small corner of a large plot of land: the rest was taken up with a vegetable patch and an orchard of fruit trees – oranges, bitter lemons, pomegranates, figs, yellow plums, pink guavas and luqu'at, also known as Japanese plums. I have no personal recollection of reading in the garden, but I do remember how much pleasure I got from roaming around the orchard, climbing trees and gorging myself on ripe fruit, especially figs and guavas.

Sometimes I went to visit Nana on my own after school. She was always pleased to see me. I was her favourite because I was a boy. But, as with my mother when she was a child, Nana did not give physical expression to her feelings with hugs and kisses. Her main way of showing affection was by plying me with food. Verbal communication between us was minimal: she could hardly speak any Hebrew and I was reluctant to speak in Arabic. As soon as I arrived, she would make me sit at a table and start piling on my plate food of different kinds: cheese-filled pastries, chocolate cookies, cakes, nuts, dates and bananas. Some of the food was pretty stale and the bananas were brown. Dalia reminded me that Nana used to hoard food for me and say to her 'This is for Abi, and this is for Abi'. Small wonder that Dalia felt she was not getting her fair share. My main recollection is of Nana saying to me '*Kool, kool! Ashu makatakool?'* – 'Eat, eat! Why are you not eating?' The answer, which I was far too polite to utter, was that much of the food she tried to force on me had seen better days. No doubt I received preferential treatment, but it was preferential treatment I could have done without. The orchard was a different story: it was paradise.

In the fifth grade I had a new form teacher who refused to tolerate my lack of commitment. Sara Greenberg, a Holocaust survivor, was highly-strung and melodramatic in manner but deeply committed to education and an effective communicator. She had high expectations of all of us and may have felt that we did not realise how lucky we were to be able to lead a normal life, free from persecution. She certainly thought that I had failed to grasp the educational opportunities that, as she saw it, had been presented to me on a silver platter. This exasperated her, and she said so. My father never attended parent-teacher meetings because his Hebrew was not good enough but my mother attended without fail and took them very seriously.

At these meetings, my mother was regularly subjected to a cascade of complaints about me: I was indolent, introverted, cut-off, phlegmatic to a rare degree, and I made no effort whatsoever to contribute. The criticism reached its crescendo with an exclamation: *'ha'adishut shelo mefotsetet oti!'* – 'his indifference makes me explode!' I was never allowed to live down this comment. For years and decades to come, my mother would repeat it to me, imitating Mrs Greenberg's high-pitched voice and melodramatic manner. The comment bore repetition because it went to the heart of the matter – I internalised the inferior status that I thought society had assigned to me and I behaved accordingly. Not applying themselves to schoolwork and not being interested in excelling are habits many children have. My case was different. Being an Iraqi gave me a continuous sense of estrangement, both inside and outside the classroom. Estrangement bred passivity and reluctance to play a part in any collective endeavour. Mrs Greenberg wanted to make me repeat the fifth grade, but my mother persuaded her to give me another chance. At the end of the sixth grade, the same scenario repeated itself:

Mrs Greenberg thought that I should repeat the year and my mother prevailed on her to give me one more chance.

One of the strategies my mother deployed was to promise to hire private tutors for me to help me catch up with the rest of the class. And hire private tutors she did – although we could ill afford it, my parents spent a fair amount of money on tuition. Some tutors were subject-specific and some were not. Some of them came to our house, while others held the private lessons in their own houses. All of them were paid by the hour. If they came to our house, they would take both Dalia and me together, allowing our parents to benefit from the economies of scale. If the teachers preferred to hold the lessons at their house, I went alone. Among our teachers were Itzhak Azouri, an economist, the nephew of my father's accountant in Baghdad, who taught us maths; Ezra, a very tall and very bright high-school graduate who taught us a range of subjects; and Niazi, a Cambridge graduate who taught us English. All three were of Iraqi origin and therefore close to us in culture and custom.

One teacher, by contrast, was quintessentially Ashkenazi. She was a young schoolteacher named Ora. She was tall, thin as a rake, with long blond hair and blue eyes. She lived with her parents and I used to go to their flat for private lessons in a range of subjects. The flat was spotlessly clean and tastefully arranged with mahogany furniture, silk rugs, chandeliers and bookshelves lined with books from floor to ceiling. Ora was soft-spoken and well-mannered. An air of calm and serenity pervaded the flat. Going there allowed me to take a peek at another culture and another world and one that I secretly envied.

From the above description it should be obvious that as a young boy in Israel I did not feel at home in an Ashkenazi environment. I respected this environment, but I was not part of it. To be frank, I felt out of place on account of being a Sephardi, an Oriental, a Jew from the East, a Mizrahi. The term Mizrahi was not commonly used at the time; it took another couple of decades for it to become established as the main designation for all emigrants from the Arab world, including North Africa. The most widely used term at the time was *yots'ei edot ha-mizrah*, descendents of the Eastern communities, *mizrah* being the Hebrew word for the East. This was how Israeli society labelled me and, more importantly, this was how I saw myself.

Sometimes one aspect of one's identity dominates and overshadows all others. In my case being Iraqi was the dominant, ever-present, restricting, even stifling sense of myself. Throughout my time in Israel, I carried a chip on my shoulder because I was an Iraqi. I did not experience direct discrimination and I did not encounter overt racism, except on rare occasions. But I could not rid myself of the subjective feeling that I was not as good as the Ashkenazi kids in my class. This feeling was a barrier to realising my potential. The preferential treatment received at home on account of my gender made no difference. I was particularly ashamed of speaking Arabic in public, because Arabic in Israel was considered an ugly language, a primitive language, and, worst of all, the language of the enemy. Subconsciously, I assimilated these crass prejudices. This helps to explain why, in my first year in Israel, I hardly spoke at all until I was able to speak Hebrew properly. And it certainly explains why I was so acutely embarrassed when my father spoke to me in Arabic in front of my friends.

My mother, on the other hand, did not embarrass me in this way because she was careful not to address me in Arabic outside our home. She may also have sensed that my self-consciousness as an Iraqi held me back in my studies at school. Once, after a meeting with Mrs Greenberg, and after hearing the usual litany of complaints, she tried to get to the bottom of why I was not doing better at school. She looked me in the eye and asked me directly, 'Do you feel inferior because you are an Iraqi?' I felt deeply uncomfortable, looked away and wished she had not asked me this question. In reply, I made some inarticulate noises, rejecting this notion completely. But deep inside I knew it was true: I was ill at ease because I was an Iraqi and I just wanted to be left in peace without grown-ups prodding and prying into my psyche.

Ironically, the one grown-up I did not find intrusive was a psychiatrist. The school must have referred me to him because they were concerned about me, but no one informed me about the precise nature of their concern or the purpose of the referral. In those days there were no school counsellors with exclusive responsibility for dealing with the mental health of pupils. If a child persistently misbehaved in class, they were sent to see the headmaster or the deputy head. The purpose of the appointment was to punish and to warn, not to offer psychological support. It was rare to refer a pupil to an expert outside the school but that is what happened to me. One day, when I was twelve or thirteen, the form teacher informed me of an appointment that had been set up for me at a clinic whose name I do not remember. Slightly anxious, I turned up at the clinic at the appointed time. The psychiatrist who met me was a middle-aged man who wore a suit and a tie, and exuded kindness and sympathy. He asked me many questions and elicited honest answers. He also invited me to play chess with him. At the end of the hour, he thanked me for my time, and I went back to school. No doubt the psychiatrist submitted a report to the school after the session, but I never heard another word about it. For my part, I would have been happy to go back to the clinic, because I appreciated the psychiatrist's benign disposition as well as his calm and courteous manner.

Life at home went on as normal with very little excitement and virtually no intellectual stimulation. Our material circumstances were much diminished compared with Baghdad but that did not bother me. The flat we bought was pretty modest, with basic facilities and no luxuries. It had an entrance hall, a sitting room, two bedrooms, a kitchen, a toilet, a bathroom and two very small balconies. In the hall there was a table where we had our family meals. In the sitting room there was a large Persian rug on the floor, a bed covered with another rug and cushions which served as a sofa, some chairs, a big radio/record player and a smarter dining table and chairs where Dalia and I did our homework and had our private lessons. One bedroom belonged to our parents: it had a double-bed, an old-fashioned wardrobe and a movable washing machine with three legs on wheels that lived in a corner. The other bedroom had to be shared by my sisters and me with our paternal grandmother Lulu – 'Yuma'. There was only room for one cupboard and three metal beds in the room. A fourth bed was low and on wheels so it could be kept under one of the other beds and brought out into the middle of the room at night. There were no bookshelves in the house and no books except for schoolbooks and children's books.

Yuma was in her late sixties or early seventies when she joined us in Israel. She had moved from Iraq to Israel with her middle son Ezra and his family in the 'Big Aliyah' and lived with them in a ma'abara until my father joined us and we bought a flat in Ramat Gan. Yuma was a slight and frail woman with very long white hair, tied into a bun. The move to Israel constituted a painful severance from her home. In Iraq she had an extensive network of family and friends. In Israel she was almost totally isolated. Illiterate and unable to speak Hebrew, she rarely left the flat. Like our other grandmother, she missed the old country terribly, which she regularly extolled as *jana mal allah* – paradise. Although I was not aware of this at the time, Yuma became a sleepwalker following the move to Israel. On three or four occasions she walked in her nightgown out into the street and my parents had to go and look for her. My sisters and I liked her company. She had a store of Arabic folk tales which she enjoyed telling and we never tired of hearing. Coming from her within the safety of our home, Arabic was not the language of the enemy but our own language.

I particularly liked the story of Rapunzel, the princess who was locked up in a tower and lowered down her hair to enable her prince to climb up. In the Arabic folk tale Rapunzel was called *Anka bint al-rih* – 'Anka, Daughter of the Wind'. Like many Iraqis of her generation, Yuma was superstitious. She believed in the evil eye, for example. When we had fish at home, she would gouge out their eyes, wrap them in newspaper and ask me to step on them and repeat after her, '*nfakset ein al ra'a!*' – squash the evil eye!

Yuma would spend hours cracking sunflower seeds: she would put the kernels in three equal little bundles and give them to each of us individually, telling us '*hayi hisitak*', this is your share. Sometimes there was a failure of communication due to our inability to appreciate the nuances of the Arabic language. Once Yuma, sitting on a low stool on the kitchen floor, asked me to give her what I understood to be a couple of grapes, so I did as she requested. In Arabic there is the dual, which she had used – *inbaytain* – to make her request. She immediately castigated me for taking her so literally and giving her just two grapes.

The division of labour was for my mother to do the shopping and for Yuma to do the cooking. Yuma prepared the food on a thick chopping board and cooked it on a kerosene stove. With these primitive facilities she produced the most delicious meals: chicken and rice with peas or beans was the staple diet but her repertoire included meatballs in tomato sauce, lamb and aubergines, stuffed vegetables, potato croquettes with fried mincemeat, and sweet and sour dishes. The main meal of the day was lunch. Yuma, unlike other close family members, was an observant Jew, so she did not cook on the Sabbath, the day of rest. Instead she used to prepare the traditional Jewish dish of chicken and rice called *t'beet*, placing it on a very low heat to cook overnight in a big pot. On top of the chicken and rice Yuma placed eggs which by the morning had turned brown outside and tender inside. The eggs were the basis for the special Saturday breakfast. This consisted, in addition to the brown eggs, of slices of fried aubergines, shredded onions and parsley, finely chopped salad, hummus, mayonnaise and a very spicy mango pickle called *amba*. All the ingredients were mashed together and eaten with flat, round bread. In restaurants, this concoction is served in pitta bread, like falafel, and is called *sabih*.

We had fresh milk delivered to our flat every other day by a milk-woman who lived near us in a simple, one-storey house. She had a small plot of land and a chicken coop. Early every morning, before the heat of day, she set off on her milk round in a narrow horse-drawn cart, carry-ing three large and heavy urns. To deliver the milk to her customers in our building, she had a container that she carried on her back and an aluminium jug she used to measure and pour out what was probably a litre or a litre and a half of milk. Occasionally, Yuma would give the milkwoman bits of leftover bread to feed to her chickens. For Yuma, as for other simple folk in the Arab world, bread was a symbol of life – one of several Arabic words for bread, and the most common in Egypt, is *iish*, which literally means life. Yuma never threw bread away. If she or anyone else dropped a piece of bread on the floor, she would pick it up and kiss it, and tap it on her forehead as a mark of respect. Yuma and the milkwoman could not communicate because Yuma spoke no Hebrew, but they did not need words for the basic transaction: delivering the milk and collecting the stale bread. Even without a common language, the two women seemed to like one another. Just occasionally, my sisters and I were called upon to act as interpreters.

I cannot remember exactly when Yuma died but I was probably about ten years old. One day I came back from school and bumped into Vilma at the bottom of the stairs. She said only two words to me in Hebrew: '*Yuma meta*' – Yuma died. I remember vividly the exact spot and the expression on Vilma's face – outwardly blank but conveying a sense of pride that she, the youngest, had some momentous news to share with her older brother. I also remember that I made no reply of any kind: I was struggling in my own mind to process what I had just heard. I was not distraught; I just did not know what to think. This was my first encounter with death; it was not frightening so much as strange and confusing. My sisters and I did not go to the funeral. Our parents acted as if nothing had happened, no doubt to minimise our pain. Whether right or wrong, their attempt to shield us from the natural grief of losing a grandparent was largely successful. One day Yuma disappeared, and life went on as usual.

When Yuma was alive, my mother did the shopping and after Yuma passed away, she did the cooking as well. She quickly emerged as an excellent cook in her own right. There were no supermarkets in those days. We did the bulk of our shopping in two stores. One was a grocery store owned by the parents of a friend of ours called Ruhama. Dalia fell out with them over a trivial matter and refused to set foot in their store, so it fell to me to do the additional shopping we needed on top of the bulk buys by my mother. All our purchases were on credit. Ruhama's parents had a black exercise book and in it they recorded the date and the total of each of our purchases. We had no budget and no self-imposed quotas so our debt to them mounted very rapidly. At the end of every month we would settle up. After our money ran out, it became increasingly difficult to pay our bills so my mother turned to her mother to bail her out. Nana was well-off but tight-fisted, so a certain amount of pressure had to be applied. My mother was not above pointing out to Nana that she had forced her to marry against her will and that she had to take responsibility for the consequences. It usually did the trick. On one occasion, when Ruhama's parents pressed for payment and Nana refused to help, they cut off our credit facility. Ever resourceful, my mother sold a gold coin to a jeweller, settled the debt and reopened the line of credit. We never went hungry. But the experience of austerity left me with a residual anxiety which, seventy years later, still finds expression in a tendency to over-shop.

The other main source of supplies was a fruit and vegetable store. I often went to both stores with my mother to help her carry the heavy load back home, ending with four flights of stairs. The greengrocer was a short and stocky man from Eastern Europe who spoke Yiddish with his Ashkenazi clients. In spring and summer, he wore shorts and short-sleeve shirts. My mother had picked up some Yiddish and she enjoyed placing her orders and giving the desired quantities in Yiddish. This seemed to amuse the greengrocer, but it decidedly did not amuse me. The reason for my discomfort was that the greengrocer had a number on his arm inscribed in indelible blue ink, the tell-tale sign of a Holocaust survivor, as I had learnt at school. At one level, I realised that the inscription had originated in a Nazi concentration camp and I knew it represented an ID number but the reality behind it was still beyond my comprehension. At another level I was reluctant to face up to the macabre reality behind the number. Every time I saw the number, it would trigger dark thoughts about cruelty and bestiality, about the unbelievable depths of degradation to which human beings could sink. These were inchoate, terrifying and painful thoughts and I did not share them with anyone.

We did not have many visitors to our flat. One of them was my uncle S'hak, my father's youngest brother. He was called *S'hak al-aami*, blind S'hak, supposedly because he had very small eyes. He was generally considered to be a bit slow; in Iraq he was nowhere near as successful as my father; and my father may have been ashamed of him. S'hak never married, lived on his own in Petah Tikvah and worked as a construction labourer. He used to visit us from time to time although his relations with his elder brother were slightly strained. My mother always welcomed S'hak when he came to our house, but she was rather reserved while he, for his part, invariably addressed her as madam rather than by her first name – the difference in social status that had separated my parents from S'hak in Baghdad apparently persisted following the move to Israel. After being served a substantial meal, S'hak would spend time with my sisters and me in our room, chatting to us in Hebrew.

We enjoyed our uncle's company because he was a good storyteller, but he was an odd character and, hard as we tried, we could not make him out. He had had a good education, but it had not got him anywhere. Evidently fearful that we would look down on him, he repeatedly told us, 'You must not think that you have a primitive uncle.' As proof of his education he used to declaim a poem in French. Sixty years later, by using a search engine, I managed to track down the poem. It was '*Après la Bataille*' ('After the Battle') by Victor Hugo. It is a poem about chivalry, written in homage to his father, Joseph Hugo, who was a general in Napoleon's army.

My father's middle brother was called Ezra. When he fell in love with his first cousin Hatoun, the daughter of Yuma's sister, he inadvertently found himself in the middle of a family saga of the kind described in Sami Michael's novel *Victoria*. Yuma did not approve of the marriage, fell out with her sister and ostentatiously refused to attend the wedding. Yuma, according to my mother, had a tendency to fall out with people, sometimes over trivial matters. She was capable of inventing strange excuses, to use an Arabic expression, 'from under a chicken's feet'. Ezra and Hatoun had two boys, Avraham and Itzhak. Avraham was my age, Itzhak a year younger. In 1950 the whole family flew to Israel with Yuma as part of Operation Ezra and Nechemiah. They received the standard DDT spray on arrival and were sent to a ma'abara near Herzliya. Once notified of the name of the ma'abara, we went to visit them there. What we found was a noisy, ramshackle and pretty chaotic refugee camp in which our relatives occupied a corrugated iron shack. My cousins and I had a jolly time running around and playing games. It was raining, there was mud everywhere, and we did our best to dodge the puddles. With the randomness of childhood memories, I think I had a haircut in the ma'abara. After about a year Uncle Ezra was given a job in an arms factory and the family moved into a modest house. We stayed in touch with the cousins, occasionally paying them a visit at weekends.

My father's sister Ragina also arrived in Israel in the Big Aliyah from Iraq in 1950 but she followed a different trajectory. She and her husband, Eliyahu Hamama, were illiterate. He had run a nuts and spices shop in Hanouni market in Baghdad. Three of their children had arrived in Israel before them: Ezra, who was killed in the first Arab–Israeli war; Avraham, who left Iraq illegally with his colleagues in the Zionist underground; and Fouad, who made the hazardous journey from Iraq to Israel on his own at the age of twelve. The parents arrived in Israel with their son Itzhak and three daughters, Rena, Lebyen and Jacqueline, in 1950. In early 1948, before the war, 80 per cent of the Jewish population lived in the big cities. In the course of the war Israel expanded its borders, expelled hundreds of thousands of Arabs and refused to allow them to return to their homes. There was strong pressure from above to inhabit the whole country and much rhetoric about making the desert bloom. Government plans were drawn up to build collective agricultural settlements in the Negev and development towns in the periphery of the country, and to settle there the new immigrants from the Middle East and North Africa. This was a radical idea: to make people settle not where they wanted to but where the state ordered them to. The defence establishment decided on the location of the ma'abarot, the collective settlements, and the development towns, and the guiding principle was to redistribute the population from the big cities to the rest of the country.

After a short stay in a ma'abara, the Hamama family was sent, with no say in the matter, to a moshav, a collective settlement, in the Negev, northeast of the Gaza Strip, established in 1950 with other new immigrants from Iraq who also had no experience in farming. It was called Kokhav, meaning star, appropriating the former name of the Palestinian village it had displaced, Kawkaba. In Kokhav the Hamama family were given two houses, a plot of land, agricultural machinery, a beginners' course in farming and left to get on with it. It was arduous work in the sweltering heat, with modest yields. Literally, they had to eke out a living by the sweat of their brow. Nevertheless, they soldiered on for a number of years.

One of the happiest memories of my childhood is staying in Kokhav during the summer vacations. Proper holidays were beyond our means. Although we descended on our relatives without notice, as neither we nor they had telephones, they quickly made arrangements to accommodate us, and spared no effort to make our stay as comfortable and enjoyable as possible. The contrast between our crowded urban environment and their rural lifestyle, with open fields, clean air and fresh produce, was very striking. Rather than experiencing the harshness of the landscape, for me this was a picture of bucolic bliss. My sisters and I offered to assist our older cousins with the work of the farm and they kindly obliged by giving us some easy tasks to make us feel that we were earning our keep. It was the simplicity of life on the farm that was so appealing to us, but our cousins lived the harsh reality.

After five or six years, when the going was still tough, the Hamama family decided to pack it in and go and live in a big city. They were not the only ones. Many of the olim found it difficult to adjust to the new life that was chosen for them and started drifting to the cities. This posed a serious problem for the authorities. They resorted to various measures and sanctions to deter people from abandoning the periphery for the

centre. Books were kept with the names of those who left without permission and the lists were sent to labour exchanges to deny the escapees
employment and housing. The police were asked to set up checkpoints
and not to allow them to pass. Such draconian measures belied Israel's
claim to be a free and egalitarian society.

In the case of the Hamamas, the move out of the moshav was accomplished gradually and without getting into trouble with the authorities.
Rena, the eldest daughter, lived in Tel Aviv. She married her cousin,
Khthuri Hamama, who became a major importer of rice to Israel. There
were many Iraqi Jews in Israel whose staple diet was rice, so his business
prospered. Itzhak and Fouad, helped by the family network, moved from
the moshav to a small town called Pardes Katz and opened a shop. Then
the rest of the family joined them. In their store they sold grains, nuts,
dried fruit and spices. The whole family reverted to what they had been
in Baghdad – urban shopkeepers.

Avraham Hamama was not included in the Zionist social engineering project, which was designed to turn his family from shopkeepers
into farmers. As noted earlier, he had been an active member of the
Zionist underground in Baghdad. Soon after his arrival in Israel, he
and Tsipora got married and he found employment in the department of customs and excise. While working, he also studied for a
BA in Arabic and Middle Eastern Studies at the Hebrew University
of Jerusalem. He continued his studies for an MA in Middle Eastern
Studies and Arabic literature. Not unreasonably, he thought that his
academic qualifications would enhance his prospects of promotion at
work. But the Mossad, Israel's external intelligence agency, had other
career plans for him: they recruited him as a spy. It is not difficult
to guess why they were so determined to secure his services: he had
lived in an Arab country; he was a native Arabic speaker; he was well
versed in the history and culture of the region; and he looked like an
Arab. Avraham initially rejected the Mossad's approaches but his path
to promotion was blocked and other coercive tactics were deployed
until he gave in.

From that point on, Avraham was hardly ever in Israel. The cover story was that he was studying in Paris. His actual activities were hidden behind a thick veil of secrecy, as is the case with all spies. The little I know comes from a conversation with his younger brother, whom we continued to call Fouad even though he changed his name to Herzl on arrival in Israel. According to Fouad, Avraham's first posting abroad was to Iraq where he spent many years. On rare occasions Avraham and Tsipora met secretly in Paris. The rest of the time they communicated by letters that went through Mossad channels. In the early 1960s Avraham was sent to Cairo and, astonishingly, gained entry into Al-Azhar University, the renowned centre of Islamic learning and Sunni Islam's most prestigious university. Under Nasser, a wide range of secular faculties were added. To gain entry, Avraham posed as a mature student from Iraq. By the time he left, he knew the Qur'an inside out.

Avraham's classmates at Al-Azhar University included a group of young Egyptian air force officers and he cultivated good relations with them. By listening to their conversations, he picked up some useful pieces of information on the training of pilots, the maintenance of aircraft, the exact routines of airbases and emergency procedures. This information was apparently invaluable for the Israeli air force in planning its surprise attack on the Egyptian airbases on 5 June 1967, the first day of the Six-Day War. This attack destroyed most of the Egyptian air force on the ground and gave Israel mastery of the air, which it retained until the end of the fighting. Just before the outbreak of war, Avraham hurriedly left his post in Cairo and returned home. He knew he had come under suspicion; he had felt the noose tightening and escaped in the nick of time. After his escape, he was sentenced to death in absentia by a military court in Cairo. Eli Amir, the Iraq-born novelist, was one of Avraham's few friends. Amir wanted to write a book about Avraham Hamama and his career as a spy, but he was told by the military censor that he would have to wait forty years.

Curiously enough, my mother also attracted the attention of a talent-spotter in the Mossad. This was not long after we had arrived in

Israel. She received a letter that did not mention the Mossad by name but simply invited her for an interview at an address in Tel Aviv without indicating the purpose of the meeting. She reported to this address at the appointed hour and was received by a tall man who exuded authority, sitting behind a big desk. The man had much more information about her than the basics contained in her passport. He was well informed about her educational qualifications, family background, marital status and political connections prior to arriving in Israel. It did not take her long to realise that the purpose of the meeting was to assess her suitability and sound her out about becoming a spy. The man told her she was just the woman they were looking for: she was young and beautiful, she came from an Arab country, she had a British passport, she spoke four languages and she could operate very naturally in an Arab environment. He added that she would have an interesting time with foreign travel, glamour and adventures. My mother rejected the offer with some vehemence, pointing out that she was a married woman and had three young children to look after. She added that she was one hundred per cent Iraqi and that Iraqis are *sharifin*, people of honour, that Iraqi women had to protect the honour of their husbands and that they did not need any adventures. As she stood up to go, the man came from behind his big desk, embraced her and tried to kiss her. She gave him a mighty kick, he fell backwards and she noticed that he had a wooden leg. This explained the clattering noises he had made as he collapsed in a heap. She ran away, no doubt dashing both his desire for sexual adventures and his hope of recruiting an Israeli Mata Hari.

My mother's gloss on this episode was that had it happened in a later era, she would have complained, and she would have wanted to see her attacker go to prison. She was very glad that laws were introduced subsequently to protect women against sexual predators. But in her time men invariably got away with it. There was *farhud* – chaos with no rules and regulations to prevent the abuse of power. It was very common for men in positions of power to abuse their authority by sexually harassing their female subordinates or by soliciting sexual favours from applicants for jobs. In her day, she repeated glumly, women did not complain; they just put up with it.

As I write about my mother, I have to keep reminding myself she was only twenty-six years old in 1950 and that nothing in her earlier life could have prepared her for the trials and tribulations that awaited her in the Promised Land. Biblical mythology portrayed it as a land flowing with milk and honey: the reality could not have been more different. All of a sudden, the young woman found herself on her own in a foreign country and an alien environment, without a husband, with three children under ten to look after and a totally uncertain future. Having led a carefree life, she was suddenly forced to shoulder heavy responsibilities. She missed the lifestyle we had led in Baghdad and, oddly enough, she also missed Christmas celebrations. Once a year she and all British passport holders had been invited to a sumptuous Christmas party in the British embassy in Baghdad. I did not have the slightest idea what Christmas was all about – in Israel, Christmas day was a regular working day. Many foreign diplomats had their residence in Ramat Gan, a short distance from the embassies in Tel Aviv. One day, on the way back from school, I caught a strange sight in the sitting room of a diplomatic residence: a tree with small lightbulbs and curious decorations. When I got home and reported to my mother what I had seen, she exclaimed, 'It's a Christmas tree!' and burst into tears.

Thrust into this strange world, my mother coped remarkably well with the new challenges, but it could not have been easy. Outwardly she appeared steadfast and self-confident when in fact, as she later revealed to me, she was depressed and teetered on the verge of a nervous breakdown. Two friends came to her aid in her hour of need: Meir and Selma David. Dr Meir, as we always called him, was a distant relative and the family doctor. He had received his medical education in the American University of Beirut and later in London. In London he had met Selma, the sweet and beautiful daughter of German Jews who had emigrated to Palestine, married her and brought her back to Baghdad where he practised as a doctor. Dr Meir treated four generations of my family:

my great-grandparents, my grandparents, my parents, my sisters and myself. Selma had started teaching my mother Hebrew in Baghdad in preparation for the move to Israel and in Israel, Selma and her husband continued to take extremely good care of her, taking her with them to the beach, to picnics and to parties with their friends.

When my father arrived in Israel, the initial relief and joy of reunion soon faded away in the face of the difficulties in adapting to his new home, difficulties that were immeasurably greater than those of my mother. He was fifty years old, spoke no Hebrew, had lost his business and was pretty disoriented. My mother noted that he had aged considerably during the long and arduous journey from Baghdad to Ramat Gan. Not long after the happy reunion, they began to drift apart and to move in different social circles. She had her own circle of upper-class Iraqis with whom she played cards every Friday night while he had a smaller circle of like-minded Iraqi men who were also down on their luck. They used to meet in an open-air café and while away the time, sipping Turkish coffee, smoking and chatting.

It was common among the middle-aged men in my father's circle to boast about their past glories, about their wealth and social status in Iraq. An Arabic saying likens this kind of a man to a camel: when hungry it brings up food from inside its hump. My father was different. He never spoke about the past, at least not in my presence. Nor did he wallow in self-pity. On the contrary, he was proud and stoical – and silent. He continued to dress as he had always done: with three-piece suits he had had tailor-made in Baghdad from superior British fabrics, with a white shirt and a matching tie. But deep inside, he was a broken man. He was completely out of place in the new environment, and he was unable to adjust. Young though I was, I was well aware of the tragedy that was unfolding before my eyes. I felt sympathy for my father, laced with an incomprehensible sense of guilt for the dramatic decline in his fortunes.

To give him credit, my father did make an effort to earn a livelihood in the new land. He embarked on two business ventures, but both ended in dismal failure. The first venture was with a man called Kaplinsky who, by all accounts, was a crook. Kaplinsky was the owner of a famous café in Tel Aviv, Café Bustan, but he was deeply in debt. My father met him by chance during his first year in Israel. Kaplinsky presented himself as a wealthy merchant with a permit to import food stuffs from America. It was a period of austerity and food shortages in Israel; Kaplinsky said he needed capital to set up a food import business and promised my father high returns on his investment. Part of the money that my father had managed to get out of Iraq was delivered to him in Israel and part of it was in the custody of his brother-in-law Salih in New York. Kaplinsky flew to New York in the hope of laying his hands on some of this money only to be met with a firm rebuff from Salih. Salih told my father that Kaplinsky was clearly a crook because he wore five-dollar shoes and smoked a ten-dollar cigar. Despite this warning, my father, who was himself honest and trusting by nature, went into a partnership with Kaplinsky and invested a substantial sum of money. One of the few family papers I have is the contract that my father signed with the Herka Industrial and Trade Company of 8 Fin Street in Tel Aviv. Typed in English, which my father did not speak, and dated 21 October 1951, the contract stated that the company would import Individual Food Parcels from the Ralan Trading Corporation in New York and that the profits would be divided 40:60 in favour of Mr Joseph Shlaim. The first lot was to consist of three hundred parcels of sugar, applesauce and chicken noodle. But the partners fell out before any food parcels arrived and my father lost all the money he had invested.

The second business venture was with Ruben Nasrallah, an acquaintance from Baghdad who became a friend in Israel. He had the idea of opening a wholesale store and my father went into a partnership with him. They rented a large store in Tel Aviv in a street in which the wholesale stores were concentrated. Their clients were Iraqi retail store owners whose customers consisted mostly of Iraqi Jews. A large range of items were displayed in the store: sugar, rice, lentils, tea, coffee, chocolate, halva, nuts, dried fruit, spices and all kinds of Middle Eastern sweets. As a little boy I was impressed by the scale of things compared to an average grocery store. There were sacks of food in two straight lines on the floor, big slabs of halva and large quantities of everything. The business flourished and the partners got on well: Ruben was the buyer and he did the heavy lifting; my father was the cashier and the accountant. It was a promising start in what was clearly an expanding market.

The business continued to flourish for a couple of years, then disaster struck: my father suffered a heart attack. An ambulance took him to the hospital in Tel Hashomer where he stayed for two weeks. This was a Kupat Kholim – national health service – hospital, which was free, but we had not joined the national health service because we had Dr Meir as our family doctor and in Israel he provided his services for free. From Tel Hashomer my father was transferred to a private hospital called Assuta in Tel Aviv. There he was diagnosed with *angina pectoris*, pain caused by reduced blood flow to the heart muscles. My sisters and I visited him several times in hospital. For me this was my first visit to a hospital, and I was struck by the immaculate cleanliness, the starched white uniforms of the medical staff and the air of professionalism that pervaded the place. All this, however, was not enough to allay my anxiety about the fate of my father.

Not long after my father returned home, he suffered a second heart attack and had to be taken again to the private hospital. This time he had open heart surgery and had to stay for a much longer period for monitoring and recovery. He had complete faith in the doctors, and was especially fond of the nurse who looked after him whose name was Telma. While the service was excellent, the cost was staggering and a serious drain on our meagre resources. For my father the two heart attacks had lasting effects: they weakened him both physically and psychologically, eroding what little was left of his old self-confidence.

Financial disaster followed close on the heels of the medical setback. Ruben Nasrallah claimed he could not run the business with my father in his weakened state and he unilaterally decided to dissolve the partnership. Without consulting us, he had found another partner and offered him my father's share of the business. He offered my father 9,000 liras for his share although my father had invested 10,000 liras to set up the business, and he made the offer in an offensive manner, on a take it or leave it basis. My mother, who took part in the acrimonious negotiations, had never seen her husband so angry – at one point he took off his shoe and threw it at Ruben.

My father came out of hospital and lost his business in 1954. He was fifty-three years old and remained unemployed until his death on 3 December 1970. This was not openly acknowledged but it was the reality. My father did try his hand at brokering land deals. An Iraqi friend of his, Yaacov Sofer, was an estate agent with an office on the ground floor of our apartment block. My father spent a great deal of time there as well as in the open-air café, talking to people, trying to match a seller with a buyer in the expectation of earning a commission. But all his efforts were in vain. His demeanour also changed: he looked older, he walked more slowly, he fell silent and he turned in on himself.

One hot summer day I went with my father to Galei Gil, literally the waves of joy, a swimming pool in Ramat Gan. In the changing room there were no lockers with keys, only coat-hangers with canvas bags attached to them in which you could leave your clothes. My father had a big, flat, Swiss gold watch with a leather strap that had survived the rough journey from Baghdad. He put it in his trouser pocket, folded the trousers, put them in the bag and handed the bag to the cloakroom attendant, who gave him a disk with a number. I did the same. We had a relaxing time, swimming and sun-bathing. We then changed and started walking out of the swimming pool when my father noticed that he did not have his watch. We went back to the changing room and told the attendant that we had lost a watch, but he was offhand and dismissive, claiming he had not seen any watch. It seemed fairly obvious that the man had stolen it but my father did not challenge him, did not protest, did not demand to see the manager. He just mumbled, turned on his heels and walked away. On the way home he was visibly upset but sullen and silent. I felt extremely sorry for him but also wondered why he had been so feeble. It occurred to me that he was not more assertive because he felt an outsider, that this was not his country and that he did not have the right to complain or to raise his voice. But I kept my thoughts to myself and walked on in silence, just like my father.

The collapse of father's business had repercussions for our family finances and family dynamics. With no money coming in, we had to live on what remained from the capital we had brought with us from Iraq, which had been significantly diminished by the hospital bills. It was clear that sooner or later our capital would run out. As my father was unable to find work, my mother came under pressure to take over as the breadwinner. Dr Meir David, our faithful family doctor, went into local politics by joining the General Zionists and ended up as deputy mayor of Ramat Gan. This was a centrist political party which advocated *laissez-faire* economics and counted many middle-class Iraqis among its supporters. My mother joined the party and worked for them as a volunteer. This brought her into contact with other members of the party who worked in the town hall. Dr Meir then gave her the idea of applying for paid employment.

In 1955 my mother started work as a telephonist in the town hall. This had the advantage of a short working day of only five hours, starting at 8 a.m., compared with eight hours for other posts. Although this was a lowly job, my mother was proud of it and made the most of it. To the new job she brought patience, flexibility, good manners, platinum-grade social skills and willingness to help. This made her popular and won her friends at every level, from the mayor down to the messenger boys. In the course of her work, she got to know many of the employees of the town hall, their powers, remit and responsibilities. This enabled her to exert influence and wield patronage out of all proportion to her actual position. Iraqi friends used to come to her for help with all kinds of problems to do with council taxes, utility bills, parking fines, planning permissions and so on. As an Iraqi woman exclaimed in awe: 'Your word is like a sword!'

One close friend my mother made at work was Miriam Yakim, the daughter of the mayor and the head of the department of children's welfare. She was also the chair of the committee for the twinning with the Israel Defense Forces' Paratrooper Corps; the big cities in Israel had twinning arrangements with one of the branches of the IDF and Ramat Gan's twin were the paratroop brigade. Mrs Yakim invited my mother to serve as a member of the committee. This committee was very active in raising money, organising events and throwing parties for the paratroopers. I remember these parties as very jolly affairs, in the garden of the mayor's house, with food and drink that were considered lavish by the standards of the day.

Of all the officers who came to these parties, one stood out because he was a showman. His name was Ariel Sharon. He was a young lieutenant-colonel, plump, with a shock of blond hair and piercing blue eyes that exuded self-confidence. On one outing we stopped by a bridge along the Jordan River. A Jordanian soldier from the other side of the bridge shouted something at us. Sharon shouted back in Arabic: '*Uskut, ya aswad!*' – shut up, you black! My mother was evidently impressed with this macho Israeli way of treating Arabs because she kept repeating the offensive words afterwards. Sharon became a major-general, a leader of the right-wing Likud and eventually prime minister. He was embroiled in controversy throughout his career because of his mendacity and brutality towards Arab civilians. As a student of the Arab–Israeli conflict I would pass extremely harsh judgement on Sharon, but as a teenager I had a much warmer impression of him. Much later I reflected on the paradox that even war criminals can be perfectly pleasant company.

When I reached the age of thirteen, I had a Bar-Mitzvah. According to Jewish law, at the age of thirteen, boys become fully-fledged members of the community and, as such, accountable for their actions. They must fast on the Day of Atonement, and they may be counted towards a *minyan*, a prayer quorum of at least ten men. A Bar-Mitzvah consists of both religious rituals and secular festivities. My father took care of the former and my mother the latter. My father gave me the three basic items worn during Jewish prayer: a kippa or skullcap; a tallit or prayer shawl; and tefillin or phylacteries. Tefillin consists of two black leather boxes and straps to hold them on to the left arm and to the hairline on the forehead. We were a secular rather than an orthodox Jewish family and I was not at all religious, so I opted to keep this side of the coming of age to a minimum. I practised putting on the tefillin and I went to the Serphardi synagogue with my father on the Saturday after my thirteenth birthday, but rather than going up to the podium to read a portion of the law (Torah), I only recited a benediction after the reading by the rabbi and the adults.

My mother really pushed the boat out when it came to the festivities. A Bar-Mitzvah normally includes a joyous *se'udat mitzvah*, a celebratory meal for family and friends. My mother hired a hall and invited all of our relatives and friends. Being rather status-conscious, not to say snobbish, she arranged a top table for distinguished guests. These included Mayor Avraham Krinitzi, his daughter Miriam Yakim, Dr Meir David, and Shalom Zisman, another leader of the General Zionists party and deputy mayor. Although it was a time of austerity, there was plenty of food at the party: pittas filled with chicken, salads, hummus and tahini, lamb-filled pastries, Middle Eastern sweets and fruit. There was also a range of spirits and soft drinks. My mother presided with aplomb. Her brother Isaac had sent her a green velvet dress from England. She wore it with a red chiffon belt. Mr Krinitzi reportedly told his daughter 'Look at Aida, how beautiful she is!' My mother never tired of repeating this remark well into her nineties.

An exceptionally exciting present I received for my Bar-Mitzvah was a Raleigh bicycle that my uncle Isaac sent me from England. It came in a wooden box, and I still remember the thrill of prising open the planks and discovering a shining, brand new bicycle. Many years later, Uncle Isaac told me that he had not paid a penny for this princely gift. A rich Jewish friend, who had stayed in Iraq after the exodus of 1950, had asked him to buy two upmarket English bikes for his teenage sons. Isaac had gone into a shop and bought three identical bikes, two for his Iraqi friend and one for me, and the invoice was fudged so that the friend ended up paying for all three bikes. I had no idea at the time about the murky origins of the gift and, had I known, it would probably have made no difference. I was ecstatic to own this fantastic bike, and quickly learnt to ride it, using it every day and becoming very attached to it.

With growing proficiency as a rider came the urge to do stunts. One of my favourites was to ride the bike with my back facing the direction of travel; another was to stand on the seat with one leg in the air, like a prima ballerina. Many of my friends in the neighbourhood learnt to ride on this bike and I was happy to let them take it out for a spin; because I was the owner, I felt a cut above the rest. In time I became quite skilled in carrying out minor repairs and fixing punctures, a skill that remained with me for the rest of my life. At Oxford I had a 1950 green vintage Raleigh to which I was similarly attached but had to abandon when it could no longer be repaired. No other bike has given me as much pleasure as these two green Raleighs, one in my early teens, the other in the twilight of my career as a cyclist.

Avi in class in seventh or eighth grade

TEN

ADRIFT

IN MY LAST TWO YEARS IN PRIMARY SCHOOL, IN THE SEVENTH and eighth grades, I was increasingly afflicted by what today might be described as existential angst. What I experienced on a small scale was what Iraqi Jews experienced all over Israel: disrespect for our Iraqi provenance; ignorance of our history; disdain for our culture; denigration of our language; and social engineering to make us fit into the new European-Zionist-Israeli mould. There was a dominant Ashkenazi nationalist narrative which contrasted our life as a humiliated minority in exile with the bright present of Jewish freedom and independence in the Promised Land. A systematic process was at work to delegitimise our heritage and erase our cultural roots. The unstated aims of the official policy for schools were to undermine our Arab-Jewish identity and to turn us into loyal citizens of the new Israeli nation-state.

The clash of cultures was dramatised by my relationship with our new form teacher. She clearly disliked me, and the feeling was mutual. Her name was Miriam Lentz. She came from Germany and spoke Hebrew with a German accent. She lived near us with her only son whom she often mentioned in class and to whom she was closely attached. There was never any mention of a Mr Lentz. Mrs Lentz was not a 'happy bunny'. She looked severe, she never laughed and rarely even smiled. What I disliked about her, however, was not her austere countenance but her apparent prejudice against those of us in her class who came from Arab countries.

Mrs Lentz made no attempt to conceal her hostility towards me. It may have been because I was a bad student: I was not motivated; I was a minimalist when it came to homework; and my performance across the board was well below average. My school certificate at the end of seventh grade recorded that my behaviour was 'very good'; my mark for Maths was 'good'; my marks for Hebrew, Bible, History, Biology and Geography were 'nearly satisfactory'; and my mark for English was 'unsatisfactory'. I was not inspired and made no special effort in any subject, but I found English particularly difficult and began to fall badly behind in class. That the child of an Anglophone mother ended up failing in English in Israel seems remarkable in retrospect. Mrs Lentz had no complaint about my general behaviour, hence the mark of 'very good'. Had she complained about my laziness and lack of commitment, she would have been fully justified. But my sense was that there was another factor at play.

Roughly a quarter of the children in the class came from Iraq or other Arab countries. Collectively we were known as Sephardim, Orientals or Mizrahim, and I shall use these terms as if they were interchangable although, strictly speaking, they are not. Mrs Lentz was from Europe and we felt a lack of empathy in the way she treated us. She favoured the Ashkenazi kids in the class, especially those who came from upper middle-class families. There was an element of class snobbery mixed with intra-ethnic antipathy in her attitude towards us. Once a term, on a Friday evening, we used to have a gathering of the entire class and the form teacher in the house of one of the kids. The parents had to volunteer to host us and to do so they had to have a large house or flat. They were usually also successful members of the economic or cultural elite. Mrs Lentz used to ingratiate herself with the parents and hold them out to the rest of us as model citizens. In this subtle intersection of class and culture, those of us who came from less affluent or less educated backgrounds were made to feel as if we were the poor cousins or worse still – inferior.

One episode that seemed to suggest prejudice against Iraqis on the part of Mrs Lentz involved me directly. She dressed very soberly: she wore no make-up and no jewellery of any kind. Women from Arab lands, by contrast, tended to wear jewellery, especially gold jewellery, of various kinds: necklaces, brooches, bracelets and rings. It was also an Arab-Jewish custom to give b'nei mitzvah items of gold and silver as presents. I received for my Bar-Mitzvah a gold necklace with the Star of David and a gold ring with the English initials of my name, AS, inscribed on it. Innocently, I wore both the chain and the ring at school, being unaware of their cultural and ideological signifiers.

Zionism was a stern ideology which rejected the legacy of the Diaspora and aimed to build a Jewish Sparta in the Middle East. Jewellery, especially when worn by men, did not sit comfortably with this austere ideology. Mrs Lentz, a committed Zionist, said so to the class. Addressing the entire class, she made some disparaging remarks about Orientals and their decadent habit of wearing jewellery. Then she turned to me and ordered me to remove my necklace and ring. Taken aback, I took the ring off my finger but had difficulty opening the clasp of the necklace. My neighbour came to my aid and after a tense minute or two I succeeded in removing the second offensive object. All this time, Mrs Lentz stood opposite me, glowering at me with a look of disgust. It was a deeply humiliating experience, made worse by the fact that I did not fully understand what she was on about. This was my equivalent of being sprayed with DDT, but I remained silent.

Another encounter was even more painful. One day, when Mrs Lentz was writing something on the blackboard and had her back turned to the class, someone threw up a crumpled piece of paper which landed on the floor. Hearing the commotion, Mrs Lentz turned around, picked up the piece of paper and scrutinised its content. Looking very stern, she demanded to know who had written it. No one owned up. She asked again, and again no hand went up. She asked a third time and again no one pleaded guilty. She then divulged that the piece of paper contained obscenities and declared her determination to find out the culprit. Switching roles from teacher to detective, she asked six of us in the area where the paper ball had landed to go up to her with an exercise book containing a sample of our handwriting. After a cursory examination, she declared that I was the culprit. I cannot remember whether I protested my innocence. I probably did not because I was stunned and speechless. What I remember clearly, however, is that I put down my head on my folded arms on the desk and cried silently. The injustice of the accusation stabbed me in the heart. I thought it was cowardly of the perpetrator not to own up, but my deepest rage was directed at the teacher who I believed had deliberately framed me for a crime I had not committed.

In the eighth grade, the final year of primary school, nothing changed. The form teacher persisted in her negative attitude towards the Oriental children in general and towards me in particular, while I continued to feel alienated and to lag behind the rest of the class. The performance recorded in the school certificate for the first term of the eighth grade was almost identical to the previous year: 'good' for Maths; 'barely satisfactory' for most subjects; and 'unsatisfactory' for English. Towards the end of the school year, however, something unexpected and momentous happened: I passed the *seker*, the national exam that determined one's subsequent path or, more specifically, whether one could go to an academic high school, a vocational school or the job market. This was a country-wide system of selection that divided the fourteen-year-olds into three levels of ability and three streams. The purpose of the *seker* was two-fold: to identify those suited for post-elementary academic education, and to provide them with scholarships to cover their fees. Only elementary education was free at that time.

The pass mark of the *seker* for children of Asian and African origins was slightly lower than that for Ashkenazi children. The exam was set by the Ministry of Education. It reflected the outcome of a debate between two schools of thought: those who thought that intellectual ability was innate and those who thought that material and environmental conditions affected educational performance. The second group argued that such conditions were all-important and that the high percentage of failure among Asian and African children at primary school was due to factors such as poverty, overcrowding and uneducated parents. Accordingly, a system of very limited reverse discrimination was put in place under the heading of *Norma Bet* or Norm B.

The *seker* exam consisted of seventy-eight questions. Those at the receiving end complained that it was unusually difficult, but experts thought it was intelligently composed. The good news for me was that I passed the exam. It was a huge boost to my self-esteem. Mrs Lentz, my nemesis, apparently resented my success. She discussed the results in general in front of the whole class. But at the end of the session, she came up to me and said: 'I hope you realise that you only passed the *seker* because of the concessions made to Mizrahi children.' I made no reply, but I remember thinking to myself, 'Why is she saying this to me?' In retrospect, I think that this was an appalling way for a teacher to behave towards a young child in her care. In the first place, this was a national exam and she had no way of knowing whether I had passed only because of the allowance made to Mizrahi children. Secondly, even had she known for certain that this was indeed the case, there was no need for her to rub it in. All she needed to do was to congratulate me on my success and wish me good luck. The actual line she took only fuelled my anger and reinforced my suspicion that she was prejudiced.

What I did not know at the time was that many experts considered the entire Israeli educational system, including the *seker* exam, to be unfair to Mizrahim and socially divisive. The minister of education from the mid-1950s was Zalman Aran, a prominent member of the ruling Labour Party, or Mapai as it was called in those days. Aran saw himself as the son of a superior Ashkenazi elite and looked down on Asian and North African Jews as an inherently inferior race. He believed that their poor performance at school reflected low native intelligence rather than external socio-economic factors. His aim was not to close the educational gap but to direct as many Mizrahim as possible towards vocational schools and the labour market; he wanted a large proletariat to support the country's industrial and agricultural development. Although he did not use the biblical phrase, the role he envisaged for Asian and African Jews in Israeli society was 'the hewers of wood and the drawers of water'. The effect of his policy was to hold back the Mizrahim by restricting their access to higher education and to the 'white collar' and well-paid occupations that went with it.

In 1959–60, Mizrahi children constituted 50% of their age group in the country at large, but only 18.8 per cent of their cohort in academic secondary schools. Aran saw nothing wrong with that. In March 1964, he told the Board of Trustees of the Hebrew University that 'The children of the olim from Islamic countries were not equipped with all that was necessary to assume their full part in post-elementary and higher education.' He reported that this group constituted 60% of the populations of kindergartens, 50% of primary schools, 25% of academic secondary schools and 12% of higher education. Again, these statistics were not a cause for concern for the minister of education but a reflection of the natural order of things. The limited measure of reverse discrimination in the *seker* was not Aran's idea and, in any case, it did not make much difference. The great majority of Mizrahim still failed the *seker*. Some teachers did not enter their Mizrahi children for this exam at all because they thought they had no chance of passing.[1] I was one of the few lucky ones. But the pleasure I derived from this one and only academic distinction of my first ten years at school was irremediably marred by Mrs Lentz's sour comment.

Having painted such a comprehensively dismal portrait of Mrs Lentz, I feel duty-bound to add that there is a very different contemporary view of her. This view comes from Arlette Sha'ya, an Iraqi girl who was my classmate in the last six years of primary school. After writing the present chapter, I came across a letter she wrote me on 14 August 2005 with comments on a long interview with me, published in the liberal daily *Ha'aretz*. The title of the article was 'Our hand is stretched out for war'. The author was a left-wing journalist named Meron Rapoport and the occasion for the interview was the publication of the Hebrew edition of my book *The Iron Wall: Israel and the Arab World*. Rapoport was intrigued by my background as an Arab-Jew, and consequently, almost half the article consisted of personal recollections of my early life in Israel, including the story of Mrs Lentz and the *seker*.

Arlette Sha'ya was surprised and pleased to read the article about me and my book and tried to contact me by phone. There was only one Shlaim in the Ramat Gan telephone book, but when she called, they told her that they did not know me. So she wrote me a long letter and asked Meron Rapoport to forward it. In the letter Arlette stated that she had found my thesis about Israel's intransigence both interesting and well-founded but not entirely new. She herself had always held this view because her Communist elder brother had exposed her to alternative explanations of Israel's behaviour. At the same time, she noted, courage is needed to say these things openly and to challenge the false theses propagated by the establishment. She congratulated me on my bravery in going against the current and on my impressive trajectory since our days in primary school.

The rest of the letter concerned Mrs Lentz. Arlette was surprised by what I had told Meron Rapoport about her hostility towards Iraqi children. She too was Iraqi, she wrote, but she had never sensed any hostility. On the contrary, in Arlette's experience Mrs Lentz had been sympathetic and supportive. On one occasion, two girls, who were probably jealous of Arlette, had called her *iraqit masriha* – a stinking Iraqi. Mrs Lentz had overheard them, got extremely angry and reprimanded them in no uncertain terms. So exercised was Mrs Lentz by this solitary incident that she devoted a whole civics class to the subject, stressing repeatedly that racial stereotyping was a fascist and a Nazi practice that had no place in the state of Israel. Against this background, Arlette wondered whether Mrs Lentz was hostile to me not because I was an Iraqi but because, by my own admission, I was singularly uncooperative and uncommunicative.

Despite the passage of time, I remember Arlette very vividly. In the eighth grade she sat two rows in from of me. She was top of the class in

most subjects and a wizard in Maths. She was strikingly self-confident
and unusually assertive. She contributed frequently and knowledgeably
to class discussions. No sooner had a teacher finished putting a question
to the class than Arlette would be thrusting her hand high up in the air.
Arlette was also a leading light in the drama society. When our class
was invited to put on a play about Hannah Szenes, a Zionist national
hero, in front of the whole school, Arlette was given the lead role. In
short, in every way, except our common Iraqi provenance, Arlette was
the opposite of me. I secretly admired her, and I was very proud of
her. Here was an Iraqi girl who more than held her own against all the
Ashkenazi children in the class. Yet I never made friends with Arlette
and hardly ever spoke to her. I was far too shy and tongue-tied. As for
solidarity based on the Iraqi connection, that was something I felt deep
inside me but could not bring out into the open.

After re-reading Arlette's letter, I called her on the landline at her
home in Rehovot. In her letter she had given her telephone number
and her married name – Mintzer. A long conversation ensued which
helped me to better understand some of the issues with which I had
grappled but only dimly grasped during this difficult phase in my life.
Arlette herself had had a successful career as an actor, theatre director,
clinical psychologist and poet. She remembered me from school as 'an
extreme case' of quietness. Not only was I silent in class but even during
the breaks I hardly said anything. It was obvious that I was lazy and
negligent when it came to homework but because I was so taciturn, she
and the other children thought that I was probably a bit dim. Children,
after all, she remarked, only see what is on the surface; they rarely delve
underneath the shell.

The other quality for which Arlette remembered me was that I was
adin, delicate, refined. This she attributed to my being a child of the East.
Iraqis, she observed, attach great importance to being courteous towards
other people. But there was evidently more to me than met the eye. How
come she was so confident as well as courteous? I asked. Surprisingly,
Arlette's response also revolved around her Iraqi background. She was

six years old when she arrived in Israel. She had six siblings who were considerably older than her. They ranged from eighteen to twenty-four years of age on arrival. Her brothers were university graduates. One of them was a member of the Communist party and an outspoken critic of the Israeli establishment. At home, generally, there was a high level of political consciousness and debate. Her siblings educated and empowered her, and this cancelled out any sense of inferiority she might have otherwise had on account of being an Iraqi.

Arlette's observations about the climate of opinion in the Israel of the 1950s struck me as perceptive. There was racism, she said, towards all new immigrants. This manifested itself in the widespread resort to national stereotypes. Romanians, for example, were commonly seen as a nation of thieves and there were endless jokes based on this stereotype. In this hostile climate, it was not unusual for new immigrants to develop a sense of inferiority compared to the *sabras*, the Israeli-born. Prejudice, however, was particularly pronounced in the case of the Mizrahim. They were widely regarded by the Ashkenazim as different, as alien, as having a low intelligence quotient, as backward and primitive. Even some of the teachers shared these views. To emphasise the pervasiveness of anti-Mizrahi prejudice, Arlette confessed that even she had been contaminated. She had not wanted to marry an Iraqi when she grew up and looked down on her sisters because they spoke Hebrew with an Iraqi accent. Today she feels an acute sense of shame at the prejudices she internalised as a child.

The conversation with Arlette led me to reflect more deeply on the roots of my failure at school. When I thought about it, it seemed to me that the main reason for my inability to do well at school was my Iraqi identity and the continuous sense of inferiority that it bred in me. The intellectual poverty of my home environment was another contributory factor. Arlette's home environment was intellectually stimulating, promoted political awareness and inspired independence of spirit. I had none of these advantages. We had no books at home, no university graduates and no encouragement to think more critically, let alone to challenge the premises and the prejudices of the society around us.

My sister Dalia was a year ahead of me at Yahalom primary school. She too passed the exam for entrance to secondary school and in her case too, the result came as a surprise to her superiors. She was very quiet in class, kept a low profile and did not distinguish herself in any subject. Given her past record, she was expected to fail the *seker* exam. According to her account, the form teacher was asked to explain the discrepancy between her low grades in class and the high grades she received in the *seker*. His inability to do so gave rise to the suspicion that she had cheated. She was asked to resit the exam and once again she got high marks. Her explanation of the discrepancy was that the *seker* was an intelligence test, not a test of academic knowledge. Success in the *seker* did something for her self-esteem but it was not enough to propel her into an academic secondary school. Instead, she did a two-year course at an ORT college, part of a network of vocational schools, where she trained to be a hairdresser. She settled for this career path because she received no encouragement from either the school or our parents to pursue academic studies. In our community a good education was considered highly desirable for boys but much less important for girls. Girls were expected to be pleasant, pliant and polite. They were badgered to get married early, to look after the home and to bring up children. My other sister, Vilma, who was nearly three years younger than me, got no encouragement either. At the age of fourteen she enrolled for a two-year secretarial course and then started work as a receptionist in a doctor's clinic.

My two sisters were very different in temperament. Vilma was chubby and cheerful, friendly and outgoing, and she took life as it came without worrying too much about her identity or her future. Was she aware of the preferential treatment I received? I think so. In Ramat Gan, as in Baghdad, our mother acted on the theory that nuts stimulated the development of the brain. So every Friday she would buy a bag of roasted ground nuts for me and hide them on the top of the wardrobe. If Vilma tried to reach them, our mother would say to her: 'These nuts are not for you. They are your brother's nuts'. Vilma's retrospective gloss on our mother's motives was characteristically generous: she thought that our mother kept her away from the nuts because she did not want her to put on weight. Dalia was a more complex and troubled adolescent. From the age of eight onwards, she was expected to wash the floors in our flat in Ramat Gan every Friday in preparation for the Sabbath, and this was a source of resentment. She felt unappreciated and unloved at home. At school, she probably suffered from an inferiority complex on account of being Iraqi, though, like me, she would not admit it. Both she and Vilma had to endure me being the favoured child, but for Dalia this was more of a problem than for Vilma. Dalia used to fight with me and on one occasion, on holiday with our cousins in their agricultural settlement in the Negev, cracked a whip and hit me hard, reducing me to tears. Vilma was passive and malleable, whereas Dalia was truculent and rebellious.

Vilma got on well with our father and he was very fond of her. Because he couldn't find employment, he had time to spare. During the summer holidays he would sometimes take her to the beach in Tel Aviv. They would buy fruit on the way, hire deck chairs, swim in the sea and sunbathe. Vilma does not recall any disagreements or any issues that could have soured her relationship with our father. She thought he did his share of looking after us, that he was a kind of house husband while our mother became the breadwinner. This sort of role reversal was nowhere as common in those days as it is today. Staying at home when his wife went out to work did nothing for his self-esteem.

Through Dalia, social pressure to cut ourselves off from our Arab roots, and to leave behind the habits of the Diaspora, was exerted upon our household. Dalia refused to speak Arabic even in the comfort zone of the family home because she regarded it as the language of the despised Diaspora. Her obstinate refusal added to the tensions between her and our father. He was a news addict and he also liked to listen to Arabic music. He used to listen to the news bulletins in Arabic several times a day. When it was time for the news, he would shout '*Oh, al-akhbar*' – 'Oh, the news' – and rush to switch on the radio. We, the children, used to look at each other and repeat the words in Arabic as if it was something strange: *Oh, al-akhbar*! His favourite singer was Umm Kulthūm, the legendary Egyptian singer. One day the conflicting linguistic preferences produced a real explosion. We had an old-fashioned Zenith radio, both a radio and a record player. Dalia wanted to hear a drama in Hebrew whereas our father wanted to listen to the news in Arabic. They had a multilingual row, Dalia got very angry, and she stopped speaking to our father for a long, long time to come. Like Yuma, she had developed a habit of falling out with people. The impasse between Dalia and our father was awkward for the rest of us. However, when she visited us in Oxford in her early seventies, she told my wife that our father was the only person who ever really loved her. It was only in the last few years of her life that our mother's attitude towards Dalia changed markedly for the better. The selfless way in which Dalia attended to all her material and medical needs finally earned her our mother's respect and appreciation.

The unstable home environment inevitably affected my performance at school, but it was only one factor. The main factors were lack of inner motivation and low self-esteem. Success in the *seker* increased my self-esteem to some extent but it did not guarantee a place in secondary school. In Israel in those days state education was compulsory and free up to the age of fourteen. Secondary education was not compulsory and most secondary schools were in private hands. This meant one had to apply for admission and, if admitted, the government would pay the fee. I was unlikely to be accepted to any secondary school in Ramat Gan because of my low grades.

One of these schools, a rather prestigious one, was called Gimnasia Dvir. This school appealed to me, but I had no chance of getting there under my own steam. Embarrassing as it is to admit, I only got a place there through nepotism. My mother's determined intervention secured my entry. She went to see the mayor, Avraham Krinitzi, and pleaded for his help in resolving the problem of an allegedly brilliant son with unjustifiably low school grades. The mayor called Mr Halevy, the owner of Gimnasia Dvir, and demanded I be given a place. The owner replied that they could not possibly accept me as they had already rejected other applicants with better grades than mine. The mayor then offered a 'compromise': that I be accepted on probation for one term and thrown out at the end of term if my progress was not satisfactory. It was on this ethically questionable basis that I gained admission.

The range of subjects taught at Gimnasia Dvir was broader than in the state school, the classes were smaller and the standard of teaching much higher. One phase in my life had ended and a new one had begun. I made new friends among my classmates. Whereas most of my friends in our neighbourhood at home were of Iraqi origin, many of my new friends were Ashkenazi. The gulf between Mizrahi and Ashkenazi children in the new school was not as pronounced as before. The ethos of the school was liberal and progressive and all pupils, boys and girls, were treated as equal. Despite this inclusive atmosphere, I was still self-conscious of being an outsider. Having Ashkenazi friends helped, to a limited extent, to attenuate this feeling. All my friends were boys; I was too shy to talk to the girls.

There were several good school friends. My closest friend was Gil Sadan, a bright and articulate fellow who excelled at school and showed early signs of aptitude for journalism by publishing articles in a national youth magazine. He lived near us, we often went to each other's homes and we co-operated in doing our homework, with Gil always in the lead. Another friend was Jeki Alkalai. Unlike the Iraqi friends who lived in flats in our enormous building, Jeki lived in a villa with a large garden that became our playfield. I was touched when one day, walking home after school, Jeki put his arm around me and told me I was his best friend. Placing friends in rank order is nothing unusual among teenagers, then or now, but Jeki's casual remark meant a great deal to me.

Another Ashkenazi friend from Gimnasia Dvir whom I remember with particular affection was Benny Ambach, who later changed his surname to Arbel. I sat in the corner at the far end of the classroom and he sat at the desk in front of me. Next to him sat Amnon Barzilai who later became a prominent journalist at *Haaretz*. Benny came from a wealthy family and lived in a villa not far from the school. His father owned Elite, the famous chocolate factory. I was a stamp collector and Benny used to give me envelopes bulging with stamps that he got from the factory. He was exceptionally bright, a star student, but also a kind and generous individual with a friendly manner and a good sense of humour. If I had any questions on any subject, I would ask him, and he invariably knew the answer. He helped me a great deal with my school-work, always patient, never patronising. Benny was a charming fellow and the best of friends. He later became a professor of Early Modern History at Tel Aviv University. I regret that I did not stay in touch with him, especially as I too eventually became a historian.

Although I liked the new school better than the old one, I still did not work hard, I continued to daydream at the back of the classroom and my academic achievements were well below average. Daydreaming about worldly success and heroic exploits was something I indulged in a lot in my childhood because, as a shy boy, I found it difficult to face up to the real world. In one dream I featured as the commander of a tank regiment in the IDF, leading it in a column in the Negev and stirring a whirlwind of desert sand as we charged forward. Daydreaming was harmless enough, but it did nothing to improve my academic perfor-mance. The end of year report shows that I did slightly better in the humanities than in the natural sciences. On a scale of 1–10 my average score was 6.1 where 6, if I am not mistaken, was the pass mark. I scored 7 for Bible, Hebrew and Geography; 6 for French, History, Physics, Biology and Maths; and 4 for English. English was my weakest subject as reflected in the outright Fail mark. I had fallen so far behind that I was unable to follow what the teacher was saying in class. There was a lot of catching up to do. I failed to bestir myself from my habitual lethargy and I eventually paid the price. English was going to be the principal cause of my academic downfall.

French was a new subject in the curriculum; I did not find it as diffi-cult as English, and it was the subject I enjoyed most. My mother, who had studied everything through the medium of French in her Alliance school for girls in Baghdad, took great pleasure in reading aloud stories from my textbook and translating them for me in a curious mixture of English, Arabic and Hebrew. Having a charismatic teacher made all the difference. Our French teacher was a middle-aged woman, a new immigrant from France, short and stocky, with dramatic flair and boundless energy. Her Hebrew was limited but that did not matter because she preferred to do all her teaching in French. She had us sing French songs and resorted to a range of other techniques to bring the language to life. For the first time in my young life, I became an active participant in the learning process.

The promotion of Zionist values, which had begun in grade one, continued and intensified in secondary school. But it was a subtle process. Forging a nation and a common sense of national identity for Jews who came from all over the world, spoke different languages and at times seemed to have little in common, was the overriding goal of the state of Israel. Education was a major tool in pursuit of this goal. The whole school curriculum was geared to generating pride in belonging to the Israeli nation and confidence in the justice of its cause. History was the main but not the only subject through which this ideological agenda was driven. The way history was taught at school was more closely related to the project of nation building than to the disinterested pursuit of truth.

It is only in retrospect that I became aware of the tendentious and selective nature of the history I was taught at school. In the first place, the geographical scope of this history was largely confined to the Jewish experience in Europe – there was virtually nothing about the history of the Jews in the Arab and Islamic countries. By implication, these Jews were considered marginal to the broad sweep of Jewish history. The rich cultural legacy of the Arab-Jews was not just ignored; it was erased. The impression purveyed by the educational system therefore was that Jewish-Arab culture was of little value; our distinct cultural heritage was sacrificed at the service of Israel's 'melting pot' ideology. Moreover, the connecting thread that ran through school history was the story of Jewish suffering – in line with the 'lachrymose conception of Jewish history' that Zionism happily adopted.

Oddly enough, the Holocaust, the supreme example of Jewish suffering and victimhood, was not emphasised at school, nor outside school for that matter. At least that was the case until the trial of Adolf Eichmann. Eichmann was a middle-ranking Nazi official who had played a pivotal role in the implementation of the 'Final Solution'. He was captured by Mossad agents in Argentina and brought to trial in Jerusalem in April 1961. The trial sparked international interest and heightened public awareness of the horrors of the Nazi genocide. There were more reporters to cover the trial than at the Nuremberg trials of German war criminals at the end of the Second World War. At Nuremberg the prosecutors had relied mainly on written documents; in Jerusalem the survivors were placed at centre stage. Day after day the survivors talked, in some cases for the first time, about the horrors they had endured. By sharing their experiences, they helped to create a new openness in Israeli society.

Prime minister David Ben-Gurion saw the trial as an opportunity to unify the nation by educating it about this traumatic chapter in its history. He also wanted everyone to recognise that 'whatever the world owes to the victims, they now owe to Israel.' Chief prosecutor Gideon Hausner told the court in his opening speech: 'When I stand before you, I don't stand alone. Here, with me at this moment, stand six million prosecutors.' The speech sent shivers down his listeners' spines. Eichmann testified from behind a glass booth to protect him from physical violence. His main line of defence was that he had not made policy but merely implemented it. 'My heart was light and joyful in my work', he said, 'because the decisions were not mine.' The judges rejected this claim and condemned him to death by hanging. His body was cremated, and the ashes were spread at sea, beyond Israel's territorial waters. This was the only time in its history that Israel officially enacted the death penalty.

The Eichmann trial made a huge impression on me as a fifteen-year-old child. If the aim of the people who put Eichmann on trial was to sear the memory of the Nazi genocide on the consciousness of mankind, they were entirely successful in my case. The lesson of the genocide was also repeatedly drilled into us: Never again will Jews be led like sheep to the slaughter. 'Never Again! Never Again! Never Again!' The trial went on for five months. Its proceedings were reported very loudly and prominently, on a daily basis, on the radio and in the press. I still carry in my mind the image of the man in the grey suit with the thick-rimmed glasses, sitting there silently and impassively inside the glass booth, listening through earphones to the German translation of the court proceedings. What struck me repeatedly was how ordinary he looked. In my mind's eye I expected a major Nazi war criminal to be huge and to look like a monster in human form. And here was this small, middle-aged, slightly balding and utterly unimpressive man.

Decades later, reading Hannah Arendt's 1963 book on the Eichmann trial helped me resolve some of the conundrums that had troubled me as an adolescent, notably the disconnect between the underwhelming figure of the man in the dock and the enormity of the crimes of which he stood accused. The full title of the book is *Eichmann in Jerusalem: A Report on the Banality of Evil*. Arendt was critical of the way the trial was conducted, seeing it as a 'show trial' rather than an honest attempt to review the evidence and administer justice. She charged Hausner with resorting to hyperbolic rhetoric to further Ben-Gurion's political agenda and dismissed his parade of Holocaust survivors as having 'no apparent bearing on the case'. Above all, Arendt was critical of the way Israel framed Eichmann's crimes as crimes against a nation-state rather than crimes against humanity. To cap it all, she rejected the claim that a strong Israel was necessary to protect world Jewry.

Arendt's book was greeted with a storm of protest from various Jewish quarters. Much of the protest related to the subtitle of the book – about the banality of evil. She was accused of coldness and lack of sympathy for the victims of the Nazi genocide. Her attempt to explain how ordinary people become actors in totalitarian systems was construed, or rather misconstrued, as an apologia for their deeds. It is true that she wrote that Eichmann was 'terribly and terrifyingly normal'. But she did not exonerate him as a man who simply followed orders and she considered the death penalty served on him by the judges to be fully justified. The deeper question she set out to examine was whether evil is inborn or simply the result of the tendency of ordinary people to go with the flow, to conform and to obey orders without thinking about the consequences of their actions. During the trial Eichmann struck her as a dull bureaucrat who had found a role for himself in the Nazi party and who lacked the capacity to evaluate the ethical implications of his actions. His example led Arendt to conclude that going along with the rest and wanting to say 'we' were enough to make war crimes possible. Even the most horrific crime committed by totalitarian regimes, she argued, can have mundane origins. This was the real meaning of the phrase 'the banality of evil'. Whether Arendt was right or wrong about SS-Obersturmbannführer Adolf Eichmann, she certainly grasped an important truth about the nature of evil.

In post-war Israel, survivors of the Holocaust were harshly and unfairly criticised for not resisting, for allowing themselves, in the biblical phrase, to be led like sheep to the slaughter. Jewish nationalism reacted against this passivity and glorified armed resistance. The heroism of the fighters in the 1943 Warsaw Ghetto Uprising, the outstanding example of Jewish armed resistance to the Nazis, was appropriated by Israeli propagandists to portray other Diaspora Jews as passive and weak in contrast to Israel's 'new Jews'. Jewish history, as it was taught in my school, lavished praise on individuals who resisted foreign oppressors and fought for Jewish independence. One of them was Simon Bar Kokhba, who led a revolt of the province of Judea against the Roman Empire in the second century CE. Bar Kokhba was held out as a national hero although the revolt he led was crushed, Judea was devastated and its population was killed, exiled or sold into slavery. The lesson we were expected to draw from the history of this revolt was that it is more honourable to go down fighting than not to fight at all.

Another hero, from the Zionist phase of Jewish history, was Joseph Trumpeldor. Trumpeldor was a proud Jew who volunteered for the

Russian army, became an officer and lost his left arm to shrapnel in the Russo–Japanese war of 1905. He moved to Palestine in 1912 where he advocated collective agricultural settlement and armed Jewish self-defence. In the First World War he helped organise volunteers to the Jewish Legion within the British Army and to bring Jewish immigrants to Palestine. Trumpeldor died defending the settlement of Tel Hai in northern Galilee against Arab attackers in 1920 and subsequently became a Zionist icon and a symbol of self-defence. In the standard Zionist rendition of the story, his last words were: 'It is good to die for our country.' A poster of Trumpeldor adorned the wall in our classroom and we were taught a song of praise for his heroism. It was a tender, beautiful song and we sang it so many times that I knew the words well. I could not sing for the life of me but at a birthday party for my Iraqi friend, Yosef Sofer, his father prevailed on me to sing this song in front of all the guests. Many years later I learnt that the story about Trumpeldor's last words had been manufactured. It transpired that his last word had been *yopfoyomat*, a Russian swear word which, very roughly translated, means 'motherfucker'.

Round about this time I began to develop an interest in politics. How or why this interest developed is not entirely clear to me today. I do not recall talking about politics with my friends. Nor could the stimulus have come from home. My parents did not read newspapers and they were not well-informed about either domestic politics or foreign affairs. Having grown up in an authoritarian political culture, they were not accustomed to political freedom and grasped only dimly the meaning of democracy. To be sure, the Israeli political scene was rather baffling. A pure proportional representation system had resulted in a proliferation of parties, some of them with only a handful of representatives in the 120-member Knesset. Israel thus had a well-developed – one might say over-developed – party system. As no single party ever won an absolute majority, all governments were perforce coalition governments. Mapai, representing labour Zionism, was the ruling party and Herut, a right-wing nationalistic party, was the main opposition. Mapai was led by the diminutive and pugnacious David Ben-Gurion whereas Herut was led by Menachem Begin, a Polish Jew, a disciple of Ze'ev Jabotinsky, and the former commander of the Irgun, the pre-independence National Military Organisation. The parliamentary scene was dominated to such an extent by the bitter personal and political rivalry between these two leaders that it sometimes resembled a Punch and Judy show.

My parents supported the General Zionists, a centrist party made up of merchants, industrialists, landlords and white-collar profession-als. My mother joined the General Zionists and worked for them as a volunteer in helping to organise events. Her commitment to the party, however, was only half-hearted. It had to do more with personal con-nections than with political ideology. She willingly lent her support to Dr Eliyahu, a rich Iraqi Jew who aspired to become a member of the Knesset. She could not even remember whether he was lobbying to be adopted as a parliamentary candidate by the General Zionists or by a separate Sephardi party list. All she remembered was that he held sev-eral meetings in the lead-up to the election campaign to promote his candidacy. My mother and her cousin Esperance, the daughter of Uncle Jacob, organised the refreshments. Dr Eliyahu was not successful; he was not adopted as a candidate. My mother recalls him saying, 'In politics there is a ladder to climb up. The Ashkenazim push one another up the ladder. We, Sephardim, push one another down.'

My initial leaning was not towards the left but towards Herut. I was young and struggling to make sense of the complicated political landscape around me. As far as I can remember, the initial impulse for my rightward drift came from our neighbour, Ezra Mansour, an Iraqi Jew from Basra who had been moved by Zionist convictions to immigrate to Palestine before the establishment of the State of Israel. He and his family lived at the other end of the landing on the fourth floor of our large building; our two front doors were about five metres apart. His wife Margot came from Aleppo, the second largest city in Syria after Damascus, and gave me private lessons in French at her kitchen table. She was not a trained teacher, but she helped me a great deal with my homework and thanks to her I performed much better in French than in English. Margot and my mother illustrated a little noticed paradox in the emerging Israeli society, namely, that Arab-Jewish women were often better educated and more Westernised than their Eastern European Ashkenazi sisters.

On the culinary front the difference between East and West was very striking. Syrian food is widely considered to be the best in the Middle East and Margot was an excellent cook. Wonderful aromas sometimes wafted through the kitchen when she was cooking, and I was always very grateful when she invited me to sample her dishes. Margot spoke Arabic with a Syrian dialect, very different to the Iraqi-Jewish dialect to which I was accustomed. She was a kind woman – even to the point of helping my mother tidy up our chronically messy house. After Yuma died, my mother did not keep up the labour-intensive and time-consuming custom of cooking *t'beet* every Friday. The name for this Sabbath dish comes from the Arabic *tabayit*, which means to stay overnight. We could do without the slow-cooking chicken with spicy rice, but we still all wanted the brown eggs for the traditional Saturday breakfast. Margot came to the rescue by allowing us to put our pencil-marked eggs alongside hers in the *t'beet* pot.

Ezra did not share his wife's benign qualities. He was a tough and gruff man with a definite authoritarian streak to his personality. Our apartment block had about thirty flats, four different staircases and one large, flat roof. Both we and the Mansours lived on the top floor of the four-storey building. My friends and I liked to play on the roof, and I particularly enjoyed doing stunts with my bike. We also played ball games and hide and seek. Ezra used to shout at us and chase us away, especially when we disturbed his afternoon siesta. He was not a well-educated man, having left school at fourteen. He was a picture framer, and rented a shop in Bialik Street, a few hundred metres from our apartment block. He was an ardent nationalist and a passionate supporter of Herut – Menachem Begin was his God. There was a leaflet of the local branch of Herut, and I was most impressed to see Ezra's name on a list alongside half a dozen other party activists.

Ezra kept at home a large collection of books, all written by members of what is sometimes called 'the national camp' in Israel. As far as I can remember, he had no other books. The books were mostly written by right-wing journalists, by leaders of Herut, many of them former members of the Irgun, or of the Stern Gang, the more extreme faction of the Revisionist Zionist movement whose real name was Lehi, the Hebrew acronym for the Fighters for the Freedom of Israel. The Stern Gang proudly described itself in its own literature as a terrorist organisation. Among its more famous victims were Lord Moyne, the British minister of state in the Middle East, who was assassinated in Cairo in 1944, and Count Folke Bernadotte, the UN mediator for Palestine, who was assassinated in Jerusalem in 1948. I used to borrow these books from Ezra and found them fascinating and completely absorbing. The connecting thread of this literature was the national struggle for independence. Some of the books were about the struggle against British colonialism, others were about the conflict with the local Arabs. By reading this literature, I gradually absorbed a Revisionist Zionist perspective on the Arab–Jewish conflict and the emergence of the State of Israel. Without realising it, I was moving slowly towards the right wing of the political spectrum.

Resentment against Mapai, the all-powerful ruling party, and its Ashkenazi leaders, played a large part in my political awakening. Mapai prided itself on being a socialist, progressive and egalitarian workers' party but that was not how it came across to me. Its attitude towards the Jews of the Arab lands struck me as particularly hypocritical. I have already mentioned Zalman Aran and his discriminatory educational policy. Infinitely more important was David Ben-Gurion, Mapai's leader and Israel's first prime minister. Widely regarded as the father of the nation, he set the tone in the first fifteen years of statehood. In a speech in the Knesset in October 1960, Ben-Gurion declared that the Jews in Muslim countries had 'lived in a society that was backward, corrupt, uneducated and lacking in independence and self-respect'. The older immigrants from these countries, he opined, would never change fundamentally, but the younger ones had to be imbued with the 'superior moral and intellectual qualities' of those who had created the State of Israel. 'If, heaven forbid, we do not succeed,' he warned, 'there is the danger that the coming generation may transform Israel into a Levantine state.'[2]

I was fifteen years old at the time and unlikely to have been aware of this speech. I quote it now because it captures the zeitgeist, the defining spirit and mood of that period. It cuts to the core of the Zionist conception of Israel as a European stronghold in the Middle East. This was how Herzl envisaged the Jewish state in his famous book with that title. It was also the basis on which Britain had issued the Balfour Declaration. It was the ethos of the Jewish state. And this was what we, young immigrants from Muslim countries, were up against. The passage of time did little to modify this conception of Israel as being fundamentally at odds with its environment. 'A villa in the jungle' was the insufferably arrogant description of Israel by Ehud Barak, the Labour Party leader and prime minister in 1999–2001.

On 15 August 1961, general elections were held for the fifth Knesset. Nearly all of Israel voted – with a turnout of 86.1%. Fourteen parties contested the election and eleven of them secured representation in the Knesset. Israeli elections are always raucous, no-holds-barred affairs. The 1961 campaign was prolonged, tumultuous and bitterly contested. Three elections had taken place since our arrival in Israel, but this was the first campaign which aroused my interest. My engagement in politics, however, was a solitary affair. I rarely discussed politics with my parents, my siblings or even my friends. Nor did I have any clear party preferences. I attended talks by speakers from different parties, listened, reflected on what I had heard and kept my inchoate thoughts to myself.

Mapai held no attraction for me: it was remote, alien, unsympathetic and, above all, smug and self-satisfied. It was renowned for its bigotry towards the Mizrahim and it was closely connected with the unsatisfactory status quo. The General Zionists were sensible, civil and rational but lacked any passion or exciting ideas. They catered primarily to middle-aged, middle-class and middle-of-the-road men and women; for a young person they had very little to offer. I also went to two meetings of a new party which tried to garner the support of Sephardi Jews, but I found the level of political discourse embarrassingly low. The speakers were unimpressive, and the audience largely consisted of bored-looking, elderly Iraqi Jews. For voting purposes, the party was identified by the letter Shin. A singer, accompanied by an oud player, kept intoning the signature tune of the party in a mixture of Arabic and Hebrew: '*hatha al-shin shelanu, u-hatha al-shin shelanu*' – 'this is our Shin, and this is our Shin'. The organisers evidently thought that even if the attendees got nothing else from the meeting, they would at least remember which letter to put in the ballot box. It came as no surprise when this party failed to gain a single seat in the Knesset.

The only politician who impressed me during the election campaign was Menachem Begin, the leader of Herut, the second biggest party, and the official head of the Opposition in the Knesset. Begin was a right-wing politician who advocated free-wheeling capitalism at home and a militant foreign policy in dealing with the Arabs. Neither his home policy nor his foreign policy had any particular appeal for me. What did appeal to me was the respect he apparently showed towards the large segment of Israeli society that had been shunned by the Labour establishment. Labour politicians from Ben-Gurion down typically treated the Oriental masses with disdain, seeing them as crude and primitive, 'little better than Arabs'. Begin grasped that the Orientals were sensitive and proud people and he exploited their hurt feelings to the full. He made no effort to appeal to their material interests, as politicians normally do. Instead, he related to them at the emotional level as proud, patriotic, equal fellow citizens. His success showed that people can be persuaded to sacrifice self-interest for satisfaction of a symbolic kind.

The secret of Begin's populist appeal lay more in his oratorical skills than in the substance of his policies. He was a spell-binding orator who knew how to stir a crowd. As a teenager I experienced at first-hand the tremendous emotional and psychological impact of his oratory. This was when he addressed an open-air rally in the central square in Ramat Gan in the course of the 1961 election. The square heaved with thousands of people. Begin stood on a balcony in front of a battery of microphones and delivered a powerful, passionate and fiery speech. Through his oratory he created a direct relationship with the crowd, who punctuated the speech with deafening rounds of applause. The crowd was thrilled, excited, elated. The rally reached its climax with the singing of 'Hatikva', the national anthem.

While enthralled by the speaker, I felt out of place in this crowd. Looking around me, I saw a lot of young, swarthy-looking Oriental Jews, many of them with heavy gold chains around their necks, cheering and applauding the leader. These youngsters were what Begin's political opponents called his *chakhchakhim*, a derogatory term for Mizrahi, and especially North African Jews, meaning lower-class louts or riffraff. I am ashamed to admit that I distanced myself from the *chakhchakhim*. I was shy, sensitive and introverted, but I did join the rest of the crowd in shouting '*Begin la-shilton! Begin la-shilton! Begin la-shilton!*' – 'Begin to power!' It was as if we thought that the rhythmic repetition of the slogan would help to make it a reality.

Another slogan that reverberated repeatedly through the square was '*Begin la-shilton, Ben-Gurion la-ziratron!*' – 'Begin to power, Ben-Gurion to the circus!' (On the advice of his personal physician, David Ben-Gurion used to stand on his head and there were many pictures in the press of him doing so.) In retrospect, my ambivalent attitude towards the young North African supporters of Begin stands out as a classic case of cognitive dissonance. I looked down on them, yet I was an Arab-Jew like them. Begin gave all of us a voice, and united all of us against the Ashkenazi-Mapai establishment, regardless of our country of origin in the Muslim world.

Menachem Begin became prime minister after Likud (formed by a merger of Herut and the General Zionists) won the election of 1977, bringing to an end three decades of uninterrupted Labour Party political hegemony. In my grown-up opinion, he was a disastrous prime minister who inflicted serious damage on the country he loved. He deserves some credit for the peace treaty with Egypt which won him the Nobel Peace Prize, but he was also responsible for the ill-starred and ill-fated invasion of Lebanon in 1982 and for the massive expansion of Jewish settlements on occupied Palestinian territory which undermined the prospect of a two-state solution to the Israeli-Palestinian conflict. So why was I attracted to this right-wing politician in my youth? The only honest answer is that at that time I was angry and alienated, I had no critical judgement and this made me easy prey for demagogues. Begin was a clever populist who skilfully played on my resentment of the Ashkenazi establishment. In the rally I attended he attacked mercilessly the Mapai-led government, its domestic policies, its nepotism and its complacency. He did not, as far as I can remember, engage in his usual Arab-bashing rhetoric on this occasion and had he done so, I suspect it would not have resonated with me.

My experience helps me to understand a pattern and a paradox in Israeli politics, namely, of Oriental Jews voting for Menachem Begin and his successors. The leadership of the Likud is predominantly Ashkenazi and its neoliberal policies never served the interests of the underprivileged sectors of society. Yet the Oriental communities, and particularly the Moroccans, continue to vote in large numbers for the Likud. Without their support the Likud would not be able to remain in power. So why do they vote for a party whose policies are at odds with their interests? The usual explanation is that Oriental Jews brought with them to Israel a deep hatred and mistrust of the Arabs and therefore naturally gravitated towards the overtly nationalistic, Arab-scorning parties of the right. However, this is not entirely convincing. It is not supported by my own experience nor that of my relatives. It seems to me that hatred of the Arabs was deliberately cultivated in Israel by unprincipled politicians in order to gain power and to prolong their hold on it. Menachem Begin was one of the first Israeli politicians to resort to this ugly tactic, but he was not the only one. Nor was the manipulation of anti-Arab feelings a monopoly of the Israeli Right.

My political awakening had no apparent effect, for better or worse, on my performance in school. In my second year in Gimnasia Dvir, I continued to lag behind the rest of the class. I was still not motivated to study, and I made just the minimal effort to get by. A comparison of my marks for the first and second terms reveals no progress in any subject and regression in History, Geography, Physics and Biology. My mark for these and nearly all other subjects was six out of ten or a bare Pass. My marks for Maths and English were four out of ten – an unambiguous Fail. These last two marks served a clear warning that, barring a major improvement, I would not be allowed to proceed to the next grade – I would have had to pass a special exam during the summer vacation in order to be able to go on. There was a good chance I could pass the Maths exam but only the slimmest chance of my passing the English exam.

It was in this discouraging context that my mother came up with the idea of sending me to study in England. Indifferent to my sisters' education, she was totally committed to giving me every opportunity to succeed. She was not prepared, as she told me later, to sit by and see me end up as a messenger boy, like so many Iraqis of my age. Given our strained financial circumstances, the idea of sending me to study in England seemed far-fetched in the extreme. But it was not entirely new. An argument used to overcome my mother's reluctance to marry my father was that she would be able to send her children to school in England. Now my father was unemployed and, while not opposed the idea, he felt they could not possibly afford it. But there was no deterring my mother. Once again, as so often since our arrival in Israel, she turned to her mother for financial help.

Nana owned a substantial villa in the affluent district of Karrada in Baghdad and, because she was a British subject, her property had not been confiscated by the government after she left Iraq in 1950. Her eldest son Isaac had received British nationality on joining the British Army in the Second World War and settled down in England at the end of the war. Some years after we left for Israel, Isaac had managed, with the help of two lawyers, one in London and one in Baghdad, to sell the house for

10,000 dinars. Nana had had to make a special trip to London to sign the documents, travelling on her British passport. Isaac had sent her a return air ticket to London which, as he informed my mother in an undated letter, cost £124. We do not know whether a new bank account was opened to deposit the money. But as Nana knew no English and was returning to Israel anyway, it is more likely that the money was deposited in Isaac's name. As far as Nana was concerned, she still had this money and she was willing to use it to pay for my schooling. It later transpired that Isaac had spent the money – his brother Salih, who lived in New York, fell out with him when Isaac refused to give him his share of the sale of the family home. My mother did not get involved in this dispute. She did, however, write to Isaac to say she wanted to send me to school in London and that Nana was willing to foot the bill. By this time Isaac was living in Newcastle-Upon-Tyne. Having married an English-Jewish woman called Doris Friedman, he had liquidated his failing business in London and relocated to her hometown in the north.

At first Isaac agreed to the plan. On 28 June 1961, he wrote to my mother that he had received a letter from Uncle Jacob urging him to give me a chance to continue my studies in England. Isaac agreed and told my mother to proceed with the arrangements to send me to London. He said he would meet me in London and take me to Newcastle. He then added, 'In case you can send Abi on the Orange Cargo boat to Newcastle-Upon-Tyne, it will be much better, as there are such boats from Israel.' A month later, however, under pressure from Doris, Isaac changed his mind.

The idea of going to study in England instantly captured my imagination and I became fixated. It seemed like the perfect solution to all my problems, a kind of *deus ex machina*. I did not have anything going for me in Israel and I realised it. I was bored at school, my life at home was dull and I did not have any sense of attachment to the country. Hanging over me was the fear of failing the exams, being chucked out of school and having to go into the job market without any qualifications. Against this backdrop, the prospect of going abroad and starting a new life seemed desperately appealing. So as soon as this prospect emerged, I began to work really hard to improve my English. But the way I went about it was not especially intelligent. Every time I came across an English word I did not know, I wrote it down in a small exercise book with the Hebrew translation alongside it. This expanded my vocabulary, but it did not enhance my knowledge of grammar and it did not help me to construct sentences. There were also some practical steps to be taken to plan the trip, like getting a passport and applying for a British visa. Mentally and practically, I was prepared for the trip when an unwelcome piece of news arrived from Newcastle.

One day the postman knocked on our door to deliver a telegram. My mother was not at home, only my sister Dalia, my father and me. My father could not speak English. I read the telegram aloud. It said 'Cancel Abi's trip.' Dalia and I had no idea what 'cancel' meant. My father, however, did know this word. He said with an air of authority, 'cancel means *battel*' the Arabic word for cancel. So, between us we managed to decipher the telegram. For my father the news probably came as a relief, though he did not show it. For me the news came as a crushing blow and I burst into tears. When my mother came home, we showed her the telegram. She told me not to worry and assured me of her determination to go ahead with the plan. She even started talking about selling our flat to finance my study abroad. To do so would have been utterly unfair on my father and on my sisters, but she was determined to send me to England, come what may. In my friend Sami Michael's book *The Israeli Experience*, there is a chapter about me as an example of an Oriental boy who did well, despite the odds being stacked against him in Israel. The title of the chapter is 'My mother was determined to make me a success'.[3]

Miriam Yakim, the daughter of mayor Avraham Krinitzi of Ramat Gan, played a modest part in enabling my mother to realise her plan. In her privately printed autobiography *Story of My Life* there is a short section about me with a photograph of the two of us. Mrs Yakim was the head of the department of child welfare in the town hall, where my mother worked as a telephonist. My mother sometimes went up to her office for a chat during the coffee break. My mother told her that she had a brother in England and that he had promised to help her, but his wife had vetoed the plan. In despair, my mother turned to her friend for help. At that time Mrs Yakim was hosting a group of Jewish schoolchildren from London led by a rabbi. She asked him for advice, and he gave her the name and address of the director of Hillel House, a hostel for Jewish students in London. On her ninetieth birthday I gave Mrs Yakim a book of mine with a dedication, thanking her for her encouragement and support. With a touch of melodrama, she describes in her autobiography the 'stunning story' of my rise from zero to lecturer at a prestigious British university. This story, she writes, reinforced her conviction that every child has the potential to succeed if given the opportunity.

It later transpired that Hillel House was indeed a hostel for Jewish students in London, just not for boys of my age. All that Hillel House could offer was temporary accommodation for a week or two, but this was enough to embolden my mother to resume preparations for my trip abroad. She wrote to the director to inform him that I was on my way, taking it for granted that I would be able to stay there when I arrived in London. Similarly, she wrote to my uncle in Newcastle – but only to present him with a fait accompli. Rather than protest, he commended my mother for seizing the initiative and placing the responsibility on him. Using an Arabic expression, he said he understood she was saying: 'It's on you now. You deal with it!' The next step was to buy a ticket from the ZIM shipping company for a boat ride from Haifa to Marseilles. I packed one suitcase and was given $100 in cash – the maximum foreign currency allowance for Israelis travelling abroad. On 7 September 1961, my whole family accompanied me to Haifa for an emotional goodbye and send-off. I left the Promised Land without as much as a backward glance.

Avi with his uncle, Isaac Obadiah, in Newcastle

ELEVEN

LONDON

As the ZIM cruise-liner sailed away from the port of Haifa, I experienced, for the first time in my life, a profound feeling of liberation. I was on my own now, free from the constraints of school and the pressures of an Ashkenazi-dominated society. I also felt liberated from the psychological complexities of family – not unnatural in an adolescent. I was giddy with excitement. How the journey would evolve was far from clear, but for the time being my newly gained freedom exhilarated me.

The journey from Haifa to Marseilles took six days, with stops of half a day each in Naples and Genoa. Life on the boat was for me the height of luxury with three meals a day, a coffee break in the morning and a tea break in the afternoon, excellent food in unlimited quantities and various forms of entertainment: films, singers, comedians, cafés, bars and armchairs on the deck for sun-bathing. I made a friend on the first day, a charming Ecuadorian student called Pépé, and he and I became companions for the rest of the journey. During the stops in Naples and Genoa, we amused ourselves with childish pranks like trying out on people in the street the only Italian phrase we knew, 'Dove la posta?' – 'Where is the post office?' – and then pretending to understand the answers.

The most memorable part of the trip was the long train journey from Marseilles to Paris. Next to me in the eight-person compartment sat a

most attractive, elegantly dressed and impeccably made-up woman. She
was probably in her mid-forties; she had short blond hair, blue eyes, a
smiley face and gracious manners. Her demeanour, to my untutored
eyes, was that of an affluent, upper-class woman. We spoke in French
and, to my surprise and gratification, my grasp on the language was just
about good enough to hold a conversation. The stranger bombarded me
with questions about myself, my family, my background and my plans.
She may have found my story interesting against the background of
post-war populations movements: a Jewish boy from an Arab country
who moved with his family to Israel and was now going to England
on his own. Or she may have been just a kind Frenchwoman who was
trying to befriend a foreign adolescent who was travelling through her
country. Either way, she seemed to take a shine to me. In one respect her
behaviour was slightly odd: she kept alternating between addressing me
formally as '*monsieur*' and more affectionately as '*mon petit*'. My attitude
towards her was also a bit confused: I was in awe of her because she
was so strikingly European and glamorous, but I was also very flattered
that she seemed to be genuinely interested in me. She asked me where
I planned to stay when we got to Paris. I said that I was hoping to stay
with a distant Israeli relative of mine who was a doctoral student at the
Sorbonne. She said that I would be welcome to stay with her in her
big house. In those days it was not unusual to offer travellers a place
to stay. Looking back, I wish I had taken her up on her offer. At that
time, however, I was far too shy. I was not yet sixteen and a complete
innocent abroad.

In Paris I made my way by metro to the students' residence in the Cité
Universitaire, where I had a warm welcome from Itzhak Azouri once
he got over his surprise at my turning up on his doorstep without any
prior notice. Itzhak had no father; his uncle was my father's accountant
in Baghdad. In Ramat Gan, Itzhak had given private maths lessons to
Dalia and me before going on to continue his higher degree studies in
economics in Paris. The subject of his PhD thesis was, if I remember
rightly, foreign investments in Israel. For the next week I slept on Itzhak's

floor, ate in the students' cafeteria and had a wonderful time. During the day I did intensive sightseeing, sometimes accompanied by Itzhak but mostly on my own. Among the places I visited were all the usual tourist sights: the Eiffel Tower, the Arc de Triomphe, the Champs-Élysées, the Pantheon, the Louvre and the Palace of Versailles. In the evenings Itzhak and his fiancée Perla, an Israeli from an upper-class Moroccan family, showed me Paris nightlife. The highlights were strolling in the historic artists' quarter of Montmartre and a spectacular floor show in the Casino de Paris. The letters I wrote home conveyed my excitement at being able to roam so freely around the big city. While I wanted to share all this with my mother, I also knew how painful it would be for her to be stuck in dreary Ramat Gan. Another letter was sent from Itzhak to my parents, essentially a report on my good behaviour and a reassurance that they had nothing to worry about. The section to my mother was in English and the one to my father was in Hebrew; whether Itzhak knew Arabic or not, I cannot remember. With Perla's mother, who lived in Paris, I could communicate only in French. Fortunately, my French was slightly more fluent now as a result of the intriguing, seven-hour long chat on the train journey from Marseilles to Paris.

The train from Paris took me to Victoria Station in London, from where I made my way to Hillel House, the hostel for Jewish students in Endsleigh Street, near Euston Square. There was only one person in Hillel House, an elderly secretary who was not Jewish. She informed me that it was Yom Kippur, the holiest day in the Jewish calendar, and all the men had gone to the synagogue. In Israel I used to fast on Yom Kippur and go to synagogue with my father but abroad I had lost track of the *hagim*, the holy days. To compound my delinquency in travelling on this holy day, I had brought with me from France a ham sandwich, strictly forbidden at any time by Jewish dietary laws, let alone on a day of fasting. Needless to say, I kept quiet about the sandwich. The secretary led me to a small dormitory with ten beds, one of which I was reassured to see had my name on it. After the secretary left, I surreptitiously ate the sandwich – opting to commit a new sin rather than atone for those of

last year. For better or for worse, Judaism was to play a far more prominent part in my life over the next three years than it ever had either in
Baghdad or in Ramat Gan.

Mr Henry Shaw, the director of Hillel House, had written to my
mother to say that Hillel House was not a hostel where a young person
could stay for any length of time. They had two small dormitories
where university students could pass a few nights while journeying
through London; I could stay there for just a few days until I found
better accommodation. As far as schools were concerned, Mr Shaw said
he was going to get in touch with Hasmonean Grammar School and
report the outcome. The problem was that all schools were closed for
the summer vacation, making it difficult to contact them. In a second
letter, written a week before my arrival, Mr Shaw was openly critical of
my mother. 'I must say that you are putting me in a difficult position',
he wrote. 'I do not know whether the school will accept your son as I
have no idea of his educational grades. What you have done is to send
your son to this country without making sure of any kind of preparation
for his acceptance into any school whatsoever.' In retrospect, both sides
had a point. Mr Shaw had good reason to complain but my mother had
no way of finding a suitable school for me in London; she relied on her
brother Isaac to take care of me after my arrival. And at that point he
was nowhere to be seen.

The day after Yom Kippur, Mr Shaw was back in the office and we
had our first meeting. There was no mention of my being under-age for
his establishment nor of my being foisted on him. On the contrary, he
was friendly and welcoming. Evidently, he did not hold me responsible
for my mother's supposed misdemeanours. He also informed me that
he had arranged an interview for me with his friend, Dr Conway, the
headmaster of the Jewish Free School, for that afternoon and that his
secretary would take me there. To my mother he wrote: 'Your son Abi
arrived here in the evening of Yom Kippur, and although I was annoyed
that you sent him to London before arrangements were made, I must tell
you that he seems a most delightful young man, and later today he will

have an interview with the Principal of the Jewish Free School. Doubtless he will tell you all about it in his next letter.' Hasmonean Grammar School was a school with high educational standards for bright Jewish children who had passed the 'Eleven Plus' examination. The JFS was a mixed comprehensive school for Jewish children, two-thirds of whom had failed the Eleven Plus. But the hierarchies and complexities of the British educational system eluded me at the time. I was grateful to be introduced to a headmaster so soon after my arrival in London and, as Mr Shaw had predicted, I wrote about the meeting in my next letter home.

The headmaster of the school was Dr Edward Conway. I was slightly nervous in his presence, but he did his best to put me at ease. He asked me numerous questions about my background, my interests, my educational attainments in Israel and the purpose of my trip to the United Kingdom. I had no papers and no school certificates from Israel, but he seemed willing to take me on trust and to want to facilitate my admission. At first, he said he needed to obtain the permission of the relevant authorities but, on second thoughts, he told me I could start the following day. I was to go into the GCE (General Certificate of Education) class of the Fifth Form which was due to take Ordinary Level (O-Level) exams at the end of the academic year. If I passed these exams, I would go into the Sixth Form with a view to taking the Advanced Level (A-Level) exams after two further years of study. Dr Conway asked where I proposed to live and how I would finance my stay in London. I said that for the time being I was happy to stay in Hillel House but added, somewhat optimistically, that I had an uncle in Newcastle-Upon-Tyne who was going to come down to London to help me make more permanent arrangements. Not having had any direct contact with my uncle made me anxious. But on the strength of his having sent me a Raleigh bicycle, I had faith that he'd show up eventually.

A week later my uncle, now fifty-one years old, did indeed turn up. In England some people called him Ivor, but for me he was always Uncle Isaac. He was very smartly dressed: a dark blue three-piece suit, a white shirt with a stiff starched collar, a tie, well-polished black shoes, a bowler

hat and a black umbrella. Never having met anyone who dressed like this
before, it was somewhat hard to think of him as a relative. He opened
the conversation by saying that he was very pleased at my arrival, that
I was his only relative in England, that he would take care of me like a
son and that I did not have to worry about money. We then went out
to buy school uniform, clothes, pyjamas, underwear and an item with
which I was totally unfamiliar, but he insisted was essential in England
– a dressing gown. We also went to Burton, the country's first high street
tailor, and ordered a dark blue, made-to-measure three-piece suit – my
first ever suit and my last tailor-made one.

Although Uncle Isaac told me not to worry about money, I could not
help it. Of the $100 with which I had set off from Israel, I had only $10
left and I was bashful about asking for money to meet my immediate
needs. For the next three years I had worries about money that I could not
discuss frankly with my uncle. There is an Arabic saying that something
that starts crooked, remains crooked. It was not clear who was responsible
for funding my stay in London. Clearly, my parents lacked the means to
support me abroad. No doubt under some pressure from my mother,
her mother had agreed to pay for my education. Nana had received
10,000 dinars for her house in Baghdad and left Isaac in charge of the
money in London. She now instructed him to meet all my needs from
her account. It gradually transpired, however, that Isaac had drawn out
all the money from this account. Angry words were exchanged between
Nana and her eldest son in letters written in Judeo-Arabic, that is Arabic
written in Hebrew characters – the only script that Nana could write.

Uncle Isaac never made any mention to me of Nana's money. The
impression he created was that every penny he gave me came out of
his own pocket. Although I knew the truth, I could not confront him
with it; to do so I thought would have only antagonised him without
serving any useful purpose. To make matters worse, Uncle Isaac turned
out to be extremely stingy; he soon began to begrudge the money he
had to spend on me. In the evening of his first day in London he took
me to a restaurant on the Finchley Road for dinner. We sat down at a

table facing one another and before the waiter had a chance to come to us with the menu, my uncle suggested we moved to another table. On the table in front of him stood an empty cup of coffee, and by it a small sixpenny coin, a tip left for the waiter by the last occupant. As we got up to move, I noticed that my uncle furtively picked up the coin and put it in his pocket. This incident indelibly tarnished my view of my uncle's character. At the time it was all the more shocking to me that a man dressed like an English gentleman would behave in such a shabby and shoddy manner. I had obviously internalised some ideas about the British national character before arriving in Britain.

The next day Uncle Isaac came to school to meet with the headmaster. Dr Conway described the school in general terms and then outlined his plans for my education. Towards the end of the conversation the question of permanent accommodation for me came up. My uncle asked whether the headmaster knew of a nice Jewish family with whom his nephew might live as a paying guest. Dr Conway replied that his wife had *rahmanus*, Yiddish for mercy, and that it might be possible for me to lodge with them. My uncle immediately warmed to this idea and in the evening he and I went together to visit Dr and Mrs Conway at their home in Golders Green. The unstated purpose of the meeting was for the Conways to look me over and assess my suitability as a house guest. The meeting seemed to go smoothly, and the following day Dr Conway informed me that he and his wife would be happy for me to live with them while I pursued my studies at his school.

On the appointed day, in mid-October 1961, I moved from Hillel House to the Conways' home at 193 Golders Green Road, a road that, when I drive down it now, still reminds me of being young and alone in a bleak foreign country. The Conways lived in a semi-detached Edwardian house with four bedrooms, two living rooms, a kitchen and a dining room. I was greeted warmly by Dr and Mrs Conway and their two sons, Charles and David. From the moment of my arrival, they treated me as a member of the family, even though there were many subtle indications of my different status. I did not know what they thought of me but outwardly they were all kind, friendly and welcoming. Dr Conway was the son of immigrants from Eastern Europe. He had been born in 1911 in the Welsh town of Llanelli, which had a small Jewish community of about forty families, and educated at the local grammar school and University College, Swansea. After university he changed his name from Efraim Zalman Ha-Cohen to Edward Sidney Conway and began his teaching career in Liverpool, eventually becoming headmaster of the Liverpool Jewish School. From 1951 to 1958 he served as the Principal of the Norwood Jewish Orphanage. His experience there served as the basis for a PhD thesis he wrote on the institutional care of children at the London School of Economics under the supervision of the eminent sociologist, Professor Richard Titmuss. In 1958 Dr Conway was appointed headmaster of the JFS. His two main aims were to provide high-quality general education and to make the JFS a bastion of Jewish ideals.[1]

Dr Conway was a man of rich experience and deep humanity. He was held in great esteem by the Jewish community in Britain as an educator and promoter of Jewish values. I imagine that his own background as the son of immigrants and his interest in institutional care predisposed him to want to help me. He acted as a benign if distant guardian for the next three years. At school he monitored my progress closely but tactfully, to avoid giving the impression that I was getting preferential treatment. At home I saw very little of him but, when I did, he was unfailingly kind and considerate and helped me to improve my English. One duty he fulfilled conscientiously was to write to my mother on a regular basis, to reassure her that I was well taken care of by Mrs Conway, that their sons treated me like a brother, that I was doing well at school and that all the teachers shared his high opinion of me. Ironically, given my past record, the only note of concern in his letters was that I was working too hard.

One quality of mine that apparently impressed Dr Conway was my perseverance. On reading in the *Jewish Chronicle* of my appointment as a Reader in International Relations at St Antony's College, Oxford, he wrote to congratulate me. In his letter of 22 October 1987, he wrote: 'I do not think I can recall any of the thousands of pupils I had in my charge since I started my career fifty years ago who had your degree of perseverance and determination to succeed.' In my reply I noted that I had never worked as hard as I did in the three years I spent at his school, and that everything afterwards seemed easy by comparison.

Mrs Conway's first name was Lily, but I always called her Mrs Conway. She had not had the benefit of a good education, but was well-versed in the customs, rituals and dietary laws of Judaism and ran a strictly kosher household. She did not have a profession and she did not go out to work, devoting herself whole-heartedly to looking after her children and supporting her high-profile husband. Towards me she was kind and considerate and helpful with mundane tasks like ironing. Having experienced overt discrimination in my own favour at home, it was a surprisingly welcome experience to find myself treated equally with the two other boys in my new home.

Charles was a year older than me and David a year younger. They were both highly intelligent, with impressive academic attainments. One would have expected bright Jewish boys who had passed the Eleven Plus to go to Hasmonean Grammar School; instead Charles and David went to St Olave's Grammar School, a Church of England school with an outstanding academic reputation. The school was south of the river, a long way away from Golders Green, so the boys had a long journey each day. They also had to take sandwiches with them because their school lunches were not kosher. This, however, was a minor inconvenience compared with the advantage of being in one of the top performing state schools in the country. Charles was in the Sixth Form, studying for his A-Levels; David, though only fourteen, was already in the Fifth Form, studying for his O-Levels. Their striking academic success made me worry about falling short – and so spurred me on.

On the first floor of the house were four bedrooms: one for the parents, one for each son, and one that I moved into. It was the first time I ever had a room of my own and this represented a dramatic change, a real experience of privacy compared to sharing a room with my two sisters and Yuma. My room was small and not particularly comfortable,

but it had all the basics: a sink for washing, a single bed, a wardrobe, a
chest of drawers, a bookcase, a small table and an upright chair. I did
not have high expectations. The small, square card table which served
as my desk was in the corner of the room by a window facing the back
garden. My memory of the back garden is hazy as I hardly ever set foot
in there. Nor did I have the leisure of gazing at the back garden from
my window. In marked contrast to my time at school in Israel, I was no
longer a daydreamer. I was very switched on. I spent most of my waking
hours at home sitting at this desk and doing my homework. Cold, austere
and bleak though it was, this room was conducive to study because it
gave me privacy, autonomy and peace of mind. My time was my own. No
one ever disturbed me nor was I ever asked to help with any domestic
chores. Living in an Anglophone home let me make leaps and bounds
in my English – a language I was never any good at before.

The general atmosphere in the house not only permitted but positively
encouraged, indeed compelled, all of us to concentrate on our studies.
Although we went to different schools, the daily routine at home was
similar for all three of us. We would have breakfast early in the morning, go to school, return home around 5.30 p.m., have a substantial
dinner served to us by Mrs Conway, go to our rooms and get on with
our studies. At some point in the evening each of us would go down to
the kitchen to make himself a hot drink and a snack, and then go back
to our rooms to resume work. Dr Conway did not have dinner with us.
He used to come back from work much later and Mrs Conway served
him his dinner separately. On Friday evenings we had a festive dinner
en famille. Mrs Conway would light the candles and Dr Conway would
make *kiddush* with *hala* bread and sweet wine. After dinner we were
allowed to join the grown-ups in the comfortable living room to watch
TV. This was a treat. On no other weekday were the boys or I allowed
to watch TV or even enter this sanctified domain.

On Saturday mornings we would put on our best suits (in my case
my only suit) and go with Dr Conway to the orthodox synagogue in
Golders Green for the Sabbath service. Participating in this religious

ritual was tedious and tiresome – at no point did I experience a sense of spiritual elation. After a couple of years my patience was exhausted and I asked Dr Conway if I could be excused, and he readily agreed. He said he understood that I had only been going to *shul* out of respect for himself and his boys. So I started spending my Saturday mornings at the public library on Golders Green Road instead.

Saturday night was the only night we were allowed to go out. The word 'allowed' implies rules and restrictions. In my case at least they were implicit rather than explicit; no one exactly gave orders nor were there any stated rules. But I picked up many oblique messages on what constituted good behaviour and my natural instinct was to conform. Most of the time I felt lonely and unhappy. From a warm, sun-swept country I had moved to the leaden skies of Britain with its notorious rain and cold winds. In Israel I spent most afternoons and evenings playing outdoors with my friends. In Golders Green there was no outdoor life of any kind. Our home in Israel was chaotic but relaxed; the Conways' home was super-tidy and rule bound. It was essentially a study factory. My mother was warm and loving; Mrs Conway was not much more than a caring landlady. The spontaneous physical manifestations of affection, which had been part of everyday life at home, were largely absent in the Conway household, even between the family members.

From my mother I received a stream of unsolicited advice on how to behave in my new home. She was delighted at this happy turn of events and deeply grateful to the Conways for taking me in. It was an honour and a privilege, she wrote to me, to be living with such a respectable and well-educated family. Her advice to me was to follow Dr Conway's example in all matters relating to Jewish custom, such as putting on *tefillin*. At mealtimes I was to display my best table manners and eat only what Mrs Conway served me. At all times I was urged to be polite, neat and tidy, and to offer to help in any way that might be useful to my hosts. My mother rounded off by saying that since I behaved like a prince anyway, the pieces of advice she gave me were redundant. Indeed, they were. Living with the headmaster was stressful enough without the additional dose of parental injunctions.

At the new school I had a warm reception. The JFS was a co-educational, orthodox, Jewish secondary school, situated in Camden Town. The ethos of the school was more consciously Jewish than the schools I had attended in Israel. All the pupils and the more than half the teachers were Jewish and Jewish values permeated the school. Its aim, in the words of its mission statement, was 'to produce well-educated, faithful and proud Jews who will be responsible and contributing members of society'. The school actively promoted Zionist ideology and maintained close links with Israel. Every summer a large group was taken to visit Israel. Hebrew was taught not only as a modern foreign language, but as an instrument linking Jewish history and heritage to the State of Israel. Every morning the entire school would assemble in the hall for a brief talk by the headmaster followed by Hebrew prayers.

I found the transition from the Israeli to the British educational system extremely challenging, but my path was smoothed by the sympathy and support I received in the early stages. As a new boy from Israel I attracted a great deal of interest and curiosity. Many of the pupils had been on a school visit to Israel and those who had not been bombarded me with questions about it. Considerable glamour and kudos, as I discovered, were attached to being an Israeli. But I failed to exploit this opportunity because I had hardly developed any kind of identity as an Israeli citizen. Indeed, I felt like a diluted Israeli rather than a fully-fledged one. No one at school showed the remotest interest in Iraq, my country of origin. This was a critical moment at which my various identities collided. My identity as an Arab-Jew clashed with my identity as an Israeli and left me in a something of a quandary. Back home I never felt like a real Israeli because I was an Israeli of the wrong kind, an inferior kind. Now, in the eyes of British Jewish kids, I was the authentic representative of the new kind of Jew bred in Israel. I imagined that the narrative they wanted to hear from me was that I had grown up on a kibbutz, that we had made the desert bloom, that we were constantly harassed by bad

Arabs, but that we knew how to defend ourselves and that we were all ready to stand up and fight. I could have played up to this stereotype, but I couldn't bring myself to do so – not because I had developed any sort of critique of Israel but because I instinctively could not engage with this narrative. Paradoxically, I was both the centre of attention at school and quite isolated. I yearned to talk to someone who could understand my heritage, instead of imposing their fantasies about Israel on me.

My main focus, however, was on my studies, not on Israel, and here I received generous support from several of my classmates. The teachers too gave me more than my fair share of attention, advice, help and encouragement. The fact that I was living with the headmaster was not lost on anyone – classmates sometimes suggested to me that the teachers who went out of their way to help me did so in order to curry favour with the headmaster. But this explanation struck me as overly cynical and only one side of the story. What my classmates did not appreciate was that there were disadvantages as well as advantages to living with the headmaster. At home I did not enjoy the freedom to misbehave, or even to behave like a normal teenager; I was always so anxious to do the right thing and to please my hosts. At school I felt similarly constrained. When other boys were getting up to some mischief, I refrained from participating because I didn't want to get into trouble. If I misbehaved, I would be reported to the headmaster and that would have been awkward for both of us. In those days there was corporal punishment in the school; the headmaster administered it by caning the miscreants. If he had to cane me, it would have been acutely embarrassing. I therefore had to ensure that the situation did not arise by sticking to the straight and narrow. I had to worry both about myself and the headmaster. It was a heavy psychological burden and one that was unique to me in the entire school. These were feelings that I could not have articulated at the time; they only became clear to me in the process of writing this book.

Once the decision had been made to put me in the Fifth Form, I had to quickly choose the subjects to study. My English at that stage was still

very poor. In June of the following year, nine months after my arrival
in Britain, I was due to take my O-Levels, like the rest of the class. The
pressure was thus on from day one. The five subjects I eventually settled
on were English, French, History, Maths and Religious Instruction.
The rest of the class had had five years of French previously whereas I
had only two so I had to make a special effort to catch up. The history
syllabus was nineteenth-century British social and economic history,
about which I simply did not have a clue. Mr Carr, the history teacher,
was not much help. He wore a black suit and a gown, and he had the
lugubrious look of an undertaker. At the beginning of the year, he gave
each of us a textbook, *Economic History of England* by Milton Briggs and
Percy Jordan. At the beginning of each history period, Mr Carr would
announce what pages we should read in the textbook and tell us to get
on with it. He would then pace up and down the aisles, making sure we
were all concentrating on the textbook in front of us. If anyone dared
break the silence by asking Mr Carr a question, his habitual response
was: 'It's all in the Briggs and Jordan.' Many of the objects mentioned in
the book, like the mysterious spinning jenny, were completely incomprehensible to me. Was she some kind of dancer or acrobat? And what
did she have to do with the Industrial Revolution? Messrs Briggs, Jordan
and Carr were equally unenlightening.

However, the biggest challenge facing me was English language and
English grammar. Here was the greatest gap between me and the rest
of the class. By dint of dedication and sheer hard work, I managed to
narrow the gap by the end of the year. I would not have been able to
do so without the constant encouragement I received from Mr Denis
Felsenstein, who taught English at O-Level, History at A-Level and was
also the deputy head. Mr Felsenstein was a young man, probably in
his mid or late thirties. Tall, lean and handsome, he had an impressive
physical presence and an air of natural authority. Before taking up his
post at the JFS, he had been a History master at St Paul's School, one of
the best private schools in the country. He was an outstanding teacher
by any standard and certainly the best teacher that I ever encountered.

Mr Felsenstein gave me advice and unstinting support throughout my time at the JFS. In addition to teaching me English and History, he took a close interest in my general wellbeing and academic development. He also gave me much-needed encouragement and helped me realise my potential. He was more than a teacher: he was a mentor and a role model, one of those people who can transform the life of a child. Sometimes I wonder why Mr Felsenstein went so far beyond the call of duty to help me make a success of my studies. One possible answer is that I was an Israeli boy who had come to London without his family and needed additional pastoral guidance. Another is that he knew that Dr Conway had taken a chance on me and he decided to invest in me as a joint project. Perhaps he saw how hard I was working, and how determined I was to make progress, and his natural instinct as an educator was to help me. Whatever his reasons, I owed him a huge debt of gratitude.

In addition to the five subjects I took for O-Level, I started studying Classical Hebrew at A-Level. This may sound like an odd choice for an Israeli boy who had come to study in England and indeed it was. The idea came from Reverend Joseph Halpern, our Religious Instruction teacher. Reverend Halpern, as we always had to call him, was a short man with a grey beard, a large black skull cap, a gammy leg and a nervous stammer. Behind his back, the boys used to do cruel imitations of his limp and his stammer. But no one doubted his sincerity, his devotion to teaching or his erudition. He had graduated from University College London with first-class Honours in Hebrew and Semitics and an MA with distinction in Rabbinics, and he was the author of several books on ancient Jewish history. His life-long mission was to educate and encourage people to read the Bible. At Reverend Halpern's suggestion, I began to study with him towards A-Level Classical Hebrew in a small institute in Willesden Green of which he was the director. The two-hour classes were held on Sunday mornings and there was only one other Jewish boy, from Hasmonean Grammar School, in the class. The syllabus included Jewish History, Hebrew syntax and translations from the Biblical Hebrew into English. Being a Hebrew-speaker was an enormous advantage, but I still had to work hard to reach the required level. Going to synagogue on Saturday and Classical Hebrew classes on Sunday left me even less leisure time at weekends. Altogether my life was not exactly a bundle of fun.

Just as I was adjusting to my new home, new school and new lifestyle, my family in Israel went through a difficult phase, with repercussions for me as well. One of the reasons, I subsequently discovered, for my mother's determination to send me to school in London was the expectation that I would be the vanguard of the family, enabling her to follow with one or both of my sisters. This was hardly mentioned in the lead-up to my departure, but the thought was apparently fixed in my mother's mind. My older sister Dalia was seventeen years old and she was due to enrol for national service in the IDF when she reached eighteen. Our mother was strongly against Dalia going into the army because it interfered with her own plans. She therefore put pressure on Dalia to declare that she was a practising Jew in order to get exemption from military service. Reluctantly, Dalia did so but her interview with the IDF rabbi did not go well. He asked her several questions about Jewish custom and rituals that she was, unsurprisingly, unable to answer. He then asked her whether she had ever travelled on the Sabbath. Still at a loss, she turned the question back on him and asked, 'Have you ever travelled on the Sabbath?' The rabbi said, 'Yes, to Auschwitz.' The interview ended on that chilly note. The upshot was that Dalia was denied exemption and was duly conscripted into the IDF.

This was a blow to our mother. She unfairly blamed Dalia for not giving the right answers and threatened to leave her behind and go to live in London with my younger sister Vilma, who was thirteen years old at the time. This move would have split the family further, with my father and Dalia staying behind in Israel. The prospect of half of my dysfunctional family coming to live with me in London also filled me with horror. I therefore wrote a five-page letter to my mother, trying to dissuade her. The letter reeked of hypocrisy. I began by telling her how much I loved her, how much I missed her, claiming that I had only her best interests at heart. To pre-empt the argument that she was coming to help me, I stressed that I had already landed on my feet both at home and at school. I then listed all the arguments I could think of against her plan: the cost of housing, the cost of living, the atrocious weather, the obstacles to getting employment and the difficulty of making friends. I also pointed out that the proposed move would have the effect of splitting the family in two. Although these were genuine worries, I was also determined to protect my new life, no matter how austere this life was.

To Dalia I wrote a separate letter, telling her not to be too downcast by her failure to get exemption from national service. The army's decision, I wrote, was a blessing in disguise. I acknowledged her keen desire to come to England but suggested that this was based on ignorance of the real conditions here. It would be fun to travel, but would she really want to spend the rest of her life in a foreign country, with a language barrier, alien people and a very different climate? We live only once, it is important to lead a happy life and she could only find her happiness in Israel, I wrote. By serving in the IDF, she would fulfil her duty to the motherland, like most other Israeli girls of her age. In the IDF she would meet new people, gain experience and maybe acquire a new profession. The IDF, I opined, was the best school in the world for learning about life. Rereading this letter sixty years later, I was astonished to see how much I came across as a fervent propagandist.

As it happened, neither our mother nor Dalia had any realistic chance of coming to live in London even if the IDF had not intervened. I could have therefore spared myself the trouble of writing these transparently self-serving letters. They reveal me as I was: a sixteen-year-old boy who undoubtedly missed home but at the same time dreaded the prospect of half his family turning up in London with a suitcase full of psychological problems and spoiling his dream of making a fresh start in the new Promised Land. Again, looking back, I am struck by the strength and vehemence of my reaction.

Although I did not want any members of my family to come to England, I was acutely aware of my moral debt to them. One of the reasons I worked so hard, and indeed overworked, was to prove that the sacrifice they had made in sending me to England was not in vain. I had to succeed at any cost, not just for my own sake but also to justify the faith they, and particularly my mother, had placed in me. Heading them off so emphatically compounded the sense of guilt I felt towards my family. With the approach of the national exams in the summer term, I redoubled my efforts, burning the midnight oil. After supper I went up to my room, sat down at my desk and worked without a break until I could no longer keep my eyes open. Despite all my assiduous and unrelenting efforts, however, I did not do well in these exams; there was a limit to what I could achieve in only nine months. I took five subjects at O-Level – English, French, History, Maths and Religious Instruction – and Classical Hebrew at A-Level. I passed History, Religious Instruction and Classical Hebrew and failed English, French and Maths.

Failing French came as a bit of a shock because the oral exam had seemed to go so well. I read a passage in French to the woman examiner and from my accent she guessed I was Israeli. Her first question was whether I had ever been to a kibbutz. I replied that I had been to several kibbutzim on work parties from school to help them during the fruit-picking season and that it had been a wonderful experience. She then asked me about particular individuals, and I said I knew most of them by reputation. This gave me the opportunity to ask her how she knew them, and she replied that they were students with her at Oxford. This greatly impressed me. I had hardly dared to dream of studying there. Even if I had done well in the oral exam, which I had no way of knowing, I had clearly failed in the written paper. This meant that I had to resit the three subjects I had failed the following November. To my great relief, I passed all three exams at the second attempt.

During the stressful and exhausting period leading up to the exams, I relaxed by making plans to return home for the summer vacation. Although I put a brave face on it in my letters, I was seriously homesick. I missed my family, I missed my friends, I missed the sunshine and the carefree lifestyle that went with it during long summer holidays in

Israel. I could not imagine replicating this in either Golders Green or Newcastle. I had had a tough year and I was desperate to get away from the treadmill. But I bumped into unexpectedly strong opposition from my mother. It was not that she and the rest of the family did not miss me. They did, and they kept saying so in their letters. But my mother was convinced that if I went back to Israel the IDF would not allow me to return to England to resume my studies until I had completed my military service. The first letter from the IDF to set the process in motion had in fact arrived the day after I had sailed from Haifa. Subsequent informal inquiries reinforced my mother's conviction that the army would deny me permission to leave. She therefore began bombarding me with letters to force me to change my summer plans.

Reading back, I am struck by the similarities between her letters to me and mine to her and Dalia; I had learnt manipulation from a real expert. My mother's tone became more and more hysterical as she piled on the pressure and she was not above using moral blackmail. Among the various arguments she deployed were the following: it was a miracle that our family, in its poor financial state, had succeeded in sending me to study in England; I was very lucky to have been given this chance; it was a chance to become a man of some stature like a lawyer, a doctor or an engineer; and now I proposed to blow it all away for the sake of a holiday. She conceded that it was natural for me to feel homesick but feared that I was beginning to imagine Israel as paradise rather than the 'pigsty' that it really was. To describe Israel as a pigsty was somewhat extreme, even for a secular Jew, and I thought so at the time, but I put it down to her absolute determination to dissuade me from coming. Later I came to realise just how miserable life in Israel had made her.

Unexpectedly, Dr Conway came to the rescue. He wrote to my mother to say that he checked with the Israeli embassy in London and they had assured him that there would be no difficulty about my returning to London at the end of the summer. Only then did the pressure subside and I was given permission to start planning in detail my summer holiday. I set about it with gusto and surprising competence for an otherwise unworldly sixteen-year-old. My plan was to go by train to Paris, to spend a few days there, then from Paris to get the train to Geneva, to spend a week in Switzerland, then to hitch-hike in Italy through Milan to Venice and get a boat to Haifa. I was going to travel on my own and to stay in youth hostels. In a surprisingly short time, I managed to get visas to France, Switzerland and Italy, and book the train and boat tickets. My uncle, who, despite general stinginess, was capable of occasional spasms of generosity, gave me money for the holiday – possibly, his wife did not relish the prospect of being landed with me over the holidays. I packed a small suitcase with a few essentials and set off on what promised to be an adventurous journey.

Everything went according to plan until the Swiss leg of the journey. In Paris I had a room in the students' dormitory that my friend Itzhak Azouri had arranged for me. I was in high spirits, liberated from all the scholastic and psychological pressures that had been weighing me down. I relished the freedom to roam about the city, to visit old haunts and explore new ones, like the museum and sculpture garden of Auguste Rodin and the City of Paris Museum of Modern Art. Switzerland was also exhilarating but for different reasons. In Paris the excitement came from my visits to historic sites and art museums; in Switzerland I was mesmerised by the natural scenery, lakes, mountains and picturesque villages. My base in Switzerland was the youth hostel in Geneva. I began by hitch-hiking all the way around the beautiful lake, the like of which I had never seen before. Among the places I explored were Lausanne, Vevey and Montreux. Another trip took me to Fribourg and Bern and from there I returned to Geneva. In a postcard I sent home I wrote that that was the happiest week of my life.

But on the way from Geneva to Italy, disaster struck. Unlike today, getting lifts was generally easy and I never thought of hitch-hiking as risky in any way. Most of the drivers who picked me up were men and I usually sat in the passenger's seat next to the driver. One of the drivers stopped to let me out after a long drive and a friendly chat. I thanked him, got out and closed the door behind me but before I had time to open the back door to collect my suitcase, he had driven off. I was dumb-founded and had absolutely no idea what to do. How on earth was I going to complete the long journey to Israel? Luckily, I had my wallet and my passport in the pockets of my jeans. Roughly half my money was in the suitcase and the remainder was in my wallet. I decided to go to the nearest restaurant for a substantial lunch and time to think calmly about my predicament. Blowing money on an expensive meal may not in retrospect have been very sensible but it seemed to alleviate my panic; a good lunch has never failed to have the desired effect.

Having composed myself, I stood by the road again and hitched a lift to Milan. In Milan I made my way to the Israeli consulate. I was seen by an official, explained my predicament and asked for a loan. The official said that they had helped out some Israeli students in similar circumstances but the students had not repaid the loan when they got home. The upshot was that they were either unable or unwilling to help me. Israelis usually go to university after military service. I was not a student, I was a boy of sixteen, effectively destitute, with no money and no means of getting home. But the consulate failed to acknowledge any duty of care towards me.

I left the consulate dispirited, walked around in a daze, entered a park and sat down on a bench. A man came and sat next to me and started a conversation in English. He looked in his early forties, he was well dressed and had a pleasant manner and he introduced himself as a Belgian doctor on holiday. As we talked, he spread a map of the city over both of us and put his hand on my knee. I was too naïve to pick up the signal that he might be a sexual predator. In sharp contrast to the Israeli official, the Belgian doctor was empathetic and willing to help. He took me out to dinner in a restaurant. At the end of the dinner, he said that he had a large room in a hotel with a spare bed and that I would be welcome to stay the night there. Still not suspecting anything, I accepted his offer and walked with him to his hotel room where there were indeed two single beds. But something in his behaviour aroused my suspicion.

I said I was tired and wanted to go to sleep. He then came and sat down on the bed and put his arm around me. I recoiled in horror. Putting his index finger on his lips, he then explained that what he was after was not sex but just kissing. This was hardly reassuring. I got up, thanked him for dinner, calmly walked out, without him trying to stop me, and scraped together my remaining cash for a bed in a youth hostel.

The next morning, I hit the road again, bound for Venice. This time I was extraordinarily lucky and again found a saviour – this time one with no ulterior motive. A man on a huge Harley-Davidson motorcycle stopped and asked me where I was heading. I told him the whole story, leaving out only the part about the Belgian doctor. The motorcyclist's name was Ed, he was American, he had camping equipment and no fixed itinerary or timelines. He took me under his wing. At his sugges-tion, we went to the nearest post office to send a telegram to my uncle in Newcastle to inform him of the emergency and ask him to wire me money (I think it was £15) to Post Restante in Venice. We spent a day or two camping by a lake and when we got to Venice the money was there for me. I sent another telegram to thank my uncle for bailing me out. There was one more obstacle to overcome: the boat ticket from Venice to Haifa had also been in my suitcase and I could not remember the name of the company. This involved going from one shipping office to another until one of them finally found my name on the passenger list and duly issued me another ticket. I thanked Ed profusely for all he had done and boarded the boat that delivered me to Haifa.

A warm welcome awaited me on my arrival. There was a great deal of catching up to do but also plenty of time in which to do it. The next few weeks were taken up with visiting near and distant relatives, meeting with old friends, going to the beach in Tel Aviv or to the posh swimming pool in the Accadia Hotel in Herzliya, or just reading and relaxing at home. Ramat Gan had always been a drab and lacklustre place, but it seemed all the more provincial compared to London and Paris, though this was surely an unfair comparison. On the home front little had changed: my father was still unemployed, my mother continued to work as a telephonist in the town hall, Dalia was doing her national service, Vilma was still at school and there was not much sense of purpose or progress. To me they all seemed to be drifting, but that may have been because I myself was now so determined not to drift. If anything, the family seemed more dysfunctional than it had been before I had left.

It was difficult to tell whether it was the family that had changed for the worse or my perspective that had shifted. Most probably it was both. Spending time with my friends from Gimnasia Dvir, on the other hand, freed me from my anxieties. We simply picked up where we had left off. My friends wanted to know everything about my travels and my life abroad. One thing I could sense was that I had gone up in their estimation because I was studying in England, a rare thing in Israel in those days of austerity. And as a result of my enhanced status, I was less inhibited, less painfully conscious of being an Iraqi, less silent and introverted.

Charles Conway stayed with us for part of the time that I was there. It was an opportunity for me to show him around the country and for my mother to reciprocate the hospitality that I had been receiving from his family. Our holiday in the sun was exciting and action-packed, in marked contrast to the extreme scholastic rigours that governed our lives in England. I couldn't help noticing the efforts my mother made to welcome Charles and how her warmth and vivacity contrasted with the formality of the Conways. Whether Charles noticed it too I cannot say. But before I knew where I was, it was time to get on the boat to Marseilles and then travel by train and ferry back to London.

Avi in the sixth form of the Jews' Free School in Camden Town

TWELVE

AWAKENINGS

ON MY RETURN TO LONDON I ENTERED WHAT WAS THE FIRST Sixth Form in the history of the Jewish Free School; previously most pupils had left the school at sixteen to get a job. In my year about ten pupils stayed on to do A-Levels, all of them boys. We were allocated a room for private study at the back of the stage in hall, some distance from the other classrooms. As there was no teacher to supervise us 'backstage', a great deal of time was spent in idle chatter and mucking about. Some pupils were more dedicated than others, but the general atmosphere was pretty lax and playful. One memorable episode involved the headmaster reprimanding a boy and a girl who had skipped a lesson in order to be alone. We could hear them but they could neither see us nor hear us. The headmaster asked them why they were not in class. No reply. He then asked whether they were there for a kiss and a cuddle. This was the first time I had come across this expression and I added it to my collection of English phrases for what I hoped would be future use.

For A-Level I chose History, French and British Constitution. I expressed an interest in doing, in addition, the A-Level in English litera-ture but Mr Richards, the English teacher, judged, no doubt correctly at the time, that my English was not up to it. French involved conversation, translation work and in-depth study of six French set texts: a novel, a play, a philosophical work, a collection of short stories and a volume of poetry. Each of these books was a wonderful revelation in its own way and a source of immense pleasure. Only one other boy took French and a class of two should have been easy to teach. Unfortunately, our French teacher turned out to be a real disappointment. Mrs Dawid had taught us French in the Fifth Form, so we knew that she was not the most dynamic of teachers. We assumed she would perk up as the work got more interesting, but she remained as ill-prepared as ever. She spoke French very fluently and with a perfect accent and did much to improve our conversational skills, but she tended to neglect the more demanding aspects of the course, like grammar and the set texts. By the middle of the year, I had become seriously frustrated by this slow pace of progress. I did not mention this to Dr Conway but one day I plucked up my courage and went to see Mr Felsenstein, the deputy-head. I asked if I could have free periods to study on my own instead of the classes with Mrs Dawid. Predictably, he asked about the reason for this request. I replied that we were not making much progress with Mrs Dawid and that I feared that at this pace we would not get through the syllabus in time. He listened attentively, asked me a few questions, then ordered me to continue to attend Mrs Dawid's classes until further notice. Later that day, Mrs Dawid was seen coming out of Mr Felsenstein's office with tears in her eyes.

My complaint about Mrs Dawid evinced a growing self-confidence. In the first year I had been a conformist, careful not to rock the boat, anxious to please at any cost. In the second year, academic ambition took precedence over conformity. And it was precisely because I seemed so conscientious that my complaint was taken seriously. The new French teacher was a young Jew named Ron Adelman who had recently graduated from Leeds University, and I believe this was his first job. Mr Adelman threw himself into teaching with tremendous energy and panache. He was sharp, lively and entertaining, and his enthusiasm was infectious. He made it fun to study the French language and a joy to read French literature. The contrast between him and Mrs Dawid could have hardly been greater. With Mrs Dawid we had read

Le Notaire du Havre, a novel by Georges Duhamel and *Trois Contes* by Gustave Flaubert. With Mr Adelman we studied in much more depth *Le Tartuffe ou l'Imposteur*, a theatrical comedy by Molière, *Candide, ou l'Optimisme*, a picaresque novel by Voltaire, and a selection of poems from seven nineteenth-century French poets.

My second A-Level subject was British Constitution. Despite its rather dry and technical name, this course encompassed almost all major aspects of British politics, with an emphasis on institutions. Among the topics we covered were the monarchy, cabinet government, parliament, the judiciary, the rule of law, political parties, the electoral system and local government. When I had arrived in England, I had known virtually nothing about British politics. Soon after my arrival at the Conway home, Charles had enlightened me with a broad-brush survey. Having cut my teeth in Israel whose proportional representation system encouraged the proliferation of small parties, I irritated him by repeatedly referring to the government as 'the coalition'.

By studying British Constitution for two years, I acquired a basic knowledge of the British political system as well as some useless pieces of information such as where the mace is kept in the House of Commons. Our teacher for this subject, as well as form teacher and head of Zangwill House, was Victor Eales, one of the non-Jewish members of staff. He was an extremely positive and friendly teacher. While he was kind and helpful to all the pupils, he singled me out for special attention, encouragement and praise. In his reports he wrote that my attitude to work was excellent; that my personality and character were first-class; that my attainments were very good; that the extension of my English vocabulary was remarkable; that I was obviously university material, having a keen analytical mind; that I was a pleasure to teach; and that he had no doubt I would do well. I couldn't get enough of Mr Eales! I'm aware of how self-congratulatory I sound when I quote him today, yet at the time these reports were crucial in raising my confidence.

My favourite subject at school was History. When I arrived in England my knowledge of general history was thin and patchy, and I had no particular interest in the subject. Much of the history I had been taught at school before was the history of the Jews and of the emergence of the state of Israel. The emphasis in Jewish history was on persecution and martyrdom while in Israeli history it was on heroism and redemption; the history we were taught at school was scarcely distinguishable from Zionist propaganda. In my first year at JFS I was introduced to nineteenth-century British economic and social history. Not only was the subject dull but the method by which it was taught, learning by rote, was deadly dull. It was only in the Sixth Form that I experienced for the first time the pleasure and excitement of studying history. The A-Level syllabus was divided into two papers: nineteenth-century British history and nineteenth-century European history. There were five boys in the class and the teacher was Denis Felsenstein.

Mr Felsenstein was a model teacher in every way: he was extremely knowledgeable; he always came well-prepared; he covered the entire syllabus in good time; he brought the subject alive; and he gave us detailed and constructive feedback on our written work. In short, he did whatever he could to bring out the best in us. We, for our part, had great respect for him and endeavoured, in varying degrees, to rise up to his expectations. There was no misbehaviour and no mucking around in his classes. Nor was there much laughter or light-hearted banter. One exception occurred when Mr Felsenstein asked us a question. One of the boys replied, 'Wasn't it so-and-so?' Mr Felsenstein retorted mock-angrily, 'Why is it that Jews always answer a question with a question?!' Putting on an exaggerated Yiddish accent, the boy replied 'Vy not?'

During the Christmas and Easter holidays I usually went to stay with my Uncle Isaac in Newcastle. He and his wife Doris lived in a spacious, detached Edwardian house, filled with expensive and elegant antique furniture. They had no children as Doris was already middle-aged when they got married. Isaac was now in his early fifties and to me Doris looked much older than him. In fact, she was four years older than him: she was born in 1906 and he in 1910. Doris's father was a Jewish immigrant from Tsarist Russia who had settled down in Newcastle and set up shop as a tailor. She combined ignorance and arrogance in roughly equal portions, considering Harold Wilson, the leader of the Labour Party, to be as bad as Adolf Hitler. To cap it all, Doris was also extremely stingy. In my adolescent eyes, she had no saving graces.

Doris and Isaac were an odd couple. They were temperamentally incompatible, and they spent much of their time bickering. They owned three large buildings that were divided into flats and the rent from the flats provided them with a substantial income. The one thing they had in common was parsimony. Doris bitterly resented the amount of money that my uncle spent on my education, which ran to around £50 a month: £30 a month to the Conways for my upkeep, £8 for my pocket money and the rest for additional expenses such as clothes, travel and holidays. I knew that Nana had offered to pay for my education in London from the proceeds of the sale of her house in Baghdad. But as Isaac had probably spent her money, he now had to defray the cost out of his own pocket. This was a source of perpetual tension between husband and wife.

During my stays in Newcastle, however, I was always looked after very well and even spoilt – most welcome after the rigours of the Conway household. Doris could not cook at all so my uncle had to do all the cooking. He was an excellent cook. His food was like the cuisine I had been used to in Baghdad – hot and spicy with plenty of curry and cardamom. The staple diet was chicken and rice, but his repertoire extended to lamb and aubergines, meatballs and okra in tomato sauce and *masguf*, fish broiled the Jewish-Iraqi way. After school dinners and the wholesome but dull meals of Mrs Conway, my uncle's cooking was a welcome treat and a reminder of home.

Both my uncle and aunt were kind to me but hyper-critical of one another. Each of them wanted to tell me their side of the story so, against my wishes, I was drawn into their marital squabbles. When we were alone, my uncle confessed to me that he was trapped in a deeply unhappy marriage. I asked him whether he had ever considered divorce. He replied that he had, many times, and that he had consulted a solicitor

on one occasion. He also showed me a letter he had drafted at the
solicitor's suggestion, laying out his manifold grounds for divorce. But
he had dropped the case before it had reached the courts. I asked him
why. His reply was that English law is very punitive towards a husband
who sues for divorce. In his case, the law decreed that he would have to
relinquish the marital home, divide the business assets and pay alimony
to his estranged wife. The legal arguments struck me at the time as a
cover for his cowardice, but I refrained from saying so.

I remember one incident sharply. Doris had been so cantankerous
and disagreeable (I was not exactly a neutral marriage counsellor) that
the atmosphere in the house became unbearable. My uncle suggested
that he and I went out for a drive and so we did. It was a cold winter day
with dark clouds and rain. We drove around aimlessly for about half an
hour and ended up in a garden centre. One of the features was a small
water fountain in the grounds that some customers treated as a wishing
well. My uncle tossed a coin into the well and made a silent wish. He
then gave me a coin and suggested I do the same. I did. My secret wish,
I'm ashamed to confess, was that my aunt would drop dead. My uncle
asked me, in a rather embarrassed and tentative manner, what had I
wished. I declined to answer. He said he thought that we had made the
same wish and he probably guessed right.

In the spring of 1963, Isaac took Doris for a fortnight's holiday to visit
our family in Israel. Having retired from the British Army and settled
down in the UK at the end of the Second World War, he had very little
contact with his relatives in the intervening eighteen years. On arrival in
Israel, he was utterly shocked by the deterioration in the fortunes of the
whole family. His mother, who had owned a luxury villa by the Tigris
River in Baghdad, now lived in a tiny one-room bungalow in Ramat
Gan. He remembered his uncles Jacob, Sha'ul and Joseph as prosperous
merchants and men of considerable social stature in Baghdad. Now he
saw for himself how drastically they had gone down in the world. Jacob
had a grocery store, Sha'ul had a fruit and vegetable store, while Joseph
was a taxi driver.

As my mother put it in her letter to me, Isaac, who had left behind clever, enterprising, successful businessmen, was distressed to see them as shadows of their former selves. My father was the saddest sight to behold for he had been the most prosperous of them all and now he was unemployed. Isaac was also disappointed with his younger brother Alfred, who was drifting aimlessly. Towards the end of the holiday, Isaac had a blazing row with his mother, Mouzli. It was about money or, more precisely, about paying for my education. I did not know the details; what I did know was that the row ended with Mouzli telling Isaac to his face that she did not trust him.

After my mother died, I went through all her papers and came across a letter that Isaac had written to her from Newcastle on 30 March 1963, after his return from the trip to Israel. Ever the peacemaker, my mother had written that Mouzli was sorry for the letter (in Judeo-Arabic) she had sent him and he should not worry about it. He refused to be mollified, rejected the advice, stated that the letter was not a joke, and added:

I have written to her [Mouzli] a very nasty letter and I have broken all my relations with her and will never see her dirty and very ugly face again. I am sick of her all my life. I came to the conclusion that she is really mad, and you have to be careful of her because she is jealous of her children and she wants to create disturbances amongst us... Honestly Aida if I was in Israel I would have thrown that dirty cat from the balcony into the street. She has behaved very badly with me. Her money is in London and is spent on Abi's education. I have nothing to do with it. She will not see one penny of it before Abi finishes his education and takes his degree. Although it is her money, you can rest assured Aida that I need to add twice as much for his expenses. I am determined to give Abi the chance... I blame you and Alfred for letting her write to me in this way because I see that Alfred wrote the envelope for her. Anyhow Aida I want to make it clear to you and Alfred in order to keep my love and affection towards you and the children and Alfred. I am not, repeat NOT, and will not, repeat NOT, send anything from

England to anyone of you. I want this to be clear so that there will be
no more misunderstandings.

My mother felt more acutely than Uncle Isaac the collapse in the
fortunes of our family: he was just a visitor; she had to live with the
consequences. Her letters to me contained recurrent references to the
monotony and misery of her life in Israel and to her desperate desire
to get out. She often referred to Israel as a prison: she felt suffocated
and oppressed. Her main complaint was that the entire burden of supporting the family fell on her shoulders. She was critical of Dalia for
not helping her and for wanting to study instead of going out to work
after she was discharged from the army. This was in stark contrast to
her passionate commitment and the sacrifices she was prepared to make
to give me a good education.

Regarding my father, my mother said very little but occasionally her
disappointment in him came to the surface. On 22 June 1963, she wrote:
'For the last ten years, your father has been just like a tourist in this
country. I have been struggling to look after your school, food, clothes
and this was already beyond my power. To think about furniture and a
bit of luxury was out of the question. Mother is not ready to help. She
is spending so much on you, she thinks she is doing more than enough
which is true, and I cannot ask for more. Anyway, I am terribly fed up
with the house and with those who live in it. They and everything get
on my nerves.' I heard my mother's pain but was unable to help.

This letter contained the first hint that my mother was thinking of
a divorce. In another letter she wrote that, when my sisters and I were
young, she kept her mouth shut and suffered without complaining.
Now she hoped I was old enough to understand that a woman could
not carry all the burden of looking after a family alone, that she could
not be like a slave, that she needed a partner to help her shoulder the
responsibility. The implication was clear: my father was no longer that
partner. My parents were granted a divorce by a rabbinical court in Tel
Aviv on 18 March 1964. I was not there to witness the chain of events

that led to the final separation. All I know is what I heard from my mother, first briefly in letters and in more detail later, when I returned to Israel. According to her, in Israel their marriage had never been the same again. While my father sat idly at home, my mother had to go out to work as a telephonist in the town hall; she was the sole breadwinner, and she became depressed. She was a young woman at the height of her power, and he was a middle-aged man, sick and in decline. A particularly poignant moment occurred when a colleague of hers in the town hall had told her that her father had come looking for her. The man in question was not her father but her husband.

My parents' divorce was not acrimonious. My mother maintains that the first suggestion of a divorce came from her husband, not from her. In her version of events, one day he said to her: 'Look here. I am like a drowning man. I don't want to drag you and the children with me. So let me go my way and you take care of the children.' Vilma, my younger sister, who was about fourteen years old at the time, had a different version of the events. Years later she told me she believed that it was our mother who took the initiative, that the idea of separation came from her and that our father was very unhappy about it. Vilma vaguely remembers overhearing a conversation in Arabic between our father and Dalia. Vilma thought that he said to Dalia that our mother wanted a divorce and that she asked him to leave the family home and that he did not know what to do. Could Dalia help him? Dalia looked uneasy and embarrassed because there was nothing she could do. Vilma thinks she muttered, 'What can I do?' In any case, Dalia's body language conveyed that message. Dalia could not recall this conversation.

Vilma's version is difficult to reconcile with our mother's, but there may be an element of truth in both versions. The suggestion of a divorce most probably came from our mother, but father was a proud, dignified and generous man as well as a conflict-avoider – he was probably also ashamed of having become a burden and therefore put up no resistance. Once he realised that his wife had made up her mind, he chose to go quietly. His concern for the welfare of his children, as reported by our mother, certainly rings true. The divorce must have been deeply painful for him, but it progressed without ructions or remonstrations.

Once the basic agreement had been reached, the formalities were accomplished swiftly. The financial side of the agreement was that my mother would give my father a third of the value of the flat and he would move out. Nana provided my mother with the money. This was not enough for my father to buy a place of his own; besides, he needed the capital to live on as he had no other source of income. Whenever my mother was in difficulty, she went to Mayor Krinitzi for help. The mayor did not disappoint: he allocated my father social housing at a nominal rent, putting him at the head of a queue of needy families. The bungalow was on the periphery of Ramat Gan, about twenty minutes' walk from our home. It consisted of one room, a bathroom and a kitchenette. My mother helped my father furnish it. It was all pretty basic and minimalist: a bed, a small sofa, a couple of armchairs, a cupboard and a coffee table. Scattered around the room were a few non-fiction books in Arabic. The surroundings were simple but neat and tidy. There were a few rows of bungalows with pavements leading to them, with plants and trees on each side. The entire housing estate was maintained by the council. Next door to my father lived an elderly Ashkenazi couple who were kind and helpful. On Saturday, from time to time, my mother would cook Jewish-Iraqi food and either Vilma or she would take it around to my father. He lived in this bungalow on his own until his death of a heart attack on 3 December 1970, aged sixty-nine.

During my military service I sometimes went to visit my father on Saturday, when I was off duty. My mother cooked a big meal for the whole family and set aside a portion for my father. She would give me two pots, one with rice, the other with the main course, most often chicken stew with potatoes and peas. The food was always deliciously spicy and it came in generous portions. My father would warm the food on a gas stove, and we would eat it on the coffee table, facing one another. There was no dining table. We used to chat in Arabic, with my father doing most of the talking and asking a lot of questions to keep the conversation going. My Arabic had been pretty limited to begin with, but it was especially rusty after three years in London. I did not say much, making the odd comment in a hesitant manner and answering as best I could with my limited vocabulary all the questions my father put to me. It felt strange to be holding a conversation with my father in a language that was no longer my own.

Living on his own, my father was glad of company and his face lit up whenever he saw me. I felt deep sympathy for him. Yet by this time, because of my prolonged absence abroad, we had little in common, quite apart from the difficulty in communicating. We never argued, let alone rowed. What struck me most about my father was the absence of any visible sign of bitterness about the cruel blow that fate had dealt him. If he felt any resentment towards my mother, he kept it to himself. Nor was there any self-pity along the lines of 'how the mighty have fallen'. He was stoical and uncomplaining. As was the case in my early teens, he never spoke about himself, his family, his career, our life in Baghdad and the circumstances that had forced us to leave. And I, to my eternal regret, never asked.

A friend I made in the course of writing this memoir, a research fellow at Cambridge named Merav Rosenfeld-Hadad, helped me reflect on my father's silence in the last twenty years of his life. She was born in Israel to parents who had emigrated from Iraq, felt in exile in Israel and brought her and her brothers up to be proud of their Jewish-Iraqi heritage. Merav came to Oxford to interview me for a book she was writing on 'Memories, Melodies, and Muslim–Jewish Relations' and it quickly emerged that her father, Morris Hadad, had known my father in Baghdad and greatly admired him. As a young man, Morris had accompanied his father, a building contractor, to a meeting with my father at our home in Baghdad. On hearing that Merav was coming to see me, Morris had written her a letter describing the meeting in some detail. He began with a description of the house, which he said was like a palace. My father, impeccably dressed in a three-piece suit, came to the front door to greet his guests.

My father had impressed Morris as an immensely wise, courteous and dignified man who was at the same time modest and unassuming. From other sources Morris and his father learnt later about my father's generosity towards his employees, the synagogue and poor people in the Jewish community. The Arab manner of doing business is to begin with a long and wide-ranging conversation on personal and family matters unrelated to the business at hand. The purpose of the conversation is to get to know the other person and to establish a personal relationship. Business depends on mutual respect and mutual trust. Once trust has been established, the business part of the meeting is usually easy to conclude. The way my father conducted himself on this occasion was said to be a masterclass in the Middle Eastern way of doing business. But it was not the Israeli way.

My own explanation of my father's silence in Israel had been that he was a broken man. Merav suggested instead that his silence was a conscious choice, that I should think of him as a noble person and a true Arab-Jewish aristocrat – 'the noblest of the noble', was how she put it. Wealth comes and goes, she observed, but nobility of character is innate and therefore enduring, regardless of external circumstances. My father's move to Israel involved a spectacular fall. Having come from a sophisticated urban culture, he arrived in a country of European Jews who had no idea of the richness of his civilisation nor of his position and stature within it. If anything, they tended to regard him and his ilk as backward and uncivilised. What was the pointing of talking to these people? Even had he wanted to talk, he did not have a language in which to communicate with them. What was the point of complaining? What good would it do? Instead of complaining or 'banging on' about the past, my father opted for a posture of dignified silence. It was a resounding silence which derived from strength rather than weakness. Merav's hypothesis about my father's silence led me to probe the reasons for my own silence. There were clearly some parallels. Both of us had been uprooted from our natural habitat and transplanted to an unfamiliar and inauspicious environment. Both of us felt out of place. The difference was that his silence derived from inner strength whereas mine was the product of vulnerability, confusion and self-doubt.

Merav's comments also turned my thoughts to the issue of pride. My father was a very proud man. He was renowned for his generosity in Baghdad and for being ever ready to do favours for other people. But even when he had been down on his luck in Israel, he would not stoop to begging for favours. Merav's explanation of my father's behaviour in Israel was revelatory, illuminating the virtues that endured in the face of adversity: generosity, nobility of character and devotion to his family, which he took to the point of self-sacrifice. He sacrificed himself for the sake of the family not once but twice: the first time by agreeing, against his better judgement, to leave Iraq for Israel, and the second time by releasing our mother of her marital obligations towards him.

Of my own obligation to my family, I was conscious all the time. I tried to discharge it by working hard and making progress in my studies. This became easier as the work itself became a source of pleasure. My social life, on the other hand, was unexciting and unrewarding. On Saturday night I would go out with my friends from school either to a party or to a club. We had a favourite club, in Wardour Street in Soho, where a ticket cost two shillings and sixpence. In the club, we would screw up our courage, approach a girl and ask her to dance. If she turned us down, we had a ready-made retort: 'What do you expect for two and six – Marlon Brando?!' I was not a good dancer, to put it mildly, and I remained rather shy. These handicaps ensured that I had no success in 'pulling birds', to use the idiom of the day.

My social life took a massive turn for the better when I met Shai Harris in my second year in London. Shai was my first girlfriend. We were both seventeen, we met at a party, and hit it off. She had red hair, blue eyes and a permanent expression of mischief on her face. Highly intelligent, cultured and self-confident, she could hold her own in any company. Her background had something to do with her self-confidence, which occasionally verged on arrogance. Her father, Lewis Harris, was an English Jew with Zionist connections who had risen to the rank of captain in the British Army in the Second World War. After the war, he worked for the English department of the Jewish National Fund and later went into banking. When I met Shai, he was the director of the Swiss-Israel Trade Bank, which had its head-quarters in the City of London. Shai's mother, Aviva, was an Israeli: cosmopolitan in taste and internationalist in outlook, but with deep roots in Israel and a yearning to return with her family to live there. Aviva's younger brother, Amnon, was a pilot in the Israeli Air Force whose plane was shot down in the War of Independence in 1948. The death of her brother reinforced Aviva's conviction in the justice of the Zionist cause and inspired a life-long desire to serve it. She was active in promoting Israeli art and culture in the UK and formed a close rela-tionship with the British Friends of the Israel Philharmonic Orchestra. As a person, Aviva was friendly and vivacious but also volatile, liable to fly off the handle at any moment. Shai had two bright and strong-willed younger sisters: Amina, thirteen, and Ella, nine. They lived in Hampstead in a comfortable house, surrounded by grass lawns and flower beds. Together they made up a lively, dynamic, unpredictable and peripatetic family.

My friendship with Shai transformed both my social and emotional life. She had many friends, mostly trendy, upper middle-class Jewish friends, a completely new milieu for me. We were invited to parties by her friends, but we also went out on our own to movies, the theatre and concerts. Our relationship blossomed but it was not without its ups and downs. Temperamentally we were quite different. She was assertive, exuberant and something of a show-off. I was cautious, diffident and introverted. There was also a gap in social status. Underlying it all was the fact that she was an Ashkenazi and I was a Sephardi. Sometimes I could not help feeling that Shai looked down on me because I came from the Orient. Most of the time, however, we made light of these different tribal affiliations and even joked about them. Using politically incorrect terms, Shai would call me a '*frenk*' and I would call her a '*vous-vous*'. (Because Yiddish has a lot of sounds of vous and vas, Ashkenazim were sometimes called '*vous-vous*'. '*Frenk*' was an equally derogatory term that the Ashkenazim had for Oriental Jews.)

One thing that Shai and I had in common was the French A-Level. She went to the Lycée Français de Londres where the standard of teaching was incomparably higher than in my school. One of the set books was the same for both of us: *Le Tartuffe ou l'Imposteur*, the seventeenth-century play by Molière. Always ready to put at my disposal her superior knowledge of French language and literature, Shai kindly lent me her notes and essays on this play. There was never any doubt, however, that she was the dominant character in what gradually developed into a beautiful friendship.

My association with the Harris family greatly enriched my life. All of them embraced me as a member of the family and I liked each and every one of them. They often invited me to Saturday dinner or Sunday lunch at their home and I enjoyed these meals enormously. Their conversation was sprinkled with amusing anecdotes. One Israeli general who had stayed with them was asked how he liked his eggs for breakfast. 'Difficult', had been his reply – in Hebrew there is no distinction between hard and difficult, hence the bizarre answer. Among their friends the Harrises counted some world-famous musicians, like the Russian cellist Mstislav Rostropovich whom I met once at their home in Hampstead and, a couple of years later, when they took us to view Marc Chagall's twelve stained-glass windows in the synagogue of the Hadassah Medical Center in Jerusalem. Aviva's association with the Israel Philharmonic Orchestra brought a number of eminent Israeli musicians into their circle of friends. The Harrises took me to concerts in London and introduced me to their friends. As my knowledge of classical music was non-existent, I could not bring anything of value to these conversations.

At school I continued to make steady progress. The teachers' positive feedback enhanced my self-confidence and emboldened me to set my sights higher and higher. My goal had been to study for a degree at a British university, something no other JFS pupil had done before. However, as I gained in self-belief, I began to dream of Oxford or

Cambridge. Mr Felsenstein encouraged me to pursue this ambition and even suggested that the school put me forward for Oxford entrance exams in January 1964, that is to say, six months before I was due to take the A-Level exams. His thinking was that my written work was improving all the time, that I had a slim chance, but that even if I failed, I had nothing to lose: Oxford entrance exams would be good preparation for the A-Level exams the following summer.

On this basis, he and I agreed that the school would arrange for me to take the Oxford entrance exams in History and French. There was also a third paper to test general knowledge that all applicants had to take. I worked diligently and single-mindedly to prepare myself for these exams which, in the event, I was unable to take. Just as the exams were due to start, Dr Conway informed me to my horror that, due to an administrative error, I had *not* been entered for the exams. He tried to console me with the thought that I had never had a realistic chance of passing these exams anyway. He was almost certainly right but, having invested so much in preparing for these exams, intellectually, emotionally and psychologically, I felt that I had been let down by the school.

In the Upper Sixth, I made a number of applications to provincial or 'redbrick' universities, and my school reports must have been so glowing that all of them were successful. In two I was offered a place after an interview. One was Sussex University where I had applied to read History. The other was to read for a degree in International Relations at the London School of Economics and Political Science. All the time I was getting advice from my mother about the subjects I ought to study. When I informed her that I planned to do a History degree, she observed that 'there is really a lot to learn about names and dates, etc.' She therefore advised me to look for something better!

When I told my mother about the place at the LSE, she urged me to reconsider what to study. On 5 May 1964, she wrote: 'By studying political science you will be dependent all your life on our government and they will surely send you, for the best years of your life, to Africa or any barbarian hole. Don't forget that you are a Sephardi and not an

Ashkenazi, which counts very much, so they will not let you go very far no matter how clever and educated you are.' Politicians and diplomats, she continued, are very restricted in what they can say or where they can go. On the other hand, 'There are some lucky people who are making good money quietly and are free and can do whatever they like.' The advice was clear: to study a subject at university that would help me to go into business and make money. I did not bother to respond and ignored the advice. Her suspicion that I may face discrimination in Israel's diplomatic service was not entirely baseless. The Sephardim, including the well-educated among them, remained on the margins of Israeli society. They were grossly under-represented in journalism, academia, the arts and the senior ranks of the civil service. Nevertheless, I remember how shocked I was at the time by my mother's blatant racism. Ironically, it had been my mother who had aroused my interest in a diplomatic career when I was a child. This was no doubt based on the month she had spent as a sixteen-year-old in the American embassy in Baghdad during the *farhud* and her dalliance with a young and handsome American diplomat there. Her change of mind may have been the result of the change in our family fortunes. I was now her only hope of rebuilding our wealth and in her mind the path to that could only lie through a business, not a diplomatic career.

The debate on where to go and what to study was finally settled by the unexpected offer of a place to read History at Jesus College, Cambridge. I had done nothing to secure this offer – it was the work of Denis Felsenstein, my History teacher. Mr Felsenstein knew Vivian Fisher, the Director of Studies in History at Jesus College, having referred to him some of his brightest boys from St Paul's School. The college offered me a place on Mr Felsenstein's recommendation, without any entrance exams and without an interview. The place was conditional on getting two E-grade A-Levels. Grade E was the lowest pass mark, the equivalent of 40 per cent. The bar for me could not have been set any lower. There was one other requirement: a classical language at O-Level. I did not know a single word of Latin or Greek, but I had already taken and passed the A-Level in Classical Hebrew and this was acceptable to the college. I was embarrassed to receive a place through patronage, without having to meet the higher standards set for the other candidates – it reminded me that my admission to Gimnasia Dvir had only been secured by my mother's connections. This was another case of *wasta* – of influence or nepotism. But the excitement of going to Cambridge helped to dwarf the feeling of guilt.

The college agreed to hold the place for me for two academic years to enable me to discharge my obligation to do national service in Israel. Provided I met the outstanding conditions, I was assured of a place for the start of the academic year of 1966. National service in those days was two years and two months. As soon as I had taken my A-Level exams, I thanked my uncle, thanked the Conways, packed my books and belongings, and returned home where I was immediately inducted into the army. In September 1966, just a few days after completing my national service, I turned up at Jesus College, Cambridge, as a first-year History student. A new chapter in my life was about to begin.

Avi in IDF uniform with grandmother Mouzli Obadiah

THIRTEEN

EPILOGUE

My *NOM DE GUERRE* IN THE ISRAELI ARMY WAS THE PRO-
foundly unmanly 'Mademoiselle Fifi', alluding to the de Maupassant
story. Thereby hangs a tale. From 1964 to 1966, I did national service
in the Israel Defense Forces which was compulsory for all Israelis, boys
and girls, when they reached the age of eighteen. At an early stage in my
singularly undistinguished military career, my platoon was detailed to
guard a stretch of the border with Jordan. There were two night shifts,
one from 6 p.m. until midnight and the other from midnight until 6 a.m.
Our platoon was on guard duty from 6 p.m. every evening for two weeks.
We were given very old and very heavy Czech Mauser rifles left over
from the 1948 war and six bullets each. Our superiors did not expect us
to be involved in any firefights and they were right. It was all quiet on
the Eastern front – and indescribably tedious. To relieve the tedium, I
decided, after the first day, to always have a book with me. I had a stack
of French novels from the Livre de Poche series and *Mademoiselle Fifi*
seemed to offer suitably light entertainment.

In the open air I used to read until it got dark and then I sometimes
fell asleep. This was a serious offence under the army code and it also
contravened the injunction in Psalm 121 that 'he who watches over
Israel will neither slumber nor sleep.' I took the precaution of telling
my comrades to wake me up if we had visitors from across the border.

One midnight my comrades kicked me to say it was time to go back to base. Despite my sleepy state, I remembered to pick up my rifle but not the novel. The platoon that followed us discovered the tatty book in the field. There was only one soldier in Eastern Command who read French novels on guard duty, so they knew where to find me; they returned my dog-eared volume, and they conferred on me the title *Mademoiselle Fifi* amid general hilarity. Thereafter I explained to anyone who would listen that the title was inappropriate, but it pursued me until the end of my military service. By my own lights, however, I was the heroic Defender of the Eastern Front and the proof was that not a single Jordanian soldier crossed the line on my watch.

For the first three months of my time in the army, I underwent basic training in a huge army base in Sarafand al-Amar, situated on the coastal plain about five kilometres northwest of Ramla. This had been the British Army's largest base in the Middle East during the mandate era. The purpose of the IDF training was to turn boys into men, to toughen us up and to impart the basic skills that every conscript had to acquire before being assigned to a combat unit or a more specialised branch of the army. The induction ceremony will remain seared in my memory forever. It took place in the twilight in a clearing on the Judean Hills on the eastern front. Israeli flags fluttered in the wind, and a military band played the national anthem, 'Hatikva,' which means hope. We pledged our loyalty to the motherland and shouted in unison, 'In blood and fire Judea fell; in blood and fire Judea will rise again!' This was followed by a loud discharge of fire-arms that illuminated the sky. For an eighteen-year-old boy this was heady stuff. In the years that followed I was to read many academic treatises on nationalism, most notably Benedict Anderson's *Imagined Communities*. But on this occasion, I felt nationalism in my bones.

Training was physically demanding, especially long marches in the scorching heat with a rifle, a helmet, a heavy rucksack and just one canteen of water. Discipline was strict and the food was barely edible but there was an *esprit de corps*, a sense of purpose and a universal belief in the justice of our cause. We saw ourselves as a democratic little country surrounded by millions of fanatical Arabs bent on our destruction, and we genuinely believed that we had no choice but to stand up and fight. The notion of *ein briera* – there is no alternative – was frequently invoked in those days and it underpinned the broader national consensus on our position in the conflict with our Arab neighbours. Much was made of the IDF tradition of *tohar ha-neshek* – the purity of arms – which laid down that weapons could only be used in self-defence and never against civilians. Allied to this was the notion that all Israel's wars were defensive wars, not wars of choice.

We also felt that we were serving in an army that was basically decent, ethical and egalitarian, in short, a people's army. One episode in particular confirmed me in my conviction that the army had one standard for everyone, regardless of rank, ethnic origin or social class. It happened during a field exercise in which we were instructed to crawl on the stony ground, holding our rifle in both hands and shuffling forward to evade enemy fire. One chubby and spoilt lad with thick glasses complained that there were thorns on the ground and got up. The platoon commander, a young corporal, told him to lie down on the ground, then stood on his back and ordered him to carry on crawling. This was an abuse of power and the soldier lodged a formal complaint with the camp commandant. The camp commandant was a lieutenant-colonel, a short man with an artificial hand in a black leather glove. There were different versions of how he had lost his right hand but all of them enhanced our respect for him. The corporal was court-martialled, stripped of his rank and sentenced to one month in prison. On the day after the court martial, the offender was made to stand facing the entire battalion of novices on the parade ground as the camp commandant announced his verdict. This was the army's equivalent of shaming pupils by making them stand in the corner of the classroom. The message was clear: army rules applied to everyone regardless of rank; an abuse of power would not be tolerated; and all offenders would be punished.

In the army I learnt something, which was to assume greater significance later in life, concerning our neighbour to the east, Jordan.

The toughest part of the training was an exercise of two nights and three days on the Judean hills, in the hot sun, with battle rations and no hot meals, no washing facilities and very little sleep. The company was divided into teams of two and each soldier got one half of a small tent. At nightfall each team would dig a shallow foxhole and pitch its tent. We could not change our sweaty clothes or take off our boots, and we were not allowed to sleep more than a couple of hours at a stretch. A burst of sub-machinegun fire was the signal that we had five minutes to pack our tent, gather our equipment and be ready to move on to the next location to repeat the same routine. We were expected to guard our rifles with our lives but at night this was easier said than done. On the second night, when we were all exhausted, the commanding officer, a young lieutenant, managed to steal half a dozen rifles, including mine, from a total of about thirty. The whole company was woken up by the discharge of sub-machinegun fire and those of us who had their rifles stolen were ordered to stand in a row and treated to a vituperative stream of abuse, mostly unprintable. We were told that we were good for nothing, a liability to the army and a disgrace to the motherland. Our punishment was to march across what we were told was the border with Jordan in full combat gear but with no rifle and no trousers. We were also told that if Jordanian soldiers shot us, that would be a proportionate punishment and a fitting end. We duly marched about half a kilometre to the east and then came back, humiliated but unharmed.

In 1988 I published a book entitled *Collusion Across the Jordan: King Abdullah, the Zionist Movement, and the Partition of Palestine*. In the book I advanced the thesis that in 1947 the Hashemite ruler, the great-grandfather of Abdullah II, the present king, had reached a tacit agreement with the Jewish Agency to partition Palestine between themselves, and that this agreement paved the way to mutual restraint in the 1948 Arab–Israeli war and to continuing collaboration in suppressing Palestinian nationalism after the war. In retrospect, my experience as a soldier in the summer of 1964 might have given me the first inkling that the Arab–Israeli conflict was not a straightforward bipolar affair. But all I consciously concluded at the time was that the Jordanians were good Arabs because they did not bother us. The Syrians, on the other hand, were bad Arabs because they repeatedly fired on our civilians and provoked clashes with our forces on our northern front.

I was ignorant enough at the time to believe the conventional wisdom which held that force was the only language that the Arabs understood. Accordingly, I thought we should hit the Syrians hard to teach them a lesson they would never forget. The prime minister at the time was Levi Eshkol, a Labour Party moderate who tried to rein in the army. To me he looked like an appeaser who was forcing us to fight with one hand tied behind our back. Once the politicians had failed, it seemed to me self-evident that the army should be left to deal with the problem in its own way.

There was not much time for leisure reading during the three months of basic training and not much of a choice of books to read. But there was one cheap paperback, a Hebrew edition of D. H. Lawrence's *Lady Chatterley's Lover*. The juicy bits were marked so the novel could be passed quickly from hand to hand; no one was allowed to take the time to read the whole book. I was frequently ribbed for the British connection. Britain was remembered as a hostile colonial power, who had sided with the Arabs against the Jews throughout the years of British rule in Palestine. In the standard Zionist rendition of the conflict, in 1948, in the moment of truth, Britain armed and incited its Arab clients to invade Palestine and crush the infant Jewish state. This was a highly distorted version of events, but I did not know this at the time, nor did I try to put up a defence of Britain.

I was also teased for a slight lisp; my speech was frequently imitated by emphasising the way I pronounced the letter S. In addition, I was mocked for speaking slowly. To give just one example, we were taught emergency procedures in the event of coming under artillery bombardment. If one saw a shell, one had to shout '*pagaz!*' – 'shell!', a signal for everyone to take to the ground. I never actually said it, but I was repeatedly imitated as saying very slowly, 'Comrades, watch out. There is a shell coming towards us.' It was all good-humoured banter and I took it in my stride. One bad habit I picked up in the army was to tell the same old jokes and anecdotes over and over again – much to the frustration of my friends and family I have never managed to rid myself of this habit.

The rest of my military service was uneventful. I was assigned to the signal corps. Having passed the test, I came under gentle pressure to go to officers' school, but I declined since this would have meant losing three rather than two academic years and I was impatient to resume my studies in the UK. At the end of a course of three months, I was given the rank of corporal and became an instructor in communications in the signal corps. That was what I did for the rest of my time in the army. I instructed soldiers to use radio transmitters, the art of encoding and decoding, the Morse code and the use of teleprinters to transmit messages. I was placed in charge of a platoon of about fifteen soldiers of each successive intake, forming the first link in the chain of command which ended with the chief-of-staff.

I fulfilled my duties as an instructor to the best of my limited ability and rarely had cause for complaint. There was a clear hierarchy, discipline and standard operating procedures. Everything was regimented, beginning every morning with the Order of the Day which was posted on the regimental notice board. In sharp contrast to the university life I was about to experience, there was no room for debate or discussion; creativity was not encouraged, and intellectual stimulation was in short supply. There was a manual for everything, and every problem had only one IDF-sanctioned solution – everything had to be done by the book. Given that not much effort was required and I had a great deal of spare time, I used it to read books on history, politics and psychology as well as, of course, French novels. More prosaically, I also began to smoke a pipe and to experiment with various kinds of pipe tobacco. My chief reason for pipe-smoking was to impress the women soldiers on our base. Unsurprisingly this strategy bore little fruit.

Field exercises, which were the culmination of the course and lasted three days, lifted the tedium. The company consisted of three platoons of trainee wireless operators. Each platoon and platoon commander drove to a different location in a communications vehicle, while the company commander, a captain, stayed in headquarters. We pitched tents, survived on battle rations and assembled elaborate antennas by the vehicle. We had to keep the show on the road for twenty-four hours a day and that meant working in shifts. Our task was to encode messages, to transmit them to the other two groups by Morse code or teleprinter and to decode the messages we received back from them. As this was just a training exercise, we were free to choose the content. It could be a passage from a newspaper or a book or any other text. True to my Francophile leanings, I used *Les Maximes de La Rochefoucauld*, a work now ubiquitously quoted on inspirational memes online. I had great fun translating some of his maxims into Hebrew, encoding them, transmitting them to the other two platoons and waiting to see what the recipients made of them.

During my two years in the army I took part in only one real military operation. This was peacetime, and I was in Central Command, which was responsible for guarding our long border with Jordan. It was the period that preceded the June 1967 war, in the course of which Israel captured the West Bank and extended its military control over the whole area up to the River Jordan. Peacetime is a slight exaggeration; although there was no full-scale war, there was a border war as a result of incursions into our territory from neighbouring countries by the Palestine Liberation Army, the military wing of the Palestine Liberation Organization, and military reprisals by the IDF. These were sometimes carried out against villages that were suspected of harbouring Palestinian fighters. They were invariably called *mekhablim* – saboteurs or terrorists – but, in retrospect, I think they deserved the name freedom fighters.

One day I was suddenly seconded from my tranquil training base to assist a fighting force that was about to embark on a reprisal raid against a Jordanian village on the West Bank accused of aiding Palestinian 'terrorists'. My task was to maintain wireless contact with two IDF units sent on a cross-border raid to demolish some houses and a petrol station in a Jordanian village. I stayed on our side of the border and was told that if our forces needed reinforcement, they would send a message through me. There were two fully armed battalions held in reserve on our side of the border, ready to spring into action. The two units maintained radio silence throughout the operation, so I was not called upon to do anything. That was the sum total of my involvement in combat operations against the enemy. I have to confess that I longed to get in on a piece of the action. To wait as a spectator on the sidelines was mildly frustrating.

My national service in the IDF marked the high point of my identification with the State of Israel. It is a natural human instinct to want to belong to a group. During my school years, from the age of five to fifteen, I was alienated because I felt that Israeli society looked down on Orientals like me. Rightly or wrongly, I was constantly aware of being regarded as inferior on account of my Eastern provenance. In the army, by contrast, I did not have the same feeling of being out of place. The Ashkenazi-Sephardi divide existed to some extent, but it was not as acute as it had been at school. It was partially submerged by a common sense of belonging to one nation and being surrounded by enemies on all sides. This was 'fortress Israel'. It was us and them, we and the enemy. I believed in the cause, I felt I belonged and, as a consequence, I managed to shake off the debilitating sense of inferiority that dogged me throughout my childhood.

Perhaps my three years in England had given me a European dimension, making me feel the equal of any Ashkenazi member of the armed forces. Studying abroad was rare in those days and it brought some prestige home. In any case, I was much less conscious of ethnic bias in the army than I had been at school. The army came close to succeeding where Israeli society had failed. In my experience, at any rate, the army was the melting pot to which Zionist ideology had always aspired but rarely achieved.

By the end of my military service I was almost a 'normal', patriotic Israeli, perhaps even a nationalist. Nationalism, as John le Carré pointed out, is quite different from patriotism: for nationalism you need enemies. That Israel had enemies was blindly obvious; the question is who was responsible for the development of the enmity in the first place. At that time, I tended to see things in black and white, viewing Israel as the innocent victim of Arab aggression. I therefore leaned towards a hard-line posture in the conflict with the Arabs, placing more faith in military force than in diplomacy. Although I did not support any particular political party, I veered to the right of the political spectrum and shared the militant nationalism that was its hallmark. It was not until many years later that I began to question the Zionist master narrative of the conflict that I had been taught at school and which was reinforced by serving in the army. However, the fact that I once shared it has helped me to understand its powerful stranglehold on the Israeli psyche.

Four days after completing national service, I turned up at Jesus College to take up my place as a first-year History student. The transition was sudden and sharp, but it ushered in the three happiest years of my life. In May 1967, however, in the summer term of my first year, a crisis erupted in the Middle East which seemed to me to threaten the very survival of the State of Israel. On the Arab side there was blood-curdling rhetoric about the 'battle of destiny' and throwing the Jews into the sea. On the Israeli side, under the hesitant leadership of Levi Eshkol, there was an uncharacteristic mood of anxiety, and gloomy forecasts of a second Holocaust. Against the backdrop of this terrifying scenario, the patriot in me surged to the fore. I cancelled a tutorial and took the train to London to go to the Israeli embassy at Palace Green, Kensington. This was the only time I missed a tutorial in my three years at Cambridge. My tutor was very sympathetic. At the embassy I said I wanted to go back to serve in the war that we were all certain was about to break out. They took down my contact details and said they would call me if needed. War did break out: the first shot was fired by Israel, the fighting lasted six days, and ended with a resounding Israeli military victory over its Arab neighbours and the tripling of the territory under its control. The call from the embassy never came. As with all aspects of the conventional

Zionist narrative, I have since had reason to revise my original assessment of the events of 1967.

The Six-Day War marked both the crest of my Israeli patriotism and receding zeal for the State of Israel. Disenchantment did not come at once; it evolved slowly and painfully. I used to rationalise my change of heart by arguing that it was not I who changed but my country. After the 1967 war, I argued, Israel became a colonial power, oppressing the Palestinians in the occupied territories. I liked to add that during my military service, the IDF was true to its name – it was Israel's defence force – whereas after the war it was transformed into a brutal police force of a brutal colonial power. A deeper analysis, however, led me to the conclusion that Israel had been created by a settler-colonial movement. The years 1948 and 1967 were merely milestones in the relentless, systematic takeover of the whole of Palestine. Jewish colonies built on occupied Palestinian land after the Six-Day War are the extension of the Zionist colonial project beyond the 'Green Line', the pre-1967 international border.

By delving into the history of my family in Iraq I gained a better understanding of the nature and global impact of Zionism. Previously, I had studied the Zionist movement in some depth but mainly in relation to its impact on the Palestinians. The big picture was of a settler-colonial movement that proceeded ruthlessly towards its goal of building a Jewish state in Palestine even if it involved, as it was bound to, the dispossession of the native population. Looking back, it seems to me utterly indisputable that the creation of the State of Israel involved a monumental injustice to the Palestinians. In the course of the 1948 war, Israel carried out the ethnic cleansing of Palestine. Three-quarters of a million Palestinians, more than half the total, became refugees. And as the 'new historians', notably Benny Morris, have demonstrated, the Palestinians did not leave of their own free will – they were pushed out. In June 1967, Israel conquered what remained of historic Palestine by military force. Another quarter of a million Palestinians from the West Bank became refugees, some of them for the second time. Once again, as in the aftermath of the 1948 war, Israel refused to allow the Palestinian civilians to return to their homes.

The occupation, said to be temporary, pending a political resolution of the conflict, became permanent. Formal annexation of the Palestinian territories was eschewed but creeping, de facto annexation never stopped. Prolonging the occupation, slowly but surely, turned Israel into an apartheid state. Some of Israel's apologists maintain that the Zionist movement was derailed from its proper course by the military victory of 1967, that the Zionism of values was replaced by the Zionism of territory. But since Zionism was an avowedly settler-colonial movement from the outset, the building of civilian settlements on occupied land was only a new stage in the long march. Either way, there could be no doubt that the Palestinians were and continue to be the victims of the ongoing Zionist project.

What the story of my family brought home to me, however, was that there was another category of victims of the Zionist project: the Jews of the Arab lands. Moreover, there was a link between the way that the Zionist movement treated the Palestinian Arabs and its treatment of the Arab-Jews. Both groups were a means to an end: the construction of an exclusive Jewish nation-state in the heart of the Middle East. The ethnic cleansing of Palestine created empty spaces, and these spaces had to be filled by Jews from anywhere they could be found, including Jews from the Middle East, even those who had no desire whatsoever to relocate to Israel. The same colonial institutions that displaced the Palestinians were tasked with absorbing the Jewish migrants from the Arab lands. And the same arrogant, Eurocentric, Orientalist mindset greeted the Jewish newcomers from the East.

The most crucial turning point was not the war of 1967 but the establishment of the State of Israel in 1948. Until then the Jews of Iraq, among them my family, were just one of the several minorities that made up the country. We were not aliens; we were natives; and we were looked upon as natives. Unlike Europe, Iraq did not have a 'Jewish problem'. We were not singled out for special treatment. We were a minority, not *the* minority. As Jewish Iraqis, our status was not fundamentally different to that of the other Iraqi minorities. Until the rise of nationalism in the interwar period, the main criterion for differentiating between Jews and Arabs in Iraq was religion, and only as an identifying characteristic, not as a divisive one.

Zionism changed all that. By endowing Judaism with a territorial dimension that it did not have previously, it accentuated the difference between Jews and Muslims in Arab spaces. Whether they liked it or not, from now on Jews were identified with the Jewish state. The displacement of three quarters of a million Palestinians by Israel intensified Muslim hostility not only towards the Zionist movement but also towards the Jews in their own country. Increasingly, the Jews were treated not as sons of Iraq but as part of an alien and usurping entity. Zionism not only turned the Palestinians into refugees; it turned the Jews of the East into strangers in their own land. In 1947–49 it was not only the land of Palestine that was partitioned but also the past. The common past of Jews and Muslims in Iraq was superseded by the new reality of the Arab–Israeli conflict.

In Chapter 7 I dealt in great detail with the Jewish exodus from Iraq in 1950–51, going beyond the story of my family to the much bigger story of the uprooting and transfer of this ancient community to the new State of Israel. I noted the major part played by the official policy of oppression and persecution in driving the Jews to migrate. But I also laid out the evidence I have unearthed about Israel's involvement in the Baghdad bombs that hastened the departure of the Jews. I gave this as an example of 'Cruel Zionism', the terrorist tactics employed by Israel to promote Aliyah and of the harm it inflicted on the Jews of Iraq.

In my rendition, Operation Ezra and Nehemiah was not a noble rescue mission by the fledgling Jewish state but the self-serving instrument for the transfer of the Jews from their homeland. However, even if Israel had played no part in the displacement, what matters in the final analysis is that the great majority of Iraqi Jews believed that it did. The suspicion that Israel was behind the bombs, and that it was complicit in the confiscation of their property, had a profound effect on the attitude of the Iraqi migrants towards Israel, giving rise to a bitter and lingering feeling of betrayal. It was like an open wound.

One of the casualties of the mass migration of Jews from the Middle East and North Africa to Israel was their centuries-old identity as Arab-Jews; tellingly, one recent history of an Egyptian Jewish family is entitled *When We Were Arabs*.[1] Every human being has multiple identities. It is noteworthy that in this case the Arab identity is relegated to the past. In Israel it was difficult for Eastern Jews to sustain multiple identities. As Ella Shohat observed,

> The reconceptualization of Jewishness as a national identity had profound implications for Arab Jews. The Orientalist splitting of the Semite was now compounded by a nationalist splitting. The meaning of the phrase "Arab-Jew" was transformed from being a taken-for-granted marker of religious (Jewish) and cultural (Arab) affiliation into a vexed question mark within competing nationalisms... In a different fashion, the two nationalisms came to view one side of the hyphen suspiciously. In the Arab world "the Jew" became out of bounds, while in the Jewish state "the Arab", hence the "Arab-Jew" or the "Jewish-Arab", inevitably came to seem an ontological impossibility.[2]

In the age of ethno-nationalism, it is important to recall that the categories of 'the Jew' and 'the Arab' were not always mutually exclusive. Juxtaposing them as opposites is both a cause and a symptom of the Arab–Israeli conflict. The truth of the matter is that Israel never saw itself as part of the Middle East nor did it want to integrate into the regional environment. Oriental Jews, with their knowledge of Arabic and first-hand experience of living in Arab countries, could have served as a bridge between Israel and its neighbours. The Ashkenazi establishment, however, had no interest in building such a bridge. Under the leadership of David Ben-Gurion, it built Israel as a fortress state with a siege mentality that attributed genocidal intentions to its neighbours. It saw Israel as part of the West, and it used the 'special relationship' with the United States not to resolve its conflict with the Palestinians but to prolong and entrench its control over the occupied territories.

Today the situation is utterly bleak; it has deteriorated significantly in the course of writing this book. The occupation has eroded the foundations of Israeli democracy. Even within its original borders Israel is a flawed democracy at best because of discrimination at multiple levels against its Palestinian citizens. But in the whole area under its rule, including the Palestinian occupied territories, Israel is an ethnocracy, a regime in which one ethnic group dominates the other. There is another, more familiar, name for this type of a regime – apartheid. Apartheid is a crime against humanity under international law. Under the 1998 Rome statute, it is defined as an 'institutionalised regime of systematic oppression and domination by one racial group over any other' with the intent of 'maintaining that regime'.

The superior status of the Jews is enshrined in the July 2018 Basic Law: Israel as the Nation-State of the Jewish People. This Basic Law is the official confirmation that Israel is an apartheid state. The law states that the right to exercise national self-determination in Israel is 'unique to the Jewish people'. It establishes Hebrew as Israel's official language, and downgrades Arabic – a language spoken by the Palestinian citizens of Israel, a fifth of the population – to a 'special status'. Israel is in fact one of the very few members of the United Nations that has enshrined its racism in law.

The Israeli occupation of the Palestinian territories is one of the most prolonged and brutal military occupations of modern times. After fifty-six years, it is no longer possible to pretend that the occupation is temporary. B'Tselem, the highly respected Israeli human rights organisation, reluctantly reached this conclusion. In a carefully argued position paper published in 2021, it declared:

The Israeli regime, which controls all the territory between the Jordan River and the Mediterranean Sea, seeks to advance and cement Jewish supremacy throughout the entire area. To that end, it has divided the area into several units, each with a different set of rights for Palestinians – always inferior to the rights of Jews. As part of this policy, Palestinians are denied many rights, including the right to self-determination.[3]

For Palestinians it makes little difference whether the Israeli government is left or right or centre. Whatever the colour of the government of the day, the Israeli regime is fundamentally built on the oppression of the Palestinians. It is a deeply entrenched apartheid regime. The majority of Israelis, including my family, are outraged by the designation of their country as an apartheid state. But whichever way you slice it, Israel is an apartheid regime. I reject this regime completely, totally and uncompromisingly. Previously I supported a two-state solution to the Israeli-Palestinian conflict. In practical terms, this means an independent Palestine on the Gaza Strip and the West Bank with a capital city in East Jerusalem. The two-state solution enjoyed and continues to enjoy broad international support. By signing the Oslo Accord in 1993, the PLO explicitly accepted this solution. Its leaders hoped that in return for giving up their claim to 78 per cent of mandatory Palestine, they would get a small independent state alongside Israel. But it was not to be. Israel used the Oslo Accord not to end but to repackage the occupation. At no time since Oslo has Israel stopped expanding its settlements on the West Bank. In 2005 it withdrew unilaterally from Gaza but only in order to consolidate its grip over the West Bank. This is the Zionist colonial project across the Green Line. Its ultimate aim is Greater Israel. And Greater Israel is incompatible with any equitable solution of the conflict with the Palestinians.

When supporting a two-state solution to the conflict, I was well aware that a mini-state on a fifth of the area of mandatory Palestine fell a long way short of absolute justice for the Palestinians. But I also argued that in the harsh world of power politics, there is no such a thing as absolute justice. The partition of Palestine into two independent states was a way of providing relative justice for both parties. Israel, however, would not settle for four-fifths of Palestine. It continued to expand settlements, that is to say, to steal more and more land from the Palestinians. By its settlement expansion Israel effectively killed the two-state solution. What is left of the West Bank is a collection of Palestinian enclaves, surrounded by Israeli settlements and military bases, that cannot form a viable state. In short, the two-state solution is dead or, to be more accurate, it was never born.

The outcome I have come to favour is one democratic state between the River Jordan and the Mediterranean Sea with equal rights for all its citizens regardless of ethnicity or religion. This is the democratic one-state solution. Initially, the one-state idea appealed only to a small group of intellectuals; gradually, however, it gained a growing number of adherents on the Palestinian side. As hopes of independence faded, the emphasis shifted to the quest for equal rights under Israeli-Palestinian rule. On the Israeli side, support for the one-state idea is still confined to a tiny left-wing fringe. If forced to choose between keeping Israel as Jewish state or a democratic state, the majority of Israelis would opt for the former. Such an outcome would be a tragedy for all concerned. My preference is to replace the politics of separation and supremacy with the politics of solidarity and equality for all.

The obstacles on the path to a one-state solution should not be underestimated, but nor should its advantages. For the five million Palestinians who live on the West Bank and Gaza Strip, this would result in a dramatic improvement on their present situation. For Israel's 1.8 million Palestinian citizens, partition of the land is not much of a solution because it would distance them further from their friends and family in the Palestinian state. For Israeli Jews as well, one state would have the great merit of preserving their democracy and preventing them from going further down the road of apartheid South Africa. As Bishop Tutu pointed out, everyone was liberated, white people included, when apartheid ended in South Africa. Like the whites in South Africa, Israelis too can liberate themselves from the burden of apartheid by ending their coercive rule over five million Palestinians and granting genuine equality to the 1.8 million Palestinians who live in their midst. One democratic state is a noble vision of justice, equality and freedom for all.

For me, the one democratic state solution carries the additional attraction of renewing the relevance of the Arab-Jew. The present impasse in Israel-Palestine resulted, at least partly, from the central assumption of Zionist discourse, namely, that Jews and Arabs are exclusive and antagonistic ethnic categories. Zionism has in effect undermined the hybrid figure of the Arab-Jew. The Zionist movement was in origin and in essence a European movement led by European Jews who wanted to create a Jewish state for European Jews. It aspired to be in the Middle East but not of the Middle East. It sought not the melding of cultures but the replacement of the local culture by a European one. By its very nature, the Zionist movement deepened the divisions between Israelis and Palestinians, between Israel and the Middle East, between Judaism and Islam, between Hebrew and Arabic. The Zionist movement and the State of Israel have actively worked to erase our common past, our intertwined histories and our centuries-old heritage of pluralism, religious tolerance, cosmopolitanism and co-existence. Above all, Zionism has discouraged us from seeing each other as fellow human beings.

In this memoir I have tried to interweave and inter-relate the private and the public. In conclusion, I would like to stress once again the imperative of remembering the past. My experience as a young boy and that of the whole Jewish community in Iraq, suggests that there is nothing inevitable or pre-ordained about Arab–Jewish antagonism. The old world of Iraq, the one that my two grandmothers used to compare to paradise, cannot be rebuilt. Remembering the past, however, can help us to envisage a better future. Nationalism all but destroyed the identity of the Arab-Jew but perhaps it has left just enough of a remnant to warrant a little optimism about the future. One thing is certain: without reviving or reimagining the kind of religious tolerance and civilised dialogue between Jews and Arabs that prevailed in Iraq before the emergence of the State of Israel, we will not be able to move beyond today's impasse.

Arab-Jewish coexistence is not something that my family and I imagined in our minds; we experienced it, we touched it. Because of this experience of the possibilities of interweaving and sustaining multiple identities, I could describe my own position today as akin to that of the main character in Emile Habiby's novel *The Secret Life of Saeed*: I am a pessoptimist.[4] I am cautiously pessimistic about the prospect of progress in the short term but I am more optimistic about the chances of a peaceful solution to the Israeli-Palestinian conflict in the longer term. Apartheid in the twenty-first century is simply not sustainable. Like Abba Eban, I believe that nations, like individuals, are capable of acting rationally – after they have exhausted all other alternatives.

Notes

CHAPTER 1. *Arab-Jews*

1   Benny Morris, for example, depicts the Arab attack on Israel in 1948 as a jihad, a holy war. In the conclusion to his book on the first Arab–Israeli war, Morris writes that it was not just a contest between two national movements over a piece of territory but 'part of a more general, global struggle between the Islamic East and the West'. Benny Morris, *1948: The First Arab-Israeli War* (New Haven: Yale University Press, 2008), p. 394. Another example is Martin Gilbert, the British-Jewish historian and ardent Zionist, who devoted the last of his many books to the history of the Jews in Muslim lands. The book is ambitious in scope, covering 1,400 years of Jewish-Arab history, from the rise of Islam in the seventh century to the present day. But it is little more than a catalogue of Muslim hatred, hostility and violence towards Jews. Antisemitism is said to be the fundamental, underlying force that shaped Muslim–Jewish relations. By piling one horror story on top of another, however, Gilbert ended up painting a misleading picture. He was psychologically hard-wired to see antisemitism everywhere. The result was a distortion of the history of Muslim–Jewish relations to serve a Zionist political agenda. Martin Gilbert, *In Ishmael's House: A History of Jews in Muslim Lands* (New Haven: Yale University Press, 2010).

2   Moshe Behar and Zvi Ben-Dor Benite, 'Don't Arab Jews Have a History?', *Haokets*, 10 January 2022 (Hebrew).

CHAPTER 2. *Inventing Iraq*

1   Elizabeth F. Thompson, *How the West Stole Democracy from the Arabs: The Arab Congress of 1920 and the Destruction of a Unique Liberal-Islamic Alliance* (London: Atlantic Books, 2020).

2   Gertrude Bell, *The Letters of Gertrude Bell (Volume 2) 1921–1926* (Middlesex: The Echo Library, 1927), p. 143.

3   Ibid., p. 136.

4   Quoted in Pierre Salinger with Eric Laurent, *Secret Dossier: The Hidden Agenda Behind the Gulf War* (London: Penguin Books, 1991), p. 14.

5   Emile Cohen, 'Jewish Education in Iraq', unpublished paper, 2019.

6   Esther Meir, *Zionism and the Jews of Iraq, 1941–1950* (Tel Aviv: Am Oved, 1993) (Hebrew), pp. 1–2.

7   Abraham Ben-Yaacob, *A History of the Jews in Iraq from the End of the Gaonic Period (1038 CE) to the Present Time* (Jerusalem: The Ben-Zvi Institute, 1965) (Hebrew), p. 234.

8   Nissim Kazzaz, *The Jews in Iraq in the Twentieth Century* (Jerusalem: The Ben-Zvi Institute, 1991) (Hebrew).

9   Ibid., pp. 2–5.

10 Mordechai Bibi. *The Underground Pioneer-Zionist Movement in Iraq: A Documentary Study, Volume 1: 1941–1944* (Jerusalem: The Ben-Zvi Institute, 1988) (Hebrew), pp. 16–17.

11 Abbas Shiblak, *Iraqi Jews: A History of Mass Exodus* (London: Saqi, 2005), p. 61.

12 Quoted in ibid., pp. 61–62.

CHAPTER 4.   *Saida's Story*

1   Joseph Sassoon, *The Global Merchants: The Enterprise and the Extravagance of the Sassoon Dynasty* (London: Allen Lane, 2022).

2   Massoud Hayoun, *When We Were Arabs: A Jewish Family's Forgotten History* (New York: The New Press, 2019), pp. 163–66.

CHAPTER 5.   *The British Connection*

1   Tony Rocca, 'Inside Story: Behind the Farhud', in Violette Shamash, *Memories of Eden: A Journey through Jewish Baghdad*, edited by Mira and Tony Rocca (Surrey: Forum, 2008), p. 247. Tony Rocca provides a fascinating account of the *farhud* from the British point of view in which Sir Kinahan Cornwallis features as the ice-cold proconsul who knowingly abandoned the Jews of Baghdad to the tender mercies of the mob to deflect attention from Britain's role in violating Iraq's sovereignty. According to Rocca's account, while the *farhud* raged and Jews were being slaughtered, Cornwallis went back to his residence to a candlelit dinner and a game of bridge.

2   Ibid., p. 271.

3   Elie Kedourie, 'The Sack of Basra and the *Farhud* in Baghdad', Chapter 19 in *Arabic Political Memoirs and Other Studies* (London: Frank Cass, 1974), pp. 307–8.

4   Ari Alexander, 'The Jews of Baghdad and Zionism: 1920–1948', unpublished MPhil thesis, University of Oxford, 2002, pp. 87–96.

5 Kazzaz, *The Jews in Iraq in the Twentieth Century*, pp. 238–58.

6 Mark R. Cohen, 'Historical Memory and History in the Memoirs of Iraqi Jews', *Mikan, Journal for Hebrew and Israeli Literature*, Vol. 6, June 2012.

7 Orit Bashkin, *New Babylonians: A History of the Jews in Modern Iraq* (Stanford: Stanford University Press, 2012), pp. 112–25.

CHAPTER 6. My Baghdad

1 Merav Rosenfeld-Hadad, *Judaism and Islam, One God One Music: The History of Jewish Paraliturgical Song in the Context of Arabo-Islamic Culture as Revealed in Its Jewish Babylonian Sources* (Leiden: Brill, 2020).

2 Moshe Gat, *The Jewish Exodus from Iraq, 1948–1951* (London: Frank Cass, 1997), p. 38.

CHAPTER 7. Baghdad Bombshell

1 Itzhak Bar-Moshe, *Exodus from Iraq: Memories from the Years 1945–1950* (Jerusalem: The Sephardic Community Committee, 1977, translated from Arabic to Hebrew by Nir Shohet), p. 364.

2 Nathan Weinstock, *Une si longue présence: Comment le monde arabe a perdu ses juifs, 1947–1967* (Paris: Plon, 2008) (French).

3 David Hirst, *The Gun and the Olive Branch: The Roots of Violence in the Middle East* (London: Faber and Faber, 1977), and Shiblak, *Iraqi Jews*.

4 Marion Woolfson, *Prophets in Babylon: Jews in the Arab World* (London: Faber and Faber, 1980), p. 129.

5 Naeim Giladi, *Ben-Gurion's Scandals: How the Haganah and the Mossad Eliminated Jews* (Tempe, Arizona: Dandelion Books, 1992).

6 Tawfiq al-Suwaydi. *My Memoirs: Half a Century of the History of Iraq and the Arab Cause* (Boulder: Lynne Rienner, 2013), p. 15.

7 Mordechai Ben-Porat, *To Baghdad and Back: The Story of Operation Ezra and Nehemiah* (Or Yehuda: Ma'ariv Book Guild, 1996) (Hebrew), p. 65.

8 Al-Suwaydi, *My Memoirs*, p. 12.

9 Interview with Yaacov Karkoukli, Ramat Gan, 30 July 2017.

10 Hirst, *The Gun and the Olive Branch*; Giladi, *Ben-Gurion's Scandals*; and Shiblak, *Iraqi Jews*.

11 Ella Shohat, '"*Sant al-tasqit*": Seventy Years since the Departure of Iraqi Jews', *Orient XXI*, October 2020.

12 Hanan Hever and Yehuda Shenhav, 'Violence in Baghdad (1950–51), the Violence of the Archives', *Teoriya ve'Bikoret*, 49, Winter 2017 (Hebrew).

13 Bar-Moshe, *Exodus from Iraq*, pp. 333–34.

14 Sylvia G. Haim, 'Aspects of Jewish life in Baghdad under the monarchy', *Middle Eastern Studies*, 12:2, 1976.

15 Shlomo Hillel, *Operation Babylon: Jewish Clandestine Activity in the Middle East, 1946–51* (London: Collins, 1988), pp. 283–84.

16 Naeim Giladi, 'The Jews of Iraq', *The Link*, Volume 31, Issue 2, April–May 1998.

17 Ben-Porat, *To Baghdad and Back*, p. 147.

18 Ibid., pp. 245–46.

19 Ibid., pp. 219–20.

20 Jackie Khougi, 'Yaacov's Ladder', *Ma'ariv*, 31 March 2017. In a private conversation Yaacov Karkoukli told me that a large bribe paid by his wife to a military judge had secured his release from prison.

21 Letter in Hebrew from Yaacov Karkoukli to the author, May 2018, and a second letter with no date but probably summer 2020.

22 The Mossad was established on 13 December 1949. Mossad means 'an institute' in Hebrew. The full name for the agency in Hebrew is 'the institute for intelligence and special operations'. It is responsible for intelligence collection, covert operations and counter-terrorism.

23 Hillel, *Operation Babylon*, p. 276.

24 Shamil Abdul Qadir, *History of the Zionist Movement in Iraq and its Role in the Emigration of the Jews, 1950–1951* (Baghdad: Maktabat al-Azal, 2013) (Arabic), p. 214.

25 Avraham Shama, *Finding Home: An Immigrant's Journey: A Memoir* (Great Britain: Amazon, 2016), p. 79.

26 Ben-Porat, *To Baghdad and Back*, p. 77.

27 Gat, *The Jewish Exodus from Iraq*, pp. 153–54.

28 Telephone interview with Shlomo Hillel, Israel, 30 July 2018.

29 Emails from Shamil Abdul Qadir to the author, 26 and 27 April and 21 May 2022.

30 Yehouda Shenhav, 'The Jews of Iraq, Zionist Ideology, and the Property of the Palestinian Refugees of 1948: An Anomaly of National Accounting', *International Journal of Middle East Studies*, Vol. 31, No. 4, November 1999.

31 Joel Beinin, *The Dispersion of Egyptian Jewry: Culture, Politics and the Formation of Modern Diaspora* (Berkeley: University of California Press, 1998), p. 31.

32 Hanan Hever and Yehuda Shenhav, 'Violence in Baghdad (1950–51), the Violence of the Archives'.

CHAPTER 8.   *Farewell Baghdad*

1   Bar-Moshe, *Exodus from Iraq*, pp. 306–7.

CHAPTER 9. *Promised Land*

1 Esther Meir, *Zionism and the Jews of Iraq, 1941–1950* (Tel Aviv: Am Oved, 1993) (Hebrew), p. 215.
2 Orit Bashkin, *Impossible Exodus: Iraqi Jews in Israel* (Stanford: Stanford University Press, 2017), p. 4.

CHAPTER 10. *Adrift*

1 Zvi Tsameret, 'Zalman Aran and the productivisation of the children of the "Oriental Communities"', *Iyunim Bitkumat Israel*, No. 15, 2005 (Hebrew), pp. 295–326.
2 *New York Times*, 25 October 1960, quoted in Elie Kedourie, *The Chatham House Version and Other Middle-Eastern Studies* (London: Weidenfeld and Nicolson, 1970), p. 448.
3 Sami Michael, *The Israeli Experience* (Or Yehuda: Ma'ariv Book Guild, 2001) (Hebrew), pp. 216–21.

CHAPTER 11. *London*

1 Jerry Black. *J. F. S.: A History of the Jews' Free School, London since 1732* (London: Tymsder Publishing, 1998), pp. 205–6.

CHAPTER 13. *Epilogue*

1 Massoud Hayoun, *When We Were Arabs: A Jewish Family's Forgotten History* (New York: The New Press, 2019).
2 Ella Shohat, *On the Arab-Jew, Palestine, and Other Displacements: Selected Writings* (London: Pluto Press, 2017), p. 6.
3 B'Tselem (The Israeli Information Center for Human Rights in the Occupied Territories), 12 January 2021, https://www.btselem.org/publications/fulltext/202101_this_is_apartheid
4 Emile Habiby, *The Secret Life of Saeed, the Ill-Fated Pessoptimist* (Beirut: Dar Ibn Khaldun, 1974) (Arabic).

Bibliography

Alexander, Ari. 'The Jews of Baghdad and Zionism: 1920–1948'. Unpublished MPhil thesis, University of Oxford, 2002.

Amir, Eli. *The Dove Flyer*. London: Halban, 2010. (Translated from Hebrew to English by Hillel Halkin).

———. *Bicycle Boy*. Tel Aviv: Am Oved, 2018. (Hebrew).

Ballas, Shimon. *Arab Literature under the Shadow of War*. Tel Aviv: Am Oved, 1978. (Hebrew).

Bar-Moshe, Itzhak. *Exodus from Iraq: Memories from the Years 1945–1950*. Jerusalem: The Sephardic Community Council, 1977. (Translated from Arabic to Hebrew by Nir Shohet).

———. *A House in Baghdad*. Jerusalem: The Sephardic Community Council, 1982. (Translated from Arabic to Hebrew by Hanita Brand).

Bashkin, Orit. *New Babylonians: A History of the Jews in Modern Iraq*. Stanford: Stanford University Press, 2012.

———. *Impossible Exodus: Iraqi Jews in Israel*. Stanford: Stanford University Press, 2017.

Batatu, Hanna. *The Old Social Classes and the Revolutionary Movements in Iraq*. Princeton: Princeton University Press, 1978.

Behar, Moshe, and Zvi Ben-Dor Benite. 'Don't Arab Jews Have a History?', *Ha'okets*, 10 January 2022. (Hebrew).

Beinin, Joel. *The Dispersion of Egyptian Jewry: Culture, Politics and the Formation of Modern Diaspora*. Berkeley: University of California Press, 1998.

Bell, Gertrude. *The Letters of Gertrude Bell (Volume 2) 1921–1926*. Middlesex: The Echo Library, 1927.

Ben-Porat, Mordechai. *To Baghdad and Back: The Story of Operation Ezra and Nehemiah*. Or Yehuda: Ma'ariv Book Guild, 1996. (Hebrew).

Ben-Yaacob, Abraham. *A History of the Jews in Iraq from the End of the Gaonic Period (1038 CE) to the Present Time*. Jerusalem: The Ben-Zvi Institute, 1965. (Hebrew).

———. *The Jews of Iraq in Modern Times*. Jerusalem: Kiryat-Sepher, 1979. (Hebrew).

Benjamin, Marina. *Last Days in Babylon: The History of a Family, the Story of a Nation*. New York: Simon and Schuster, 2006.

Berg, Nancy E. *Exile from Exile–Israeli Writers from Iraq*. Albany: State University of New York Press, 1996.

———. *More and More Equal: The Literary Works of Sami Michael*. Lanham, MD: Lexington Books, 2004.

Bibi, Mordechai. *The Underground Pioneer-Zionist Movement in Iraq: A Documentary Study, Volume 1: 1941–1944*. Jerusalem: The Ben-Zvi Institute, 1988. (Hebrew).

Black, Gerry. *J. F. S.: A History of the Jews' Free School, London since 1732*. London: Tymsder Publishing, 1998.

Cohen, Haim Y. *Zionist Activity in Iraq*. Jerusalem: the Zionist Library, 1969. (Hebrew).

Cohen, Mark R. 'Historical Memory and History in the Memoirs of Iraqi Jews'. *Mikan, Journal for Hebrew and Israeli Literature*, Vol. 6, June 2012.

Cohen, Ran. *Said*. Bnei Brak: Sifriyat Poalim, 2016. (Hebrew).

De Gaury, Gerald. *Three Kings in Baghdad, 1921–1958*. London: Hutchinson, 1961.

Gat, Moshe. 'The Connection between the Bombings in Baghdad and the Emigration of the Jews from Iraq: 1950–51'. *Middle Eastern Studies*, Vol. 24: No. 3, July 1988.

———. *The Jewish Exodus from Iraq, 1948–1951*. London: Frank Cass, 1997.

Giladi, Naeim. *Ben-Gurion's Scandals: How the Haganah and the Mossad Eliminated Jews*. Tempe, Arizona: Dandelion Books, 1992.

———. 'The Jews of Iraq', *The Link*, Vol. 31, Issue 2, April–May 1998.

Gilbert, Martin. *In Ishmael's House: A History of Jews in Muslim Lands*. New Haven: Yale University Press, 2010.

Goitein, S. D. *Jews and Arabs: Their Contacts through the Ages*. New York: Schocken Books, 1955.

Gottreich, Emily. *Jewish Morocco: A History from Pre-Islamic to Postcolonial Times*. London: I.B. Tauris, 2020.

Habiby, Emile. *The Secret Life of Saeed, the Ill-Fated Pessoptimist*. Beirut: Dar Ibn Khaldun, 1974. (Arabic).

Haim, Sylvia G. 'Aspects of Jewish life in Baghdad under the monarchy', *Middle Eastern Studies*, Vol. 12: No. 2, 1976.

Hayoun, Massoud. *When We Were Arabs: A Jewish Family's Forgotten History*. New York: The New Press, 2019.

Hever, Hanan and Yehuda Shenhav, 'Violence in Baghdad (1950–51), the Violence of the Archives', *Teoriya ve'Bikoret*, 49, Winter 2017. (Hebrew).

Hillel, Shlomo. *Operation Babylon: Jewish Clandestine Activity in the Middle East, 1946–51*. London: Collins, 1988.

Hirst, David. *The Gun and the Olive Branch: The Roots of Violence in the Middle East*. London: Faber and Faber, 1977.

Horesh, Joshua. *An Iraqi Jew in the Mossad: Memoir of an Israeli Intelligence Officer*. Jefferson, North Carolina: McFarland, 1997.

Isaacs, Carol. *The Wolf of Baghdad: Memoir of a Lost Homeland*. Oxford: Myriad Editions, 2020.

Julius, Lyn. *Uprooted: How 3000 Years of Jewish Civilisation in the Arab World Vanished Overnight*. London: Vallentine Mitchell, 2018.

Kattan, Naim. *Farewell Babylon: Coming of Age in Jewish Baghdad*. London: Souvenir Press, 2009.

Kazzaz, Nissim. *The Jews in Iraq in the Twentieth Century*. Jerusalem: Ben-Zvi Institute, 1991. (Hebrew).

Kedourie, Elie. *The Chatham House Version and Other Middle-Eastern Studies*. London: Weidenfeld and Nicolson, 1970.

———. *Arabic Political Memoirs and Other Studies*. London: Frank Cass, 1974.

———. 'The Break between Muslims and Jews in Iraq'. In *Jews Among Arabs: Contacts and Boundaries*, edited by Mark R. Cohen and Abraham L. Udovitch. Princeton, NJ: Darwin Press, 1989.

Klein, Menachem. *Lives in Common: Arabs and Jews in Jerusalem, Jaffa and Hebron*. London: Hurst, 2014.

Levi, Lital. 'Historicizing the Concept of Arab Jews in the Mashriq'. *Jewish Quarterly Review*, Vol. 98: No. 4, 2008.

Lewis, Bernard. *The Jews of Islam*. Princeton: Princeton University Press, 1984.

———. *Semites and Anti-Semites: An Inquiry into Conflict and Prejudice*. New York: W. W. Norton, 1986.

Marr, Phebe. *The Modern History of Iraq*. Boulder: Westview, 1985.

Massad, Joseph. *The Persistence of the Palestinian Question: Essays on Zionism and the Palestinians*. Abingdon: Routledge, 2006.

Meir, Esther. *Zionism and the Jews of Iraq, 1941–1950*. Tel Aviv: Am Oved, 1993. (Hebrew).

Michael, Sami. *Victoria*. Tel Aviv: Am Oved: 1993. (Hebrew).

———. *The Israeli Experience*. Or Yehuda: Ma'ariv Book Guild, 2001. (Hebrew).

Moreh, Shmuel. *Baghdad My Love: Memoirs and Sorrows*. Tel Aviv: Association of Jewish Academics from Iraq, 2020. (Translated from Arabic to Hebrew by Yona Sheffer).

Morris, Benny. *1948: The First Arab-Israeli War*. New Haven: Yale University Press, 2008.

Nathan, Aharon. *From Babylon to Jerusalem: Memories and Reflections of a Wandering Jew*. London: Kew, 2020.

Neslen, Arthur. *Occupied Minds*. London: Pluto Press, 2006.

Abdul Qadir, Shamil. *History of the Zionist Movement in Iraq and its Role in the Emigration of the Jews, 1950–1951*. Baghdad: Maktabat al-Azal, 2013. (Arabic).

Rejwan, Nissim. *The Jews of Iraq, 3000 Years of History and Culture*. London: Weidenfeld and Nicholson, 1985.

———. *The Last Jews in Baghdad: Remembering a Lost Homeland*. Austin: University of Texas Press, 2004.

———. *Outsider in the Promised Land: An Iraqi Jew in Israel*. Austin: University of Texas Press, 2006.

Rose, John. *The Myths of Zion*. London: Pluto Press, 2004.

Rosenfeld-Hadad, Merav. *Judaism and Islam, One God One Music: The History of Jewish Paraliturgical Song in the Context of Arabo-Islamic Culture as Revealed in Its Jewish Babylonian Sources*. Leiden: Brill, 2020.

Said, Edward W. *The Question of Palestine*. New York: Vintage Books, 1979.

Salinger, Pierre with Eric Laurent. *Secret Dossier: The Hidden Agenda Behind the Gulf War*. London: Penguin Books, 1991.

Sassoon, Joseph. *The Global Merchants: The Enterprise and the Extravagance of the Sassoon Dynasty*. London: Allen Lane, 2022.

Satloff, Robert. *Among the Righteous: Lost Stories from the Holocaust's Long Reach into Arab Lands*. New York: Public Affairs, 2006.

Sawdayee, Maurice M. *The Baghdad Connection*. Library of Congress Catalog Card No. 78-3136.

Shaked, Gershon. *Hebrew Narrative Fiction, 1880–1980*. Vol. 4. Tel Aviv: Hakkibutz Hameuchad and Keter, 1993. (Hebrew).

Shama, Avraham. *Finding Home: An Immigrant's Journey: A Memoir*. Printed in Great Britain by Amazon, 2016.

Shamash, Violette. *Memories of Eden: A Journey through Jewish Baghdad*, edited by Mira and Tony Rocca. Surrey: Forum, 2008.

Shenhav, Yehuda. 'The Jews of Iraq, Zionist Ideology, and the Property of the Palestinian Refugees of 1948: An Anomaly of National Accounting', *International Journal of Middle East Studies*, Vol. 31: No. 4, November 1999.

———. *The Arab Jews: A Postcolonial Reading of Nationalism, Religion, and Ethnicity*. Stanford: Stanford University Press, 2006.

Shiblak, Abbas. *Iraqi Jews: A History of Mass Exodus*. London: Saqi, 2005.

Shlaim, Avi. *Collusion Across the Jordan: King Abdullah, the Zionist Movement, and the Partition of Palestine*. Oxford: Clarendon Press, 1988.

———. *The Iron Wall: Israel and the Arab World*. London: Penguin Books, 2014.

Shohat, Ella. *Taboo Memories, Diasporic Voices*. Durham: Duke University Press, 2006.

———. *On the Arab-Jew, Palestine, and Other Displacements: Selected Writings*. London: Pluto Press, 2017.

———. '"*Sant al-tasqit*": Seventy Years since the Departure of Iraqi Jews', *Orient XXI*, October 2020.

Simon, Reeva S. 'The Imposition of Nationalism on a Non-nation State: The Case of Iraq During the Interwar Period, 1921–1941'. In *Rethinking Nationalism in the Arab Middle East*, James Jankowski and Israel Gershoni, eds. New York: Columbia University Press, 1997.

Smooha, Sammy. *Israel: Pluralism and Conflict*. London: Routledge and Kegan Paul, 1978.

Snir, Reuven. 'Arabic Literature by Iraqi-Jews in the Twentieth Century: The Case of Ishaq Bar-Moshe, 1927–2003'. *Middle Eastern Studies*, Vol. 41: No. 1, 2005.

———. *Arabness, Jewishness, Zionism: A Clash of Identities in the Literature of Iraqi Jews*. Jerusalem: Ben-Zvi Institute and the Hebrew University of Jerusalem, 2005. (Hebrew).

———. *Who Needs Arab-Jewish Identity?: Interpellation, Exclusion, and Inessential Solidarities* (Brill's Series in Jewish Studies). Leiden, 2015.

Somekh, Sasson. *Baghdad Yesterday: The Making of the Jews in Modern Iraq*. Stanford: Stanford University Press, 2012.

Stillman, Norman A. *The Jews of the Arab Lands in Modern Times*. Philadelphia: The Jewish Publications Society, 1991.

al-Suwaydi, Tawfiq. *My Memoirs: Half a Century of the History of Iraq and the Arab Cause*. Boulder: Lynne Rienner, 2013.

Thompson, Elizabeth F. *How the West Stole Democracy from the Arabs: The Arab Congress of 1920 and the Destruction of a Unique Liberal-Islamic Alliance*. London: Atlantic Books, 2020.

Tripp, Charles. *A History of Iraq*. 3rd ed. Cambridge: Cambridge University Press, 2007.

Tsameret, Zvi. 'Zalman Aran and the productivisation of the children of the "Oriental Communities"'. *Iyunim Bitkumat Israel*, No. 15, 2005. (Hebrew).

Weinstock, Nathan. *Une si longue présence: Comment le monde arabe a perdu ses juifs, 1947–1967*. Paris: Plon, 2008.

Woolfson, Marion. *Prophets in Babylon: Jews in the Arab World*. London: Faber and Faber, 1980.

Ye'or, Bat. *The Dhimmi: Jews and Christians Under Islam*. Rutherford, N. J.: Fairleigh Dickinson University Press, 1985.

Zubaida, Sami. 'The Fragments Imagine the Nation: The Case of Iraq'. *International Journal of Middle East Studies*, Vol. 34, 2002.

Acknowledgements

At various stages in the long journey that led to the publication of this memoir, I received support from many colleagues, relatives and friends which it is my pleasure to acknowledge. Two friends deserve special mention.

Ella Shohat, the distinguished cultural critic, accompanied this memoir since its inception. Her own work has been a major source of inspiration. Her work covers a wide range of issues such as the colonial nature of Zionism, the Euro-centric bias in Zionist historiography, the place of Oriental Jews in Israeli society, the pivotal figure of the Arab-Jew, the displacement of the Palestinians from Palestine and that of the Iraqi-Jews from their homeland. Her work helped me to better understand the political forces that shaped my life and gave me a powerful impetus to engage with the complex existential issues that go way beyond my individual journey. In addition, Ella placed my manuscript under a sharp critical lens and made a large number of constructive comments and suggestions.

Orit Bashkin, an eminent historian of the Middle East, was another major source of instruction, enlightenment and advice. As a diplomatic historian I was used to writing about famous people and I have also published a biography of King Hussein of Jordan. But I had great doubts and inhibitions when it came to writing a book about my family and myself. Orit's book, *New Babylonians: A History of the Jews in Modern Iraq*, was an eye-opener. It offers an illuminating account of the intellectual, social and cultural life of the Jews of Iraq in the first half of the twentieth century. Orit's book not only educated me about the history of my own community; it enabled me to overcome the inhibition I felt in writing a life story and placing myself at centre stage. Even more crucially, it provided a context and a framework into which I could try to fit my individual story. Like Ella Shohat, Orit read the entire manuscript and made many perceptive comments and, again like Ella, she encouraged me to expand on the perspectives of my mother and two sisters for the sake of greater gender balance.

Two other friends read the entire manuscript, corrected factual mistakes and made helpful comments for its improvement. They are Lavinia Davenport and Emma Sky and I am grateful to both of them for their contribution.

A number of other friends read either parts of the manuscript or a detailed book proposal and made valuable suggestions. They include Erica Benner, Fawaz Gerges, Eugene Rogan, Merav Rosenfeld-Hadad and Bernard Wasserstein. Avi Raz and Tom Segev read and suggested extensive revisions to Chapter 7. To all of them I owe a deep debt of gratitude.

I also wish to place on record my thanks to Célestine Fünfgeld, my former graduate student and dedicated research assistant, for helping me to collect material and for serving as IT troubleshooter, picture researcher and proofreader.

Dr MariaLuisa Langella, the librarian of the Middle East Centre at St Antony's College, Oxford, and her assistants, Haifa Jajjawi and Caroline Davis, dealt with all my manifold requests promptly, efficiently and with good cheer.

Neil Ketchley, professor of politics at the Middle East Centre, did the maps.

My deep appreciation goes to all the staff at Oneworld and especially to Sam Carter for his wise counsel, superb editing and unwavering support for this project. His assistant, Rida Vaquas, contributed to the editorial process intelligently, imaginatively and creatively. Tom Feltham copy-edited the manuscript with a sharp eye, great skill and meticulous attention to detail.

I am deeply grateful to my daughter Tamar, a publisher by profession, for her thoughtful suggestions, practical help, and the long conversations that accompanied the writing of this book. It was her idea to produce a podcast that helped both of us to understand better our Arab-Jewish-Israeli identities. My father was silent; Tamar's father never stops talking…

Finally, I would like to thank my wife, Gwyn Daniel, a psychotherapist and passionate pro-Palestinian activist, for continuing to be interested in my work after fifty years of marriage, for her incisive criticism of the text, for her countless editorial suggestions, and for her encouragement and support throughout many seasons.

Avi Shlaim
Oxford
October 2022

Index

References to images are in *italics*; references to notes are indicated by n.